Critical Thinking & Writing

Sherry Lutz Zivley

HARCOURT BRACE ■ COLLEGE PUBLISHERS

Custom Publisher   Felix Frazier
Senior Production Manager   Sue Dunaway

Critical Thinking and Writing

Copyright ©1997 by Sherry Lutz Zivley

Printed in the United States of America

0-15-508247-7

Preface

Writing is a skill. The same recipe works for mastering any skill. Mastering a skill requires work and practice—whether or not one is blessed with any "talent." The old recipe—"99% perspiration and 1% inspiration"—also applies to learning to write.

Any college student can become a competent writer, if he or she treats writing as a skill and works at learning that skill. If a student insists that writing is a mystery, a nightmare, a punishment, and/or a genetically transmitted talent and if that student refuses to practice the basic skills of writing, he or she will not learn to write. Practice still does "make perfect."

If, however, a student is convinced that all writing is "individual" or the result of "inspiration," and if that student insists on being allowed to write "the way I like to write" and if that student refuses to work at mastering basic writing skills, he or she will not learn to write. As toddlers, nearly all of us were less than enthusiastic about using forks or spoons—much less knives. Instead, we liked to eat with our hands and to play with our food and to smear food on our faces, hands, clothes, and anything and anybody else (including the family dog or cat) within our reach. As adults, most of us do not find it overly constricting and inhibiting to eat—at least in public—without indulging in those pleasures of childhood. We have so thoroughly mastered the skill of eating with silverware that we do so without even thinking about the process (except in a few cases, such as English peas, whole pickled peaches, or spaghetti). Some of us have even mastered chopsticks. With enough of the right kind of practice, we can also become proficient at writing.

Some people are blessed with talent in writing. They are very few in number, and most of us aren't among them! And even talented writers may need practice in basic skills.

Some students have been reading books all of their lives. They have read hundreds of books, thousands of pages, and ten-thousands of sentences, and hundreds of thousands of words. Inevitably, they have learned much about the written word. They are lucky. Because they have been readers, they usually have a head start as writers. Some students have benefited enormously from spending a great deal of time around people who—even in their everyday conversation—use language maturely, logically, correctly, effectively, and even stylistically. Such students usually develop a good command of language without having to work very hard. Some students have benefited from good writing instruction in high school, intermediate school, grade school, or at home and have already mastered many or most important writing skills. Students who have already had a great deal of practice, enter a writing course with tremendous advantages. Others may have at least learned to spell and to write grammatically, have developed vocabularies, and learned to express their feelings. Unfortunately, some students have not done much reading and have had little practice at writing.

But every educated adult needs skill in writing. And the purpose of this book (and of the course in which it is being used) is to help you learn those skills essential to good writing.

If you follow the instructions you are given and practice the skills that are presented in this text and by your writing instructors, you really can become proficient in writing—and will eventually come to look on writing not as an impossible torment but as something (like jogging, washing dishes, mowing the lawn, or scrambling an egg) that you can do whenever you want to or need to. And, since I believe that we all come to like to do things that we do well, you might—just might—even begin to find some enjoyment in writing.

Good luck!

Sherry Lutz Zivley
University of Houston

Table of Contents

SECTION III: SECONDARY DISCOURSE

Chapter 7: Secondary Discourse

SECTION IV: UNITY & COHERENCE

SECTION V: COMPOUND DISCOURSE

SECTION VI: THE INTEGRATED ESSAY

Introduction

CRITICAL THINKING

People think in many ways. And often people of different cultures think differently. Even people in Western Civilization, where certain methods of thinking have prevailed for thousands of years, people utilize various methods—logical and illogical—to arrive at conclusions—some sound and some unsound. Often thinkers reach conclusions by following standard, logical thinking processes—processes which are reliable and which will inevitably yield sound conclusions. And sometimes thinkers reach conclusions through bursts of sheer, intuitive insight. Such insights usually come after long hours of logical thinking, but are not the direct result of logical thinking. (Such intuitive insights are discussed in *Chapter 7* under "Organic Conclusions.")

Critical thinking is the ability to think about thinking in general and about one's own thinking in particular. It is also the ability to analyze and evaluate the usefulness and accuracy of not only the overall thinking processes, but also of each of the specific steps in a particular thinking process. The need to not only have a record of one's work but also to do this kind of analysis and criticism of one's own thinking has led scientists to keep laboratory notebooks with very careful and specific details.

Scientific method involves understanding and being able to do deductive and inductive thinking as well; it also involves incorporating these two formal methods of thinking so that their results enhance each other and lead inevitably to sound conclusions (as Robert Pirsig demonstrates in the excerpt from *Zen and Motorcycle Maintenance* in *Chapter 2*).

How one writes and how well one writes inevitably reflects how one thinks and how well one thinks. And a person can, by improving his or her writing, inevitably improve his or her thinking. Of course the converse is true as well. The two processes—thinking and writing—exist in a reciprocal cause and effect relationship (like those reciprocal causal relationships 1) between language and politics and 2) between drinking and failing which George Orwell explains in paragraph 2 of "Politics and the English Language." (See *Chapter 5*)

Analyzing non-fiction discourses, writing non-fiction discourses, and analyzing one's own non-fiction discourses will help a student understand what kinds of things make up an effective discourse—and an effective argument. Doing such analyzing and writing will help a student know how to plan to write, how to write the discourse itself, and how to trouble-shoot and improve that discourse after a first draft of it is written. In examining one's own writing, one has the time analyze and criticize his or her own thinking after the fact and in so doing gradually learn how to self correct more quickly, until that self-correction—that critical thinking—becomes an integral part of the student's thinking processes.

To be able to think critically about writing, one must analyze and evaluate the kinds of ideas in a discourse, the elements (evidence and reasons) used to support those ideas, the structure (organization and order) in which those ideas and that support is presented, the extra-logical methods of clarifying and enhancing those ideas, and the additional coherence tactics which help to guide a reader through a non-fiction discourse.

All of these things will be explained and exemplified in this book.

The Chapters of This Book

■ Non-fiction discourse may have different purposes (*Chapter 1*).

■ Non-fiction discourse is comprised of basic materials: elements (ideas, evidence, and reasons) and components (combinations of those elements) which can be analyzed (*Chapter 2*).

■ The basic elements and components of writing are organized (*Chapters 3, 4,* and *5*) into clusters and ordered (*Chapter 6*) in various ways.

■ Primary discourse includes all the ideas, evidence, and reasons which logically support the thesis and main ideas of a discourse.

■ Secondary discourse (*Chapter 7*) is the controlled use of definitions, comparisons, analogies, and other parenthetical insertions which can clarify and enhance the primary discourse.

■ The parts of a discourse are connected by various coherence devices (*Chapter 8*) which show the relationships among the parts.

■ Compound discourse is discourse which has more than one primary subject (*Chapter 9*).

Sometimes a discourse includes material which weakens the discourse. Confusing, wordy, or overly repetitious discourse confuses and wastes a reader's time. Irrelevant discourse distracts a reader. Such discourse needs to be corrected or omitted. Confusing discourse should be clarified; wordy discourse should be condensed; and useless or damaging discourse should be deleted. Such discourse is seldom found in discourse written by professional writers. But it occurs frequently in the discourse of novice writers. Such discourse has a negative effect on the reader. Such discourse is often the primary problem with discourse written by novices because they utilize it, although it does not support their ideas, instead of using the kinds of elements which could support their ideas.

CHAPTER 1

Non-Fiction Discourse

A *discourse* is any verbal communication. It can be so long that it requires several volumes to complete or as short as a single word. It can have any purpose.

All writing is made up of the same basic elements. All writing utilizes similar patterns of organization and order. All writers must consider their purpose, audience, and persona for any given writing situation. And all writers of well-written prose follow a fairly consistent process of writing steps. Most do so on paper. Very experienced or very talented writers sometimes work out those steps in their heads. Just as all music is remarkably similar, all writing shares many of the same elements and qualities.

PROSE DISCOURSE

There are always four things involved in any written discourse: the writer, the writer's audience (the reader), the reality the writer is describing, and the written discourse itself. That situation can be described, according to James L. Kinneavy, with the following communication triangle:

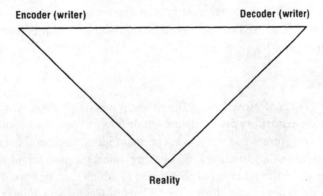

Encoder (writer)   Decoder (writer)

Reality

Notice that the writer, the reader, and the reality which is the subject of the discourse are all outside the discourse. One can never know the exact nature or purpose of the writer or of the reader or of the reality. One can only know 1) what kind of person seems to be speaking in a discourse (This fictional "person" is usually called the ***persona*** or ***speaker***), 2) the kind of person the discourse the persona seems to be talking to, and 3) the verbal reality within the discourse.

This text will focus attention on the discourse itself, and students will be encouraged to analyze the discourse in the essays published here in order to better understand what kind of elements and components are used to create discourse, how those elements and components are constructed, and what tactics are available for enhancing those elements and components—to make them easier for the reader to understand and more convincing to the reader.

Nevertheless, there are different types of prose, with different purposes and emphases.

Types of Prose Discourse

Prose discourse an be classified as ***non-fiction*** and *fiction*.

Non-fiction discourse falls into one of the following categories or may be a combination of these categories:

- *exposition* presents facts.

- *argument* presents opinions that can be argued.

- *expression* (the *personal essay*) presents, rather than argues, personal opinions and tastes.

Fiction attempts to recreate human experience as we would like it to be (*escape*), as we think it should be (*didactic*), or as it is (*experiential* or *interpretive*).

Purposes

Different types of prose have different purposes. This book will concentrate on ***expository prose***. But even different types of expository prose have different purposes, content, main ideas, uses, and content. In writing about a particular kind of thing, one's purpose might be to consider the different types of that thing, in which case one would ***classify*** the types of that thing (See "Kinds of Cakes" in *Chapter 3*).

TYPES OF PROSE

	Non-Fiction			Fiction
	EXPOSITION	**ARGUMENT**	**PERSONAL ESSAY**	**FICTION**
PURPOSE	To communicate facts	To persuade	To express personal feelings or ideas	To entertain or to provide insight into people
CONTENT	Facts	Arguable opinions and their support	Individual tastes, beliefs, and idiosyncrasies	Human experience
MAIN IDEAS	Generalizations	Assertions: 1) Are opinions 2) Imply "ought" 3) Require support	Personal opinions	Themes: Universal truths about human beings
WHERE USED	Science, news stories, and history	Most public writing essays	Personal essays and novels	Short stories
EXAMPLE	"Nuclear power can have devastating force."	"Nuclear power must be controlled."	"Nuclear power is terrifying."	"He shivered, knowing the reactor was failing."

Or one's purpose might be to examine the parts of that thing, in which case one would **analyze** that thing (See "Ingredients for a Cake" in *Chapter 4*). Or one might want to describe a sequence of events related to that thing, in which case one would write a narrative (See "A Christmas Memory" in *Chapter 6*). Or one might want to describe the process by which that thing was created (See the recipe for a chocolate cake in *Chapter 6*). Or one might want to discuss causes and/or effects related to that thing, in which case one would do some kind of cause and effect analysis (See "Causes for Cake Baking Failures" in *Chapter 6*).

In **expository essays**, the controlling ideas are *generalizations* about facts. In **argumentative essays**, the controlling ideas are *assertions*. Such ideas 1) are opinions, 2) imply "ought," and 3) require support. In **expressive (personal) essays**, the controlling ideas are *personal opinions* (personal preferences and tastes). In fiction, **central ideas** (usually called **themes**) are universal truths about human nature and are usually *implied* rather than stated.

Assertions, Generalizations, and Personal Opinions

An *assertion*, which requires support and implies "ought," is an opinion which a writer is trying to get his or her audience to accept. Sometimes all the writer wants is for the audience to agree, that is, to accept the assertion. Often the writer wants the audience to act in some way.

Assertions are the ideas used as the basis for all human negotiations.

"We should spend less money on armaments and more on social programs."

"We should spend less money on social programs and more on armaments."

"We should elect a Democrat as President."

"We should elect a Republican as President."

"We should go to a movie tonight."

"We should stay home and study tonight."

"Tom Wolfe writes great fiction."

"Tom Wolfe writes mediocre fiction."

A *generalization* is a generally accepted statement about facts.

"All organic compounds contain carbon."

"The greater a car's speed, the greater will be the destruction in a crash."

"The American population is increasing."

"The number of cases of AIDS in the United States is increasing."

A *personal opinion* differs from an assertion in that the writer may not be trying to get his or her audience to accept it. In fact, it may not be possible to support it. It may be a belief, a taste, or an idiosyncrasy. In each of the following statements of personal opinion, the writer is always implying "for me."

"Chocolate-mint is Baskin-Robbins' best flavor (for me)."

"Hot weather is wonderful (for me)."

"The beach is a better vacation spot than the mountains (for me)."

"The beach is the best vacation spot in the whole world (for me)."

"A very small college is the most comfortable and helpful (for me)."

Culturally Accepted "Truths," Warrants and Assumptions

A *culturally accepted "truth"* (sometimes called an "*a priori truth*") is a belief that a group of people believes in so completely that it is treated as if were "Truth"—as if it were an obvious, universally accepted, God-given, human, natural, and scientifically-supported truth. We not only assume that culturally assumed truths are true, but we also assume that "everyone" believes those truths and that those truths are so self-evident that they need not be defended or supported. Among the culturally accepted truths which most twentieth-century Americans accept are the following:

> "Every individual should receive equal treatment under the law."

> "Everyone has the right to life, liberty, and the pursuit of happiness."

> "Democracy is the best form of government."

A *warrant*, which Stephen Toulmin explains in *The Uses of Argument*, is a statement which will be acceptable to the audience being targeted by the writer. It is a statement the audience will permit the writer to make. The audience will be willing to grant the writer permission to make the warranted statement without supporting it.

An *assumption* is a supposition that something is true. We all make assumptions about knowledge, values, beliefs, attitudes, and even facts. Sometimes our assumptions are valid; other times they are not. As writers we make assumptions about what our audience believes and will accept, about what the audience will accept with a minimum amount of support, and about what the audience will only accept with overwhelming evidence and reasons.

The following are all assumptions which a writer may be willing to make, but which the reader or audience has no reason to accept:

> "If I try hard enough and study long enough, may teacher will pass me in calculus."

> "If I can get my teacher to like me, I can pass calculus."

> "If I let my teacher know that I have a 4.0 average in other courses, I can pass calculus."

PLANNING TO WRITE

In order to write a good essay, nearly all students need to follow these steps (although some will do so in differing orders). A very few first rate writers have so much practice and are so skilled in writing that they can do these steps in their heads; yet even they may find they can save time and avoid excessive revision if they write out these steps. Most of us, however, will find it essential to take the time to thoroughly work out each of these steps on paper in order to write a good essay.

General Preliminary Planning

Before beginning to write, a writer must consider several things: the purpose of the essay, the audience, the writer's persona (the mask or appearance the writer wants to convey to the reader), the thesis question to be answered in the essay, and the thesis sentence and correlative main ideas which will control the essay.

Before beginning to write or even outline, it is useful for the writer to make notes of anything that he or she thinks of with regard to the subject. It is especially useful to make decisions about *purpose, audience, persona, thesis question,* and *thesis sentence.*

▪ **Purpose:** Purpose involves what effect the writer wants to have on the reader. The purpose is partly determined by the writer's attitude and beliefs about the subject. Sometimes there is a specific occasion, context, or document to which the writer is responding and which influences the writer's purpose.

▪ **Audience:** The audience is the intended reader of the discourse. For most university essays, the writer should 1) assume that the audience is made up of your fellow students and 2) assume that the audience disagrees with you.

▪ **Persona:** "Persona" means "mask." Persona is the kind of person the writer wants to seem to be to the reader of the discourse. Most of the time, one should simply try to write naturally and in such a way that he or she sounds like a serious, thoughtful university undergraduate. This means that one should use language and sentence structure that is comfortable, yet sufficiently formal for the university setting. One should *not* try to sound like a professor, a minister or rabbi, a politician, a high school coach, a high school cheerleader, or a comedian. One should not try to write satire or comedy—or even to sound witty.

One should avoid ***rhetorical questions*** (A rhetorical question is a question which suggests that you are sure that your audience will answer the question in a particular way, for example, "Do we want to continue to let drug lords, robbers, and murderers control our city streets?"). Instead of using questions, one should simply assert the idea that one is presenting.

■ **Thesis Question:** Sometimes—especially when a writer is not sure initially what idea to present—it is helpful, before formulating a thesis statement, to try to think of a thesis question—the question which the essay will answer. (An example of a thesis question that has been narrowed from the assigned subject of "government budget deficits" to "city zoo fees," might be "Should the city charge an entrance fee for admission to the zoo?")

Then, as one makes notes, one can make decisions on the specific pros and cons with respect to the subject and decide on an answer to the question. Then one can use one's answer (either "The city should charge entrance fees to the zoo." *or* "The city should not charge entrance fees to the zoo.") as the thesis statement.

Since it is difficult for most writers to utilize questions effectively in an essay, you should not include your thesis question in your essays. As stated above, you should also avoid rhetorical questions or other kinds of questions in your essays.

■ **Thesis Sentence:** The thesis should be stated as a sentence, usually at the beginning of an essay. A thesis sentence helps the writer to define his or her topic or point of view, to exclude unrelated material, to commit oneself to developing a theme in a particular manner and direction, and to signify major points in your discussion.

Since a thesis sentence, a section sentence or a topic sentence states an idea, it must be stated as a complete sentence or clause.

Expository writing:

"Many varieties of Texas flora and fauna are threatened with extinction."

"Americans believe in dozens of different cures for colds."

Persuasive or argumentative writing:

"Hunting is good for the deer population."

"Good high school coaches stress other things besides winning."

Personal writing:

"Nothing makes me as angry as people who cut in line."

"Daydreaming that I am skiing always cures me of depression."

The thesis is a one-sentence summary of the essay. It limits the subject to a specific, concrete idea. It should be a declarative sentence, not a question. The thesis should discuss the topic ("Pollution is a serious problem . . ."), not about the essay itself ("This paper will discuss . . .").

The thesis and essay should not include references to the writer either in the third person ("The writer of this paper is convinced . . ." or "It appears to this writer that . . .") or in the first person ("I intend to discuss . . ." or "My thesis is . . ."). The thesis and essay should never use the first person plural pronoun ("We can see that . . ." or "It is obvious to us that . . ."). The thesis and essay should not use second person pronouns, either to address the reader or to mean "everyone" except in writing directions—like this book—for your reader to follow. One should, therefore, omit phrases like "You can see that . . ." or "On a busy freeway you feel . . . ."

■ **Main Ideas and Structure of a Discourse:** Any nonfiction discourse should be controlled by main ideas and developed with subordinate ideas, evidence, and reasons.

■ **Other Preliminary Considerations:**

Size of subject and *narrowing*: The subject should be narrowed until it is small enough to be fully developed in the length of discourse the writer plans to write. Nearly always the writer will need to narrow whatever subject he or she initially considers.

Emphasis: The emphasis a writer decides upon for a discourse involves making decisions analogous to the decisions a photographer must make before shooting a photography.

> *Lens:* Through what lens or from what perspective will the subject be viewed? The writer may choose to consider the subject from a personal, political, sociological, ecological, economic, or other perspective.
>
> **Focus:** To what does the discourse draw the reader's attention?
>
> *Foregrounding:* What in particular will be brought to the front and center of the discourse; i.e. will be stressed as most important?

Sample Thesis Questions

Example 1

[People have said that beasts do not think.] Could abstract thought be a matter not of kind but of degree? Could other animals be capable of abstract thought but more rarely or less deeply than humans?

From "The Abstractions of Beasts," Carl Sagan

Example 2

Why do I want a wife?

From "Why I Want a Wife," Judy Syfers

Sample Thesis Sentences

Example 1

For Chaucer and his contemporaries . . . lived in terms of time. But their calender and time-piece was that sky through which moved immutably along pre-destined tracks the planets and the constellations. And no change, perhaps, wrought by the five centuries between us is more revealing of material differences than that shift of attitude towards 'this brave o'erhanging firmament,' the sky. And it is that change . . . that I wish . . . to make clear.

From "Time in the Middle Ages," John Livingston Lowes

Example 2

Death is still a fearful, frightening happening, and the fear of death is a universal fear even if we think we have mastered it on many levels. What has changed is our way of coping and dealing with death and dying and our dying patients.

From "On the Fear of Death," Elizabeth Kübler-Ross

Example 3

Like Denmark, Sweden, Italy, and Bulgaria proved to be nearly immune to anti-Semitism, but of the three that were in the German sphere of influence, only the Danes dared speak out on the subject to their German masters.

From "Denmark and the Jews," Hannah Arendt

Example 4

How very often this sort of thing [discoveries made by intuition] must happen, and what a shame that scientists are so devoted to their belief in conscious thought that they so consistently obscure the actual methods by which they obtain their results.

From "The Eureka Phenomenon," Isaac Asimov

Example 5

Let half a dozen of the prestigious universities—Chicago, Stanford, the Ivy League—abolish grading and use testing only and entirely for pedagogic purposes as teachers see fit.

From "A Proposal to Abolish Grading," Ellen Goodman

Specific Planning

Although different writers follow different sequences in working their way through the basic writing steps, they nearly always do each of the following steps. Some proficient writers can easily do some of these steps in their minds, without writing them down, but most writers have to make preliminary notes and outlines.

1) Doing preliminary work: considering the rhetorical situation (purpose, audience, and persona), narrowing the topic, formulating a thesis, and main ideas.

2) Developing ideas: Determining subsidiary ideas. Developing ideas with evidence and/or reasons. Providing specific subsidiary evidence and/or reasons.

3) Organizing material (using classification, analysis, or another organizational method).

4) Ordering material.

5) If necessary, adding secondary discourse by providing definitions, comparisons, analogies, and/or explanations in other language systems.

6) Adding introductions, transitions, and conclusions.

7) Organizing compound and multiple discourse.

8) Completing, revising, and editing the final integrated essay.

Section I:
Materials: Elements
& Components

The materials of a discourse are the building blocks of which that discourse is constructed. The three basic elements of discourse are *ideas, evidence,* and *reasons.* These three elements can be combined in a variety of ways to make up the components with which the discourse is developed.

CHAPTER 2

Development: The Elements & Components

ARISTOTLE'S EVIDENCE AND ENTHYMEMES

In the last two thousand years rhetoricians have given a remarkable amount of attention to the ideas Aristotle (384-322 B. C.) presented about rhetoric—attention that is often focused on his topics—common and special. In focusing on the topics, many rhetoricians neglect his most basic assertions about rhetoric—assertions that were apparently so obvious to and so fully accepted by Aristotle and his peers that he apparently felt he had to only mention them. Only after presenting those basic assertions briefly does Aristotle then list all the other tactics, devices, techniques, and tricks he knows of with which a speaker can enhance a strong argument or compensate for a weak one. That list is what he calls the *topics*—which serves as a kind of handbook to remind a speaker of all of the tactics that might be used to enhance an argument. Aristotle assumes that a speaker will fully utilize all of the basic methods of argument at his command and only then enhance his argument with appropriate and effective topics. In focusing on the topics, subsequent rhetoricians have been analyzing the bath water while leaving the baby unattended in the bath.

At the heart of his *Rhetoric* Aristotle explains the basic methods of argument—doing so very briefly, apparently because those methods were known and accepted by his peers. In Book I, Chapter 2, Paragraph 1356, he speaks in "regard to the persuasion achieved by proof or apparent proof," saying—and this is so important that I want to quote it rather that merely summarize or paraphrase it:

> Just as in dialectic there is induction on the one hand and syllogism or apparent syllogism on the other, so it is in rhetoric. The *example* is an induction, the *enthymeme* is a syllogism, and the *apparent enthymeme* is an apparent syllogism. I call the enthymeme a

rhetorical syllogism, and the example a rhetorical induction. Everyone who effects persuasion through proof does in fact use either enthymemes or examples: there is no other way. (my emphasis)

He then repeats these assertions in slightly different words, then continues:

When we base the proof of a proposition on a number of similar cases, this is induction in dialectic, *example in rhetoric;* when it is shown that, certain propositions being true, a further and quite distinct proposition must also be true in consequence, whether invariably or usually, this is called *syllogism in dialectic, enthymeme in rhetoric.*

Aristotle then explains that

in some oratorical styles examples prevail, in others enthymemes; and in like manner, some orators are better at the former and some at the latter.

He then explains the tastes of his day—preferences for reasoning over evidence which prevailed in Western culture until after the Renaissance:

Speeches that rely on examples are as persuasive as the other kind, but those which rely on enthymemes excite louder applause.

(I, 2, 1356, Translator 26)

But twentieth century preferences have changed. Grounded in a science of measurement and analysis, we find evidence more persuasive then enthymeme; like Jack Webb of "Dragnet" we tend to say, "Just give me the facts, ma'am."

Aristotle also takes into account that some assertions require no support—either assertions which some have called "a priori assertions" and which Toulman calls "grants" or assertions which are self-evident. Aristotle says that a statement is persuasive and credible either because it is directly self-evident or because it appears to be proved from other statements that are so.

It is only after laying down these basic premises that Aristotle goes on to consider, first, the modes of persuasion (ethical, moral, and logical) and, still later, the common and special topics (topics for use in particular situations).

What is significant about his insistence that evidence and enthymeme are the bedrock—the foundation—on which any argument must be constructed, is that he identifies the two elements that are most basic to the modern understanding of what we call scientific method. We believe that the only "scientific" support for any theory or idea must be either ***evidence*** (what Aristotle calls "example") or ***reasons*** or ***logical deductions***—about general ideas or about the evidence itself (what Aristotle calls "enthymeme").

Over 2,000 years later, evidence and reasons are still the building blocks on which thinkers and scientists construct logical arguments. Evidence and reasons are the building blocks of the scientific method. In the following analysis of the scientific method by Robert Pirsig, notice that

- *observed results of experiments* produce *evidence*
- *hypotheses* correspond to *reasons*
- *statement of the problem* corresponds to *thesis question*, and
- *conclusion* corresponds to *thesis sentence*

"Scientific Method"
from *Zen and Motorcycle Maintenance*
Robert Pirsig

Two kinds of logic are used, inductive and deductive. Inductive inferences start   1
with observations of the machine and arrive at general conclusions. For example, if the cycle goes over a bump and the engine misfires, and then goes over another bump and the engine misfires, and then goes over another bump and the engine misfires, and then goes over a long smooth stretch of road and there is no misfiring, and then goes over a fourth bump and the engine misfires again, one can logically conclude that the misfiring is caused by the bumps. That is induction: reasoning from particular experiences to general truths.

Deductive inferences do the reverse. They start with general knowledge   2
and predict a specific observation. For example, if, from reading the hierarchy of facts about the machine, the mechanic knows the horn of the cycle is powered exclusively by electricity from the battery, then he can logically infer that if the battery is dead the horn will not work. That is deduction.

Solution of problems too complicated for common sense to solve is   3
achieved by long strings of mixed inductive and deductive inferences that weave back and forth between the observed machine and the mental hierarchy of the machine found in the manuals. The correct program for this interweaving is formalized as scientific method.

Actually I've never seen a cycle-maintenance problem complex enough   4
really to require full-scale formal scientific method. Repair problems are not that hard. When I think of formal scientific method an image sometimes

comes to mind of an enormous juggernaut, a huge bulldozer—slow, tedious, lumbering laborious, but invincible. It takes twice as long, five times as long, maybe a dozen times as long as informal mechanic's techniques, but you know in the end you're going to get it. There's no fault isolation problem in motorcycle maintenance that can stand up to it. When you've hit a really tough one, tried everything, racked your brain and nothing works, and you know that this time Nature has really decided to be difficult, you say, "Okay, Nature, that's the end of the *nice* guy, and you crank up the formal scientific method.

For this you keep a lab notebook. Everything gets written down, formally, 5 so that you know at all times where you are, where you've been, where you're going and where you want to get. In scientific work and electronics technology this is necessary because otherwise the problems get so complex you get lost in them and confused and forget what you know and what you don't know and have to give up. In cycle maintenance things are not that involved, but when confusion starts it's a good idea to hold it down by making everything formal and exact. Sometimes just the act of writing down the problems straightens out your head as to what they really are.

The logical statements entered into the notebook are broken down into six 6 categories: (1) statement of the problem, (2) hypotheses as to the cause of the problem, (3) experiments designed to test each hypothesis, (4) predicted results of the experiments, (5) observed results of the experiments and (6) conclusions from the results of the experiments. This is not different from the formal arrangement of many college and high-school lab notebooks but the purpose here is no longer just busywork. The purpose now is precise; guidance of thoughts that will fail if they are not accurate.

The real purpose of scientific method is to make sure Nature hasn't misled 7 you into thinking you know something you don't actually know. There's not a mechanic or scientist or technician alive who hasn't suffered from that one so much that he's not instinctively on guard. That's the main reason why so much scientific and mechanical information sounds so dull and so cautious. If you get careless or go romanticizing scientific information, giving it a flourish here and there, Nature will soon make a complete fool out of you. It does it often enough anyway even when you don't give it opportunities. One must be extremely careful and rigidly logical when dealing with Nature: one logical slip and an entire scientific edifice comes tumbling down. One false deduction about the machine and you can get hung up indefinitely.

In Part One of formal scientific method, which is the statement of the 8 problem, the main skill is in stating absolutely no more than you are positive you know. It is much better to enter a statement "Solve Problem: Why doesn't cycle work?" which sounds dumb but is correct, than it is to enter a statement "Solve Problem: What is wrong with the electrical system?" when you don't absolutely *know* the trouble is *in* the electrical system. What you should state is

"Solve Problem: 9

What is wrong with cycle?" and *then* state as the first entry of Part Two: "Hypothesis Number One: The trouble is in the electrical system." You think of as many hypotheses as you can, then you design experiments to test them to see which are true and which are false

This careful approach to the beginning questions keeps you from taking a   10 major wrong turn which might cause you weeks of extra work or can even hang you up completely. Scientific questions often have a surface-appearance of dumbness for this reason. They are asked in order to prevent dumb mistakes later on.

Part Three, that part of formal scientific method called experimentation, is   11 sometimes thought of by romantics as all of science itself because that's the only part with much visual surface. They see lots of test tubes and bizarre equipment and people running around making discoveries. They do not see the experiment as part of a larger intellectual process and so they often confuse experiments with demonstrations, which look the same. A man conducting a gee-whiz science show with fifty thousand dollars' worth of Frankenstein equipment is not doing anything scientific if he knows beforehand what the results of his efforts are going to be. A motorcycle mechanic, on the other hand, who honks the horn to see if the battery works is informally conducting a true scientific experiment. He is testing a hypothesis by putting the question to nature. The TV scientist who mutters sadly, "The experiment is a failure; we have failed to achieve what we had hoped for," is suffering mainly from a bad scriptwriter. An experiment is never a failure solely because it fails to achieve predicted results. An experiment is a failure only when it also fails adequately to test the hypothesis in question, when the data it produces don't prove anything one way or another.

Skill at this point consists of using experiments that test only the hypothe-   12 sis in question, nothing less, nothing more. If the horn honks, and the mechanic concludes that the whole electrical system is working, he is in deep trouble. He has reached an illogical conclusion. The honking horn only tells him that the battery and horn are working. To design an experiment properly he has to think very rigidly in terms of what directly causes what. This you know from the hierarchy. The horn doesn't make the cycle go. Neither does the battery, except in a very indirect way. The point at which the electrical system directly causes the engine to fire is at the spark plugs, and if you don't test here, at the output of the electrical system, you will never really know whether the failure is electrical or not.

To test properly the mechanic removes the plug and lays it against the   13 engine so that the base around the plug is electrically grounded, kicks the starter lever and watches the spark-plug gap for a blue spark. If there isn't any he can conclude one of two things: (a) there is an electrical failure or (b) his experiment is sloppy. If he is experienced he will try it a few more times, checking connections, trying every way he can think of to get that plug to fire. Then, if he can't get it to fire, he finally concludes that a is correct, there's an electrical failure, and the experiment is over. He has proved that his hypothesis is correct.

In the final category, conclusions, skill comes in stating no more than the 14 experiment has proved. It hasn't proved that when he fixes the electrical system the motorcycle will start. There may be other things wrong. But he does know that the motorcycle isn't going to run until the electrical system is working and he sets up the next formal question: "Solve problem: what is wrong with the electrical system?"

He then sets up hypotheses for these and tests them. By asking the right 15 questions and choosing the right tests and drawing the right conclusions the mechanic works his way down the echelons of the motorcycle hierarchy until he has found the exact specific cause or causes of the engine failure, and then he changes them so that they no longer cause the failure.

An untrained observer will see only physical labor and often get the idea 16 that physical labor is mainly what the mechanic does. Actually the physical labor is the smallest and easiest part of what the mechanic does. By far the greatest part of his work is careful observation and precise thinking. That is why mechanics sometimes seem so taciturn and withdrawn when performing tests. They don't like it when you talk to them because they are concentrating on mental images, hierarchies, and not really looking at you or the physical motorcycle at all. They are using the experiment as part of a program to expand their hierarchy of knowledge of the faulty motorcycle and compare it to the correct hierarchy in their mind. They are looking at underlying form. (p. 103)

TYPES OF PARAGRAPHS

In non-fiction discourse there are two kinds of paragraphs, with quite different functions. **Coherence paragraphs** (*introductory paragraphs*, *concluding paragraphs*, and *transition paragraphs*) help the reader follow the ideas of the discourse. They serve as signposts guiding the reader and do not usually contain development.

Development paragraphs (usually called *body paragraphs*), on the other hand, have the responsibility of clarifying, explaining, and supporting the ideas the writer is presenting to the reader.

A well-made development paragraph is a group of sentences, often eight or more, supporting and explaining the idea expressed in its topic sentence with evidence and reasons. A well-made development paragraph develops an idea (usually called a *topic sentence*), which is usually the first sentence in the paragraph. For expository discourse, the topic sentences are usually generalizations. (Ex.: "Many people used to smoke in public places.") For argumentative discourse, the topic sentences are usually assertions (Ex.: "Smoking should be banned in public places.") For expressive discourse, the topic sentences are usually personal opinions (Ex.: "I hate to breathe cigarette or cigar smoke." or "I should be allowed to smoke wherever I want to.")

ELEMENTS

Expository prose is comprised of certain basic *materials*. Those materials include the three basic *elements* of which non-fiction discourse is constructed—ideas, evidence, and reasons—and of a variety of components which can be constructed from those elements.

Effective paragraphs are usually *developed* with traditional content and ordered in a traditional manner. The *topic sentences* and *sub-topic sentences* (main ideas which may be generalizations, assertions, or opinions) are supported and developed with the following *elements*:

- *Ideas*

- *Evidence:* facts, examples, details, statistics

- *Reasons:* explanations, interpretations, logical deductions

- Developmental paragraphs also usually include some *coherence devices* which guide the reader by indicating the relationship between the elements.

Evidence

Evidence is any presentation of facts—of empirically verified or verifiable data. Evidence includes *examples, facts, statistics,* and *details.*

For evidence to be effective, it must be specific. If one wants to argue that college students surround themselves by too many distractions to be able to study well, one must provide very specific examples.

The following statements are so general that they are not examples; in fact they are so general that they are virtually meaningless:

1) They surround themselves with many luxuries.

2) They overcrowd their rooms.

3) Dorm rooms are so messy that they would be hard to study in.

4) They try to study with too many distracting things going on.

5) They try to do two or more things at once.

All of these statements suggest that the writer is beginning to think about some ways of developing his or her paper, but the writer has only begun. Some writers may even think these statements are examples, but they are only somewhat narrower generalizations.

In order to provide examples that are convincing, the student must offer some very specific examples, such as the ones below:

1) They have refrigerators and microwave ovens.

2) They crowd reclining chairs in spaces that were intended for a desk chair.

3) They leave coats, shoes and socks, and books in piles on the floor.

4) They try to study while other students are in the room talking.

5) They try to study while watching television.

These examples could be made even more specific. If they were more specific, they would be even more effective. What could you do to make each of them more specific?

The following essays all contain some paragraphs which are developed by example.

In analyzing these paragraphs and essays, try to identify the main ideas of each developmental paragraph and the evidence which is used to support each of those ideas. Nearly all of these readings contain material other than ideas and evidence, but for the time being, only identify the ideas and evidence.

Samples with Evidence

The following paragraphs utilize coordinate, subordinate, and mixed levels of development, and the paragraphs utilize differing numbers of levels of development. In some of the paragraphs, the function of various parts of the paragraph is indicated by type face:

Ideas are in bold-face type	(RED)
Evidence is in plain type	(ORANGE)
REASONS ARE IN SMALL CAPS	(YELLOW)
~~Irrelevant material will be marked out~~	(BROWN)
~~Repetitious and overly wordy discourse~~	(BLACK)
Secondary discourse is in italics	(GREEN)

Example 1

We hunted old bottles in the dump, bottles caked with dirt and filth, half buried, full of cobwebs, and we washed them out at the horse trough by the elevator, putting in a handful of shot along with the white water to knock the dirt loose, and when we had shaken them until our arms were tired, we hauled them off in somebody's coaster wagon and turned them in at Bill Anderson's pool hall, where the smell of lemon pop was so sweet on the dark pool hall air I am sometimes awakened by it in the night even yet.

From "The Town Dump," *Wolf Willow*, Wallace Stegner

Example 2

It was as an extension, a living suburb, as it were, of the dumpground that we most valued those camps. We scoured them for artifacts of their migrant tenants as if they had been archaeological sites full of secrets of ancient civilization. I remember toting around for weeks the broken cheek strap of a bridle. Somehow or other its buckle looked as if it had been fashioned in a far place, a place where they were accustomed to flatten the tongues of buckles for reasons that could only be exciting, and where they made a habit of plating the buckle with some valuable alloy, probably silver. In places where the silver was worn away that buckle underneath shone dull yellow: probably gold.

From "The Town Dump," *Wolf Willow*, Wallace Stegner

Example 3

We have waited for more than 340 years for our constitutional and God-given rights. *The nations of Asia and Africa are moving with jetlike speed toward gaining political independence, but we still creep at horse and buggy pace toward gaining a cup of coffee at a lunch counter.* Perhaps it is easy for those who have never felt the stinging darts of segregation to say, "Wait." But when you have seen vicious mobs lynch your mothers and fathers at will and drown your sisters and brothers at whim; when you have seen hate filled policemen curse, kick, and even kill your black brothers and sisters; when you see the vast majority of your twenty million Negro brothers smothering in an airtight cage of poverty in the midst of an affluent society; when you suddenly find your tongue twisted and your speech stammering as you seek to explain to your six-year-old daughter why she can't go to the public amusement park that has just been advertised on television, and see tears welling up in her eyes when she is told that Funtown is closed to colored children, and see ominous clouds of inferiority beginning to form in her little mental sky, and see her beginning to distort her personality by developing an unconscious bitterness toward white people; when you have to concoct an answer for a five-year-old son who is asking, "Daddy, why do white people treat colored people so mean?"; when you take a crosscountry drive and find it necessary to sleep night after night in the uncomfortable corners of your automobile because no motel will accept you; when you are humiliated day in and day out by nagging signs reading "white" and "colored"; when your first name becomes "nigger," your middle name becomes "boy" (however old you are) and your last name becomes "John," and your wife and mother are never given the respected title "Mrs."; when you are harried by day and haunted by night by the fact that you are a Negro, living constantly at tiptoe stance, never quite knowing what to expect next, and are plagued with inner fears and outer resentments; when you are forever fighting a degenerating sense of "nobodiness"—**then you will understand why we find it difficult to wait. There comes a time when the cup of endurance runs over, and men are no longer willing to be plunged into the abyss of despair.** *I hope, sirs, you can understand our legitimate and unavoidable impatience.*

Paragraph 14 from "Letter from Birmingham Jail," Martin Luther King, Jr.

Example 4

I am thankful, however, that some of our white brothers in the South have grasped the meaning of this social revolution and committed themselves to it. They are still all too few in quantity, but they are big in quality. Some—such as Ralph McGill, Lillian Smith, Harry Golden, James McBridge Dabbs, Ann Braden, and Sarah Patton Boyle—have written about our struggle in eloquent and prophetic terms. Others have marched with us down nameless streets of the South. They have languished in filthy, roach-infested jails, suffering the abuse and brutality of policemen who view them as "dirty niggerlovers." *Unlike so many of their moderate brothers and sisters,* THEY HAVE RECOGNIZED THE URGENCY OF THE MOMENT AND SENSED THE NEED FOR POWERFUL "ACTION" *antidotes* TO COMBAT *the disease of* SEGREGATION.

Paragraph 32 from "Letter from Birmingham Jail," Martin Luther King, Jr.

Example 5

I was going to be lovely. A walking model of all the various styles of fine sewing and it didn't worry me that I was only twelve years old and merely graduating from the eighth grade. Besides, many teachers in Arkansas Negro schools had only that diploma and were licensed to impart wisdom.

From "Graduation," Maya Angelou

Example 6

Rungsted is a sea town on the coast road between Copenhagen and Elsinore. Among eighteenth-century travelers the otherwise undistinguished village was well known for the handsomeness of its Inn. The Inn, though it no longer obliges coachmen and their passengers, is still renowned: as the home of Rungsted's first citizen, the Baroness Blixen, alias Isak Dinesen, alias Pierre Andrezel.

The Baroness, weighing a handful of feathers and fragile as a *coquillage* sprinkled bouquet, entertains callers in a sparse, sparkling parlor sprinkled with sleeping dogs and warmed by a fireplace and a porcelain stove: a room where she, an imposing creation come forward from one of her own Gothic tales, sits bundled in bristling wolfskins and British tweeds, her feet fur-booted, her legs, thin as the thighs of an ortolan, encased in woolen hose, and her neck, round which a ring could fit, looped with frail lilac scarves. Time has refined her; this legend who has lived the adventures of an iron-nerved man: shot charging lions and infuriated buffalo, worked an African farm, flown over Kilimanjaro in the perilous first planes, doctored the Masai.

From "Isak Dinesen," Truman Capote

"Nothing to Report"
Jonathan Schell

Whereas most conventional bombs produce only one destructive effect—the shock wave—nuclear weapons produce many destructive effects. At the moment of the explosion, when the temperature of the weapon material, instantly gasified, is at the superstellar level, the pressure is millions of times the normal atmospheric pressure. Immediately, radiation, consisting mainly of gamma rays, which are a very high-energy form of electromagnetic radiation, begins to stream outward into the environment. This is called the "initial nuclear radiation," and is the first of the destructive effects of a nuclear explosion. In an air burst of a one-megaton bomb—a bomb with the explosive yield of a million tons of TNT, which is a medium-sized weapon in present-day nuclear arsenals—the initial nuclear radiation can kill unprotected human beings in an area of some six square miles. Virtually simultaneously with the initial nuclear radiation, in a second destructive effect of the explosion, an electromagnetic pulse is generated by the intense gamma radiation acting on the air. In a high-altitude detonation, the pulse can knock out electrical equipment over a wide area by inducing a powerful surge of voltage through various conductors, such as antennas, overhead power lines, pipes, and railroad tracks. The Defense Department's Civil Preparedness Agency reported in 1977 that a single multi-kiloton nuclear weapon detonated one hundred and twenty-five miles over Omaha, Nebraska, could generate an electromagnetic pulse strong enough to damage solid-state electrical circuits throughout the entire continental United States and in part of Canada and Mexico and thus threaten to bring the economies of these countries to a halt. When the fusion and fission reactions have blown themselves out, a fireball takes shape. As it expands, energy is absorbed in the form of X-rays by the surrounding air, and then the air re-radiates a portion of that energy into the environment in the form of the thermal pulse—a wave of blinding light and intense heat—which is the third of the destructive effects of a nuclear explosion. (If the burst is low enough, the fireball touches the ground, vaporizing or incinerating almost everything within it.) The thermal pulse of a one-megaton bomb lasts about ten seconds and can cause second-degree burns in exposed human beings at a distance of nine and a half miles, or in an area of more than two hundred and eighty square miles, and that of a twenty megaton bomb (a large weapon by modern standards) lasts for about twenty seconds and can produce the same consequences at a distance of twenty-eight miles, or in an area of two thousand four hundred and sixty square miles. As the fireball expands, it also sends out a blast wave in all directions, and this is the fourth destructive effect of the explosion. The blast wave of an air-burst one-megaton bomb can flatten or severely damage all but the strongest buildings within a radius of four and a half miles, and that of a twenty-megaton bomb can do the same within a radius of twelve miles. As the fireball burns, it rises, condensing water from the surrounding atmosphere to form the characteristic mushroom cloud. If the bomb has been set off on the ground or close enough to it so that the fireball touches the surface, in a so-called ground burst, a crater will be formed, and tons of dust and debris will be fused with the intensely radioactive fission products and sucked up into the mushroom cloud. This mixture will return to earth as radioactive fallout, most of it in the form of fine ash, in the fifth destructive effect of the explosion. Depending upon the composition of the surface, from forty to seventy per cent of this fallout—often called the "early" or "local" fallout—descends to earth within about a day of the explosion, in the vicinity of the blast and downwind from it, exposing human beings to radiation disease, an illness that is fatal when exposure is intense. Air bursts may also produce local fallout, but in much smaller quantities. The lethal range of the local fallout depends on a number of circumstances, including the weather, but under average conditions a one-megaton ground burst would, according to the report by the Office of Technology Assessment, lethally contaminate over a thousand square miles. (A lethal dose, by convention, is considered to be the amount of radiation that, if delivered over a short period of time, would kill half the able-bodied young adult population.)

Essays with Examples

Notice that the following paragraphs from "Morocco's Ancient City of Fez" have mixed purposes—primarily to describe a place, but also to include some narration.

"Morocco's Ancient City of Fez"

Harvey Arden

Night doesn't fall in Fez. It rises. Hardly has the glaring African sun dipped 1
behind the hills than the darkness wells up from the deep bowl in which the city
huddles. The shadows seep quickly upward through claustrophobically narrow
streets, pooling inside the thick walls that hug this 1,200-year-old spiritual capital of Morocco in a crumbling stone embrace.

For a few moments only the tops of the minarets remain sun struck. Then 2
they too, like candles on a cake of stone, are snuffed out from below by the rising darkness.

Elsewhere it is still afternoon; in Fez it is night. Elsewhere it is still the 3
20th century; in Fez it is the Middle Ages.

The city has many names, many identities: Fez el Bali, or Fez the Old, 4
founded about A.D. 800; Fez the Holy, one of the most renowned religious cen-
ters of the Muslim world; Fez the Imperial, one of the four great capitals (along
with Marrakech, Rabat, and Meknés) of Morocco's ruling dynasties; Fez the
Secret, city of political intrigue and labyrinthine streets whose dizzying turnings
seem always to lead to a windowless wall and a locked door with its iron grating
rusted shut.

Add to these one modern title: Fez the Endangered, a city fighting for its 5
very survival as it threatens to implode from age, disrepair, and staggering population pressures.

Night had already risen when I arrived, hot and dusty, after the four-hour 6
taxi ride from Casablanca. It was mid-September; tail end of the hot season that
moves up here in summer from the Sahara, some 250 miles south. Temperatures in July and August routinely hit 110°F, and even now hovered in the
mid-90s—reminder of the lingering years-long drought that had driven tens of
thousands of mountain Arabs and Berbers out of the flanking Rif and Atlas
ranges into already desperately overcrowded Fez.

We dipped out of the late afternoon daylight into a deep pool of dark blue 7
shadows at the bottom of which the old walled city—Fez el Bali—submerged
like some ethereal Atlantis, its few electric lights winking fitfully as if about to
sputter out. Our headlights gave dim glimpses of a timeworn stone wall on the
right and, on the left, a vast cemetery whose ghost-white tombstones marched
up a hill to the skeletal remains of some shattered building.

We came at last to a weathered Moorish gateway, and I wondered where in 8
this medieval world my modern hotel could possibly be located. Honking some
donkeys out of the way, we drove inside.

I blinked my eyes. There, indeed, was the hotel—the Palais Jamai— 9
a gracious pink building rising amid the pleasure gardens of a 10th-century
vizier's palace. The taxi door was opened by a tall, fiercely mustachioed man in

a white toga-like djellaba. A paradigm of Moroccan traditional dress, he sported   10
a long, curving, silver-sheathed dagger; pointed yellow slip-ons, or babouches,
and a black-tasseled fez—the cylindrical Islamic headgear whose distinctive
bright red color (today simulated with chemicals) in ancient times derived from
natural dyes now lost to memory.

    Taking one fleeting look at my dusty visage and disheveled clothes, the   11
impeccably attired doorman smiled imperiously, sniffed, and allowed a bellboy
to wrestle with my luggage.

    After dining on French haute cuisine—France, it must be remembered,   12
ruled Morocco from 1912 to 1956—I walked outside for an introductory stroll.
It was already past eight, and the little hotel plaza was all shadows. One of
these shadows now detached itself from the others. The tall and gangling figure
of a man in jeans, T-shirt, and sneakers materialized before me.

    "A big welcome to you, sir!" came his husky voice. "You are American,   13
yes? May I have the honor of showing you our city?"

    I mumbled, "No, thank you," and turned down a small dark street. He   14
followed.

    "Very easy to get lost in Fez," he persisted. "May I walk with you?   15
Please, no money. I am not an official guide. But you can help me with my
English, and I can help you with the streets. We can be friends, yes? Is good
to have a friend who knows the way."

    I glanced warily down the long-shadowed street. This fellow's company, I   16
decided, was worth chancing for a few minutes and so I met Abdellatif, the wonderful Fezzi who was to become my constant companion. Together we strode
down that dark street, turned a blind corner; and entered the 14th century.

    We came out on a plaza at the center of the medina, the old city. It was   17
crowded with people—little girls carrying wooden trays of oven-bound bread
dough on their heads, veiled women doing the family wash at an exquisitely
tiled public fountain, a bearded old man selling caged birds, old Berber ladies
with tattooed chins squatting on the curbs with their hands held out in supplica-
tion, ragged porters lashing slow-moving donkeys loaded down with ice and
sheepskins and Pepsi-Cola cases.

    "No cars here, not even motorcycles," Abdellatif said. "The donkey is the   18
taxi of the medina!"

    The night air was clangorous with the rhythmic hammerings of the iron-   19
workers at work on their kettles, coppersmiths beating a syncopated tap-da-tap-
tap-da-tap on their ornate trays, the rasping voices of the street vendors, the
tinsely laughter of schoolgirls in their crisp pastel smocks, and, above it all, the
raucous crying of the roosters, which seem to crow all night from the rooftops
as if announcing some perpetual dawn of the spirit.

    Adding to the sensory assault were a thousand tingling aromas of spices   20
and newly cut cedarwood, of singed oxhorn (used for combs) and sizzling hot

cooking oil, of freshly baked bread and ugly-smelling animal hides—all simmer-   21
ing together, as it were, in the warm night air.

   This is Fez as it has always been—a huge emporium of craftsmen, traders   22
merchants, and hustlers of every variety, all converging on this great inland
crossroads linking the Mediterranean and the Sahara, the Atlantic and Algeria.

   Abdellatif led me through a tangled skein of dark alleyways, and suddenly,   23
turning one last blind corner, we were back—somehow—at the Palais Jamai.

   That night, a little after 4 a.m., a voice woke me as if in a dream. I stum-   24
bled out of bed and out onto the balcony. It was the muezzin of a nearby
mosque, calling the faithful to early morning prayer. His voice, a piercing tenor,
came right out of the night sky. *"allaha akba-r-r-r-r,"* it cried—"God is great!"

"China Still Lifes"
William H. Gass

If you are a visitor in Beijing, a bus will take you to the Great Wall where the   1
people clambering about on it will likely outnumber the stones. However, not
everyone in China is standing inside the circle of the buses, breathing his last, or
pushing his way up that ancient barrier's many steps and steep slopes, although
it may seem so; nor is the Great Wall this incredible country's only dragon-
shaped defender, because a billion people require the comfort of at least a million walls: walls concealing houses, safeguarding factories, lending themselves
to banks and office buildings, hotels and new construction, defining villages,
compounds, parks, and squares, protecting pagodas, temples, shrines, and
palaces; and along the top of many of these walls a snakelike creature made of
slate and tile and stucco seems to crawl, its odd equine head bearing a dog's
teeth, with thin wire flames, like antennae, breathing from its nose. For all their
apparent ferocity, the intentions of these monsters are pacific, as are the quiet
courses of fired clay they serpentine upon. The city streets themselves appear
to pass between walls and beneath trees as if they were enclosed, and the shops
open out into them as open doors pour into halls.

   In Beijing, alongside even the immediate edge of an avenue, rank after rank   2
of potted flowers have been brought to attention—thousands of salvias, for
instance, clearly a favorite—as if a pot had to be put out for every cyclist who
might possibly pass. These are protected by low wire loops or sometimes by an
iron fence of impeccable design when it is not displaying panda-covered kitsch.
Success is hit or miss. For the cyclists, too, collisions are not infrequent. I saw
a small truck run over a wheel and a leg as though they were bumps in the road.
The wheel bent like soft tin and the cyclist's mouth went "O." Cyclists *are* the
street as water is the river; and you can walk across in safety only if your movements are slow and deliberate and resemble a stone's. The bikes sail down the

dark streets at night and show no lights, though the buses like to flare theirs. The Chinese say they do it for safety's sake, but each burst is blinding. In their own much narrower lanes, which in intersections they cannot keep to, trucks and buses honk and growl; you will hear occasionally a hawker's cry; otherwise the city is silent except for the continuous ching-a-ching of the bicycle bells. Serenity is always startling. You take close hold of yourself as if your spirit were about to float away, and you say: "Perhaps it's true, and I have a soul after all, other than the one emitted by the exhaust pipe of the motorcar."

Near the long red line of blooming plants, as if to root them for as many   3
seasons as the trees shall persevere, there is a grand row or two of weeping birch or sycamore, then a handsome wide walk—crowded of course—and finally the rich red or yellow plastered wall of a public garden or royal house, the whitewashed wall of a simple shop, or often, in the poorer quarters, one of loosely stacked brick in both alternating and parallel courses, in chevrons, on edge, at length, sometimes like a pattern book they lie so side by side in every posture, frequently free of mortar too, the builder expressing his mastery of economics, gravity, and tradition in the humblest stretch of work. These are walls against which the spangled shadows of the trees fall like a celebration, and through which the light runs like driven rain.

In China, to understand some of its most appealing aspects, necessity   4
should be the first stop for the mind. The comparative freedom of the streets from cars, the sidewalks from dogs, drunks, and vandals, the gutters from trash: these are a few of the slim benefits of poverty and a socialist state. The brooms of the sweepers pass beneath the feet of shoppers as if the shoppers' shoes were simply leaves. Pets compete for a desperately overstretched food supply, and are therefore only surreptitiously kept. And if an improving econo-my fills these beautiful streets with automobiles, it will be a calamity. But necessity is never to be admired; it is, at best, only the stepmother of invention; and in China, as elsewhere, it is the cause (or rather, the excuse) for hurried, cheap, high-rise buildings, which appear to repeat every greedy callous Western gesture.

One should not sentimentalize (at least not overly much) about the rich   5
street-and-alley culture of the slums, yet the cities of China are made of streets made of people—walking, biking, working, hanging out. In the paths between buildings there is a world of narrow outdoor rooms; along the walks of wider streets, goods are set out for display and sale; in the open doorways workers enjoy the air and light and sun while they repair shoes, sew, shave a round of wood for chopsticks, clean chickens, and wash pans. The edges of the street are lined with barrows, the center is filled with pedestrians, and out over every-one, from both sides, waves the household wash, hung from bamboo poles propped out of second-story windows and held firmly by a slammed sash. Hong Kong is a world away, but the poles still bristle from the windows of the

high rises there: a bit of wash can flutter away in the wind like a kite ten floors from the street; the sanitation is superior; water rises magically in hidden pipes; there is more than the personal forty square feet of living space which is Shanghai's average; and you can no longer see your neighbor, smell his fires—a situation which many planners and politicians approve. As a visitor, a Westerner, a tourist, unburdened by the local "necessities," I say, "Let the rich rot in their concrete trees like unpicked fruit, and leave the earth to the people."

For the curious passing eye, of course, these open doors and drawn shades, these tiny passageways and little courtyards, including every inadvertent jiggle in the course of the street, afford, literally, a sudden "insight." Chinese gardens, with their doorless doors, round as the eye says the world is, their Gibson girl and keyhole shaped gates, their doors framed like paintings or some times like windows, as well as every other kind of intermission in a wall that they delight in—punched, screened, glazed, shuttered, beaded, barred—have established the motif of the maze, that arena for interacting forms which seems endless in its arbitrary variety, yet one which does not entirely conceal its underlying plans, as zigzag bridges, covered paths, and pools of multiplying water make a small space large, and negligently wandering walls and their surprising openings constantly offer charming contorted eye lines, while contributing, along with the swooping roofs and undulating levels of the ground, to the ambiguity of every dimension, especially those of out and in, whose mixture is also the experience provided by the city streets. 6

The big cities now have vast blank squares like Tian Anmen in Beijing— they are people pastures, really—fit mainly for mass meetings, hysteria, and hypnotism, while the new wide and always wounding central avenues are suitable for totalitarian parades and military reviews; although it was no different in the old days, since some of the courtyards in the Imperial Palace can hold a hundred thousand heads together in a state of nodding dunder. This is one reason why it is comforting to find these streets, yards, and squares, filled with running children, strollers, and bicycles, because they are such splendid examples of free movement—of being "under one's own power." Walking, running, swimming, skating, cycling, support the moral realm, as sailing does, inasmuch as each seeks to understand and enjoy energies already present and often selfmade, whereas the horse, train, rocket, car and plane require and encourage the skills of domination on the one hand, and passivity on the other. The pedicab, alas, is coming back. And one sees people still pulling heavy loads like beasts. In such cases, the load is truly Lord and Master. But the present regime has lifted many a beastly burden from many a human back. I like to imagine that the warm blue autumn skies I enjoyed during most of my stay in China were the radiant reflection of the faces of the people. 7

That word, and the familiar image I have called back again into service—a stream of people—would not seem farfetched or even hackneyed if you were to 8 look down into Guangzhou's Renmin Road (or "street of the people") where a glut of pedestrians slowly moves, not impatiently, though shoulder to shoulder; but reflectively, as a crowd leaves after a splendid concert. It is not New Year's; it is not an occasion of any kind; it is simply midmorning, and the people twine through the streets, living as closely as fibers in cloth. In this crowded world the wall is like one of those inner skins that keeps organs from intervening in the actions of others; they corner chaos like an unruly dog and command its obedience. I saw in a park a pair of lovers fondling one another while lying perilously in the thick fork of a tree. Couples go to such places to quarrel, too, or work out their incompatibilities with one another's relatives, to play with the baby by themselves, or simply to have an unobstructed view of their spouse's face. It is that difficult to be alone.

Nor normally is the eye left empty. The tourist will have to look high and low for the fierce stone lion behind the stiff grins and adopted postures of the Chinese, one hundred of whom are having their pictures taken in the lap of a seated Buddha, on the back of a bronze ox, in front of a garden of rock, beside a still and helpless pool: by whatever seems majestical, ancient, and handy. The photographers thrust the camera toward the ground until it hangs from their arms like the seat of a swing. Taking aim from below their knees, they stare down at the viewfinder as though peering into a well. Whatever their reason (perhaps, like me, they are waiting for a clear shot), they take their time, so poses are held like bouquets.   9

That is, they try to stand as still as the burnished brass bowl or stone lamp or painted door they are leaning against. But their lips quiver and their eyes shift and the heart beats high up in their chest. Bystanders fidget and giggle. Movement, not fixity, neither of photograph or statue, is the essence of life. It is an ancient tenet. These walls that I have made the symbolic center of this piece might be thought to be in opposition to mutability and alteration, but in China this is not so. The Great Wall rolls over the mountain ridges like a coaster.   10

And within the walls, the walls walk; not slowly, according to some customary means of reckoning, but swiftly, each step of brick marking a year as sand does seconds sliding the sides of its glass; and it is perhaps this paradox we understand least when we try to understand China: how calm, how still, and how steadfastly sustaining change in China is; how quickly, like the expression on a face, even bronze can alter; how smartly the same state can come about like a sailboat in the wind; yet the bronze endures and maintains its vigil; the ship, the water, and the wind remain themselves while disappearing into their actions; so that now, as this great nation opens itself to the West and selects some Western ways to welcome, in nearly every chest, as though it shaped a soft cage for the soul, the revolution still holds its breath, while the breath itself goes in and out of its jar as anciently and as rhythmically, almost, as moods move through a man, and men move from one place to another like vagabonds.   11

The Great Wall rolls over its ridges, I dared to say, yet the Great Wall $\quad$ 12
stands. The Great Wall draws only tourists now who sometimes steal its
stones, not invaders or brigands. Still the Great Wall stands for the past. So it
is the past that rolls over the hills here; it is the past which stands, the past
which lures the tourist; and the past, when it speaks, speaks obsessively of
the present.

In China, the long dispute between tradition and revolution, rest and $\quad$ 13
motion, action and contemplation, openness and secrecy, commitment and
withdrawal, politics and art, the individual and the mass, the family and the
state, the convoluted and the simple continues with voices raised and much at
stake. That's why, perhaps, amid the crush and the closeness, the delighted yet
frantic building on a busy Shanghai street, I am brought face to face, not with
faces for a change, but with a weather-beaten wooden box, a bowl, a simple
pile of goods, all stacked so as to still life, and my sleeping sensuality is shaken
awake as it might be by an appealing nakedness.

Or perhaps I notice two women in the act of hanging out a bright banner $\quad$ 14
of wash, arrested for a moment by a thought; or I see on the sidewalk by my
feet a display of fruit or school of glistening silver fish or a spread of dried
mulberries in the center of which a butterfly has lit and now folds its black-
and-white wings.

Or it is a set of tools resting against a garden wall in such a way their $\quad$ 15
energies seem harmonized inside them; another time it is a group of whitewash
pots, jugs of wine, or sacks of grain, or an alley empty of everything but chickens, or a stretch of silent street with freshly washed honey pots, their lids ajar
to breathe, sunning themselves in the doorways. Chairs draped with bedding
may be taking the air; a brush has been thrust between a drainpipe and its
building to dry, an ooze of color down the wall like a drip of egg. Shadows of
trees, wires, wash, the tassels of lanterns: these further animate even the
busiest lanes. I fancy I see in them operatic masks, kites, the ghosts of
released balloons. Or you discover your own shadow cast across a golden
sheet of drying rice, and you realize that you are still at home in Missouri and
that this is your shade, loose in the midst of China's life.

The sill may rot, the bowl fall, but nothing is more ageless and enduring $\quad$ 16
than the simple act of sitting—simply being here or there. The alleys of every
city are creased by ledges, crannies, corners, cracks where a rag is wedged, a
pot of paint rests, or a basket hangs, a broom leans, a basin waits; and where a
plant, placed out of the way like a locked bike, is not a plant now, but will
resume its native movements later.

Down a whitewashed little lane in Suzhou, you may find white bread and $\quad$ 17
flour for sale on a white box beneath a white sheet stretched out like an
awning, and casting a shadow so pale it seems white as well. Through an open
window with blowing white curtains you will be handed your change in the
soiled palm of a white glove.

In the same lane is a teahouse where a Vermeer may be found: benches,   18
table, tray, row of glasses, teapot just so, wall right there—all composed and
rendered by the master. On top of the teahouse stove, the tools of the cook's
trade lie in a sensuous confusion akin to bedclothes. Even the steam holds its
shape and station like a spoon. In front of a few chairs, on a small stage, a
lectern for the storyteller has been placed. There is one chair on either side of
it, both draped with cloths. I make up an artificial audience, sitting there, looking at the wooden figures where the old tales are spoken, and I am truly over-
come by the richness of this world: its care for the small things; this tidiness
that transcends need and becomes art; the presence of the past in even the
most impoverished places and simplest things, for the act of recitation, too, is
as importantly immortal as the lean of a spade or a pot's rest.

China seems today in glorious and healthy tumult, but the visitor, charmed   19
by the plenitude or patient genius of the people, the vast landscape and exotic
monuments, should not neglect the corners of quiet—the resting bamboo boats
or idle ladders, the humblest honey pot or plastic purse or rouged wall—for
these things and spaces are everywhere as well, and they are easily as ancient,
fully as lively in their own interior way, and certainly as honestly and openly
sensual as any rice-ripe, yellow, autumn landscape or languorous stretch of
back or thigh.

So it is not by one of the many Buddhas one may see in China that I am   20
reminded of Rilke's poem about that figure,

> As if he listened. Silence: depth . . .
> And we hold back our breath.

nor is it while I am bemused by the admittedly similar grandeur of the burnished
bronze bowl that stands, in company with a carefully regulated tree, in front of a
bit of royal wall in the Imperial Palace Garden,

> Oh, he is fat. Do we suppose
> he'll see us? He has need of that

but during another kind of encounter entirely, in a commonplace Shanghai
street, with a bunch of baskets hung above a stone sink. There is a lame straw
fan nearby, and on the sink a blushing cup from which a watercolor brush has
been allowed to stick. What hidden field of force has drawn these objects into
their conjunction? A wooden bowl leans at the sink's feet, its rosy basin open to
the sun. Beside the sink sits a teapot, while behind it rises a pipe where a
washrag, dark still from its own dampness, dangles as though done for. There
is also a brazier by the sink's side like a sullen brother, a handled pot perched
uneasily on its head where a shiny tin lid similarly slides. On top of the sink,
again, an enameled saucer waits on a drainboard of worn wood. It contains
another jutting brush—a nice touch. It is by these plain things that the lines
about the Buddha were returned to my mind, for I was looking at the altar of a
way of life. The simple items of this precise and impertinent collection had been

arranged by circumstances so complex, historical, and social, so vagarious and yet determined, that I felt obliged to believe an entire culture—a whole people—had composed it. Vermeer indeed, or some solemn Buddha, could only hold a candle, as though they were another witness, to this peaceful and ardent gathering of things.

> For that which lures us to his feet
> has circled in him now a million years.
> He has forgotten all we must endure,
> encloses all we would escape.

Reasons

In this non-fiction discourse, *reasons* include not only reasons, but also any explanations, interpretations, or qualifying statements used to support ideas or to explain evidence of other reasons.

From the time of Aristotle until the European renaissance, most writers and thinkers preferred reasons rather than evidence as support for their ideas. But since the renaissance, Western civilization has gradually moved to a preference for evidence. Consequently it is not common to find a contemporary non-fiction discourse whose ideas are supported only by reasons. Because we still, like Aristotle in ancient Greece and scientists who use scientific method today, trust a combination of evidence and reasons, most arguments are made up of combinations of evidence and reasons. Most contemporary writers do not depend entirely on reasons even for a whole paragraph. Paragraphs 7 and 8 from William F. Buckley, Jr.'s "Why Don't We Complain?" are rare examples.

> I think it is safe to say that everybody suffered on that occasion. And I think it is safe to assume that everyone was expecting someone else to take the initiative in going back to speak to the manager. And it is probably true even that if we had supposed the movie would run right through the blurred image, someone surely would have summoned up the purposive indignation to get up out of his seat and file his complaint.
>
> But notice that no one did. And the reason no one did is because we are all increasingly anxious in America to be unobtrusive, we are reluctant to make our voices heard, hesitant about claiming our rights; we are afraid that our cause is unjust, or that if it is not unjust, that it is ambiguous; or if not even that, that it is too trivial to justify the horrors of a confrontation with Authority; we will sit in an oven or endure a racking headache before undertaking a head-on,

I'm-here-to-tell-you complaint. That tendency to passive compliance, to a heedless endurance, is something to keep one's eyes on—in sharp focus.

All of the following passages and essays all contain some paragraphs which are developed by evidence and reasons.

In analyzing these paragraphs and essays, try to identify the main ideas of each developmental paragraph, the evidence which is used to support each of those ideas, and the reasons which support the main ideas or explain the evidence. These readings contain material other than ideas, evidence, and reasons, but for the time being, only identify ideas, evidence, and reasons.

Samples with Evidence and Reasons

Reasons include *explanations, interpretations,* and *qualifications.*

Ideas are in bold-face type	(RED)
Evidence is in plain type	(ORANGE)
REASONS ARE IN SMALL CAPS	(YELLOW)
~~Irrelevant material will be marked out~~	(BROWN)
~~Repetitious and overly wordy discourse~~	(BLACK)
Secondary discourse is in italics	(GREEN)

Example 1

But again I am thankful to God that some noble souls from the ranks of organized religion have broken loose from the paralyzing chains of conformity and joined us as active partners in the struggle for freedom. They have left their secure congregations and walked the streets of Albany, Georgia, with us. They have gone down the highways of the South on tortuous rides for freedom. Yes they have gone to jail with us. Some have been dismissed from their churches, have lost the support of their bishops and fellow ministers. BUT THEY HAVE ACTED IN THE FAITH THAT RIGHT DEFEATED IS STRONGER THAN EVIL TRI-UMPHANT. THEIR WITNESS HAS . . . PRESERVED THE TRUE MEANING OF THE GOSPEL IN TROUBLED TIMES. THEY HAVE . . . [CREATED] HOPE [OUT OF] DISAPPOINTMENT.

Paragraph 43 from "Letter from Birmingham Jail," Martin Luther King, Jr.

Example 2

Sometimes a law is just on its face and unjust in its application. For instance, I have been arrested on a charge of parading without a permit. NOW, THERE IS NOTHING WRONG IN HAVING AN ORDINANCE WHICH REQUIRES A PERMIT FOR

A PARADE. BUT SUCH AN ORDINANCE BECOMES UNJUST WHEN IT IS USED TO MAINTAIN SEGREGATION AND TO DENY CITIZENS THE FIRST-AMENDMENT PRIVILEGE OF PEACEFUL ASSEMBLY AND PROTEST.

Paragraph 19 from "Letter from Birmingham Jail," Martin Luther King, Jr.

Example 3

I had also hoped that the white moderate would reject the myth concerning time in relation to the struggle for freedom. I have just received a letter from a white brother in Texas. He writes: "All Christians know that the colored people will receive equal rights eventually, but it is possible that you are in too great a religious hurry. It has taken Christianity almost two thousand years to accomplish what it has. The teachings of Christ take time to come to earth." SUCH AN ATTITUDE STEMS FROM A TRAGIC MISCONCEPTION OF TIME, FROM THE STRANGE IRRATIONAL NOTION THAT THERE IS SOMETHING IN THE VERY FLOW OF TIME THAT WILL INEVITABLY CURE ALL ILLS. ACTUALLY, TIME ITSELF IS NEUTRAL; IT CAN BE USED EITHER DESTRUCTIVELY OR CONSTRUCTIVELY. MORE AND MORE I FEEL THAT THE PEOPLE OF ILL WILL HAVE USED TIME MUCH MORE EFFECTIVELY THAN HAVE THE PEOPLE OF GOOD WILL.

Paragraph 26 from "Letter from Birmingham Jail," Martin Luther King, Jr.

Example 4

I wish you had commended the Negro sit-inners and demonstrators of Birmingham for their sublime courage, their willingness to suffer, and their amazing discipline in the midst of great provocation. One day the South will recognize its real heroes. They will be the James Merediths, WITH THE NOBLE SENSE OF PURPOSE THAT ENABLES THEM TO FACE JEERING AND HOSTILE MOBS, AND WITH THE AGONIZING LONELINESS THAT CHARACTERIZES THE LIFE OF THE PIONEER. They will be old, oppressed, battered Negro women, symbolized in a seventy-two-year-old woman in Montgomery, Alabama, who rose up with a sense of dignity and with her people decided not to ride segregated buses, and who responded with ungrammatical profundity to one who inquired about her weariness: "My feets is tired, but my soul is at rest." They will be the young high school and college students, the young ministers of the gospel and a host of their elders, courageously and nonviolently sitting in at lunch counters and willingly going to jail for conscience's sake. ONE DAY THE SOUTH WILL KNOW THAT WHEN THESE DISINHERITED CHILDREN OF GOD SAT DOWN AT LUNCH COUNTERS, THEY WERE IN REALITY STANDING UP FOR WHAT IS BEST IN THE AMERICAN DREAM AND FOR THE MOST SACRED VALUES IN OUR JUDAEO-CHRISTIAN HERITAGE, THEREBY BRINGING OUR NATION BACK TO THOSE GREAT WELLS OF DEMOCRACY WHICH WERE DUG DEEP BY THE FOUNDING FATHERS IN THE FORMULATION OF THE CONSTITUTION AND THE DECLARATION OF INDEPENDENCE.

Paragraph 47 from "Letter from Birmingham Jail," Martin Luther King, Jr.

Example 5

A newly invented metaphor assists thought by evoking a visual image, while on the other hand a metaphor which is technically "dead" (e.g. Iron resolution) has in effect reverted to being an ordinary word and can generally be used without loss of vividness. But in between these two classes **there is a huge dump of worn-out metaphors which have lost all evocative power and are merely used because they save people the trouble of inventing phrases for themselves.** Examples are: Ring the changes on, take up the cudgels for, toe the line, ride roughshod over, stand shoulder to shoulder with, play into the hands of, no axe to grind, grist to the mill, fishing in troubled waters, on the order of the day, Achilles' heel, swan song, hotbed. MANY OF THESE ARE USED WITHOUT KNOWLEDGE OF THEIR MEANING (WHAT IS A "RIFT," FOR INSTANCE?), AND INCOMPATIBLE METAPHORS ARE FREQUENTLY MIXED, A SURE SIGN THAT THE WRITER IS NOT INTERESTED IN WHAT HE IS SAYING. SOME METAPHORS NOW CURRENT HAVE BEEN TWISTED OUT OF THEIR ORIGINAL MEANING WITHOUT THOSE WHO USE THEM EVEN BEING AWARE OF THE FACT. For example, "toe the line" is sometimes written "tow the line." Another example is the hammer and the anvil. IN REAL LIFE IT IS ALWAYS THE ANVIL THAT BREAKS THE HAMMER, NEVER THE OTHER WAY ABOUT: a writer who stopped to think about what he was saying would be aware of this, and would avoid perverting the original phrase.

From "Politics and the English Language," George Orwell

Decide the function of each part of the following paragraphs, and underline with the appropriate color.

Example 6

The idea of the child as property has always bothered me, for personal reasons I shall outline. I lack the feeling that I own my children and I have always scoffed at the idea that what they are and do is a continuation or a rejection of my being. I like them. I sympathize with them. I acknowledge the obligation to support them for a term of years—but I am not so fond or foolish as to regard a biological tie as a lien on their loyalty or respect, nor to imagine that I am equipped with preternatural powers of guidance as to their success and happiness. Beyond inculcating some of the obvious social protocols required in civilized life, who am I to pronounce on what makes for a happy or successful life? Can we do better with our children? I am unimpressed, to say no more, with parents who have no great track record, presuming to oracular power in regard to their children's lives.

From "Confessions of an Erstwhile Child," Anonymous

Example 7

Like so much of this country, Banyan suggests something curious and unnatural. The lemon groves are sunken, down a three- or four-foot retaining

wall, so that one looks directly into their dense foliage, too lush, unsettlingly
glossy, the greenery of nightmare; the fallen eucalyptus bark is too dusty, a
place for snakes to breed. The stones look not like natural stones but like the
rubble of some unmentioned upheaval. There are smudge pots, and a closed
cistern. To one side of Banyan there is the flat valley, and to the other the San
Bernadino Mountains, a dark mass looming too high, too fast, nine, ten, eleven
thousand feet, right there above the lemon groves. At midnight on Banyan
Street there is no light at all, and no sound except the wind in the eucalyptus
and a muffled barking of dogs. There may be a kennel somewhere, or the dogs
may be coyotes.

From "Some Dreamers of the Golden Dream," Joan Didion

Example 8

Gifts from parents to children always carry the most meaningful messages. The way parents think about presents goes one step beyond the objects
themselves—the ties, dolls, sleds, record players, kerchiefs, bicycles and
model airplanes that wait by the Christmas tree. The gifts are, in effect, one
way of telling boys and girls, "We love you even though you have been a bad
boy all month" or "We love having a daughter" or, "We treat all our children
alike" or "It is all right for girls to have some toys made for boys" or, "This
alarm clock will help you get started in the morning all by yourself."
Throughout all the centuries since the invention of a Santa Claus figure who
represented a special recognition of children's behavior, good and bad, presents
have given parents a way of telling children about their love and hopes and
expectations for them.

From "The Gift of Autonomy," Margaret Mead

Example 9

But nothing in that end of town was as good as the dumpground that scat-
tered along a little runoff coulee dipping down toward the river from the south
bench. Through a historical process that went back, probably to the roots of
community sanitation and distaste for eyesores, but that in law dated from the
Unincorporated Towns Ordinance of the territorial government, passed in 1888,
the dump was one of the very first community enterprises, almost our town's
first institution.

More than that, it contained relics of every individual who had ever lived
there, and of every phase of the town's history.

The bedsprings on which the town's first child was begotten might be
there; the skeleton of a boy's pet colt; two or three volumes of Shakespeare
bought in haste and error from a peddler, later loaned in carelessness, soaked
with water and chemicals in a house fire, and finally thrown out to flap their
stained eloquence in the prairie wind.

Broken dishes, rusty tinware, spoons that had been used to mix paint; once a box of percussion caps, sign and symbol of the carelessness that most of those people felt about all matters of personal or public safety. We put them on the railroad tracks and were anonymously denounced in the *Enterprise*. There were also old iron, old brass, for which we hunted assiduously, by night conning junkmen's catalogues and the pages of the *Enterprise* to find how much wartime value there might be in the geared insides of clocks or in a pound of tea lead carefully wrapped in a ball whose weight astonished and delighted us.

Sometimes the unimaginable outside world reached in and laid a finger on us. I recall that, aged no more than seven, I wrote a St. Louis junk house asking if they preferred their tea lead and tinfoil wrapped in balls, or whether they would rather have it pressed flat in sheets, and I got back a typewritten letter in a window envelope instructing me that they would be happy to have it in any way that was convenient for me. They added that they valued my business and were mine very truly. Dazed, I carried that windowed grandeur around in my pocket until I wore it out, and for months I saved the letter as a souvenir of the wondering time when something strange and distinguished had singled me out.

From "The Town Dump," *Wolf Willow*, Wallace Stegner

Sample 10

They ate economically, but when he got diabetes in his forties and subsisted on lean meat and lettuce leaves, he remembered suet puddings, treacle puddings, raisin and currant puddings, steak and kidney puddings, bread and butter puddings, "batter cooked in the gravy with the meat," potato cake, plum cake, butter cake, porridge, with treacle, fruit tarts and pies, brawn, pig's trotters and pig's cheek and home-smoked ham and sausages. And "lashings of fresh butter and cream and eggs." He wondered if this diet had produced the diabetes, but said it was worth it.

From "My Father," Doris Lessing

"Why Don't We Complain?"

William F. Buckley, Jr.

It was the very last coach and the only empty seat on the entire train, so there   1
was no turning back. The problem was to breathe. Outside, the temperature was below freezing. Inside the railroad car the temperature must have been about 85 degrees. I took off my overcoat, and a few minutes later my jacket, and noticed that the car was flecked with the white shirts of the passengers. I soon found my hand moving to loosen my tie. From one end of the car to the other, as we rattled through Westchester County, we sweated; but we did not moan.

I watched the train conductor appear at the head of the car. "Tickets, all   2
tickets, please!" In a more virile age, I thought, the passengers would seize the
conductor and strap him down on a seat over the radiator to share the fate of
his patrons. He shuffled down the aisle, picking up tickets, punching commu-
tation cards. No one addressed a word to him. He approached my seat, and I
drew a deep breath of resolution. "Conductor," I began with a considerable
edge to my . . . . Instantly the doleful eyes of my seatmate turned tiredly from
his newspaper to fix me with a resentful stare: what question could be so
important as to justify my sibilant intrusion into his stupor? I was shaken by
those eyes. I am incapable of making a discreet fuss, so I mumbled a question
about what time we were due in Stamford (I didn't even ask whether it would
be before or after dehydration could be expected to set in), got my reply, and
went back to my newspaper and to wiping my brow.

The conductor had nonchalantly walked down the gauntlet of eighty   3
sweating American freemen, and not one of them had asked him to explain
why the passengers in that car had been consigned to suffer. There is nothing
to be done when the temperature outdoors is 85 degrees, and indoors the air
conditioner has broken down; obviously when that happens there is nothing to
do, except perhaps curse the day that one was born. But when the temperature outdoors is below freezing, it takes a positive act of will on somebody's
part to set the temperature indoors at 85. Somewhere a valve was turned too
far, a furnace overstocked, a thermostat maladjusted: something that could
easily be remedied by turning off the heat and allowing the great outdoors to
come indoors. All this is so obvious. What is not obvious is what has happened to the American people.

It isn't just the commuters, whom we have come to visualize as a supine   4
breed who have got on to the trick of suspending their sensory faculties twice a
day while they submit to the creeping dissolution of the railroad industry. It
isn't just they who have given up trying to rectify irrational vexations. It is the
American people everywhere.

A few weeks ago at a large movie theatre I turned to my wife and said,   5
"The picture is out of focus." "Be quiet," she answered. I obeyed. But a few
minutes later I raised the point again, with mounting impatience. "It will be all
right in a minute," she said apprehensively. (She would rather lose her eyesight
than be around when I make one of my infrequent scenes.) I waited. It was
just out of focus—not glaringly out, but out. My vision is 20-20, and I assume
that is the vision, adjusted, of most people in the movie house. So, after hec-
toring my wife throughout the first reel, I finally prevailed upon her to admit
that it was off, and very annoying. We then settled down, coming to rest on the
presumption that: a) someone connected with the management of the theatre
must soon notice the blur and make the correction; or b) that someone seated
near the rear of the house would make the complaint in behalf of those of us up

front; or c) that—any minute now—the entire house would explode into cat-calls and foot stamping, calling dramatic attention to the irksome distortion.

What happened was nothing. The movie ended, as it had begun just out 6 of focus, and as we trooped out, we stretched our faces in a variety of contor-tions to accustom the eye to the shock of normal focus.

I think it is safe to say that everybody suffered on that occasion. And I 7 think it is safe to assume that everyone was expecting someone else to take the initiative in going back to speak to the manager. And it is probably true even that if we had supposed the movie would run right through the blurred image, someone surely would have summoned up the purposive indignation to get up out of his seat and file his complaint.

But notice that no one did. And the reason no one did is because we are 8 all increasingly anxious in America to be unobtrusive, we are reluctant to make our voices heard, hesitant about claiming our rights; we are afraid that our cause is unjust, or that if it is not unjust, that it is ambiguous; or if not even that, that it is too trivial to justify the horrors of a confrontation with Authority; we will sit in an oven or endure a racking headache before undertaking a head-on, I'm-here-to-tell-you complaint. That tendency to passive compliance, to a heedless endurance, is something to keep one's eyes on—in sharp focus.

I myself can occasionally summon the courage to complain, but I cannot, 9 as I have intimated, complain softly. My own instinct is so strong to let the thing ride, to forget about it—to expect that someone will take the matter up, when the grievance is collective, in my behalf—that it is only when the provo-cation is at a very special key, whose vibrations touch simultaneously a com-plexus of nerves, allergies, and passions, that I catch fire and find the reserves of courage and assertiveness to speak up. When that happens, I get quite car-ried away. My blood gets hot, my brow wet, I become unbearably and uncon-scionably sarcastic and bellicose: I am girded for a total showdown.

Why should that be? Why could not I (or anyone else) on that railroad 10 coach have said simply to the conductor, "Sir"—I take that back: that sounds sarcastic—"Conductor, would you be good enough to turn down the heat? I am extremely hot. In fact, I tend to get hot every time the temperature reaches 85 degr—" Strike that last sentence. Just end it with the simple statement that you are extremely hot, and let the conductor infer the cause.

Every New Year's Eve I resolve to do something about the Milquetoast in 11 me and vow to speak up, calmly, for my rights, and for the betterment of our society, on every appropriate occasion. Entering last New Year's Eve I was for-tified in my resolve because that morning at breakfast I had had to ask the waitress three times for a glass of milk. She finally brought it—after I had fin-ished my eggs, which is when I don't want it any more. I did not have the manliness to order her to take the milk back, but settled instead for a cowardly sulk, and ostentatiously refused to drink the milk—though I later paid for it—

rather than state plainly to the hostess, as I should have, why I had not drunk it, and would not pay for it.

So by the time the New Year ushered out the Old, riding in on my morning's indignation and stimulated by the gastric juices of resolution that flow so faithfully on New Year's Eve, I rendered my vow. Henceforward I would conquer my shyness, my despicable disposition to supineness. I would speak out like a man against the unnecessary annoyances of our time. *12*

Forty-eight hours later, I was standing in line at the ski repair store in Pico Peak, Vermont. All I needed, to get on with my skiing, was the loan, for one minute, of a small screwdriver, to tighten a loose binding. Behind the counter in the workshop were two men. One was industriously engaged in servicing the complicated requirements of a young lady at the head of the line, and obviously he would be tied up for quite a while. The other—"Jiggs," his workmate called him—was a middle-aged man, who sat in a chair puffing a pipe, exchanging small talk with his working partner. My pulse began its telltale acceleration. The minutes ticked on. I stared at the idle shopkeeper, hoping to shame him into action, but he was impervious to my telepathic reproof and continued his small talk with his friend, brazenly insensitive to the nervous demands of six good men who were raring to ski. *13*

Suddenly my New Year's Eve resolution struck me. It was now or never. I broke from my place in line and marched to the counter. I was going to control myself. I dug my nails into my palms. My effort was only partially successful. *14*

"If you are not too busy," I said icily, 'would you mind handing me a screwdriver?" *15*

Work stopped and everyone turned his eyes on me, and I experienced that mortification I always feel when I am the center of centripetal shafts of curiosity, resentment, perplexity. *16*

But the worst was yet to come. "I am sorry, sir," said Jiggs deferentially, moving the pipe from his mouth. "I am not supposed to move. I have just had a heart attack." That was the signal for a great whirring noise that descended from heaven. We looked, stricken, out the window, and it appeared as though a cyclone had suddenly focused on the snowy courtyard between the shop and the ski lift. Suddenly a gigantic army helicopter materialized, and hovered down to a landing. Two men jumped out of the plane carrying a stretcher, tore into the ski shop, and lifted the shopkeeper onto the stretcher. Jiggs bade his companion goodbye, was whisked out the door, into the plane, up to the heavens, down—we learned—to a near-by army hospital. I looked up manfully-into a score of man-eating eyes. I put the experience down as a reversal. *17*

As I write this, on an airplane, I have run out of paper and need to reach into my briefcase under my legs for more. I cannot do this until my empty lunch tray is removed from my lap. I arrested the stewardess as she passed *18* empty-handed down the aisle on the way to the kitchen to fetch the lunch trays for the passengers up forward who haven't been served yet. "Would you please take my tray? "Just a moment, sir!" she said, and marched on sternly. Shall I tell her that since she is headed for the kitchen anyway, it could not delay the feeding of the other passengers by more than two seconds necessary to stash away my empty tray ? Or remind her that not fifteen minutes ago she spoke unctuously into the loudspeaker the words undoubtedly devised by the airline's highly paid public relations counselor: "If there is anything I or Miss French can do for you to make your trip more enjoyable, please let us—" I have run out of paper.

I think the observable reluctance of the majority of Americans to assert themselves in minor matters is related to our increased sense of helplessness in an age of technology and centralized political and economic power. For generations, Americans who were too hot, or too cold, got up and did something about it. Now we call the plumber, or the electrician, or the furnace man. The habit of looking after our own needs obviously had something to do with the assertiveness that characterized the American family familiar to readers of American literature. With the technification of life goes our direct responsibility for our material environment, and we are conditioned to adopt a position of helplessness not only as regards the broken air conditioner, but as regards the overheated train. It takes an expert to fix the former, but not the latter; yet these distinctions, as we withdraw into helplessness, tend to fade away. 19

Our notorious political apathy is a related phenomenon. Every year, whether the Republican or the Democratic Party is in office, more and more power drains away from the individual to feed vast reservoirs in far-off places; and we have less and less say about the shape of events which shape our future. From this alienation of personal power comes the sense of resignation with which we accept the political dispensations of a powerful government whose hold upon us continues to increase. 20

An editor of a national weekly news magazine told me a few years ago that as few as a dozen letters of protest against an editorial stance of his magazine was enough to convene a plenipotentiary meeting of the board of editors to review policy. "So few people complain, or make their voices heard," he explained to me, "that we assume a dozen letters represent the inarticulated views of thousands of readers." In the past ten years, he said, the volume of mail has noticeably decreased, even though the circulation of his magazine has risen. 21

When our voices are finally mute, when we have finally suppressed the natural instinct to complain, whether the vexation is trivial or grave, we shall have become automatons, incapable of feeling. When Premier Khrushchev first came to this country late in 1959 he was primed, we are informed, to experience the bitter resentment of the American people against his tyranny, against 22 his persecutions, against the movement which is responsible for the great number of American deaths in Korea, for billions in taxes every year, and for life everlasting on the brink of disaster; but Khrushchev was pleasantly surprised, and reported back to the Russian people that he had been met with overwhelming cordiality (read: apathy), except, to be sure, for "a few fascists who followed me around with their wretched posters, and should be horsewhipped."

I may be crazy, but I say there would have been lots more posters in a   23
society where train temperatures in the dead of winter are not allowed to climb to 85 degrees without complaint.

1961

COMPONENTS

Good paragraphs have logical and recognizable developmental structures; they are constructed from one or more of six *components* (structures constructed from the basic elements).

1	2	3	4	5	6
Idea	Idea	Idea	Idea	Idea	Idea
EVIDENCE	Reasons	EVIDENCE	Reasons	(unsupported)	Combination
		Reasons	EVIDENCE		of components
		(which explain	(which supports		
		the evidence)	the reasons)		

Examples of Components

1) Idea supported by evidence:

> **Flying on airplanes is safer than downhill skiing.**
> One is 300 times more likely to be killed skiing than flying.

> **I have always thought horses were dangerous.**
> When I was a toddler, my cousin was thrown from a horse and killed.

2) Idea supported by a reason:

> **I hate to fly on airplanes.**
> I DESPISE ANY ENCLOSED AREA THAT SMELLS OF STALE CIGARETTE SMOKE.

> **I am terrified of horses.**
> I AM AFRAID OF ALL LARGE ANIMALS.

3) Idea supported by evidence which is supported by a reason:

> **As a child I was terrified of a large, red chow dog that
> lived on the route I had to walk to get to elementary
> school.**
>
>> The dog always wagged his tail, dangled his black tongue
>> out of the side of his mouth, and loved to have children pet
>> him.
>>
>>> BUT ITS BLACK TONGUE MADE ME THINK THE DOG
>>> WAS A SATANIC BEAST.

4) Idea supported by a reason which is supported by evidence:

> **I hate to fly on airplanes.**
>
>> I DESPISE TO BE IN ANY ENCLOSED AREA THAT SMELLS
>> OF STALE CIGARETTE SMOKE.
>>
>>> The last time I flew to and from Dallas, I had to have
>>> my brand new suit dry-cleaned to get rid of the smell
>>> of smoke.

6) Unsupported ideas: Each of the following ideas is so self-evident—at least to twentieth-century Americans—that it does not need
support. (From *All I Really Need to Know I Learned in Kindergarten*
and *Aunt Erma's Cope Book* by Erma Bombeck)

> Don't hit people.
> Thou shalt not covet thy neighbor's dessert.
> Thou shalt not kill for chocolate.
> Clean up your own mess.
> Flush.

Ideas, evidence, and reasons are the *elements* of which developmental paragraphs are constructed. But they are used in various relationships to the topic sentence and to each other. Those relationships
can be called *levels of development*. Each element in a paragraph is
in a hierarchal relationship to the topic sentence and to the other elements of that paragraph. Usually, all of the evidence and reasons in a
paragraph is subordinate to the topic sentence; that is, it functions to
support and develop the topic sentence.

The elements, which may be sentences, clauses, phrases, or single words, can be numbered to show their relationship to the other elements in the paragraph. They are numbered with small Arabic numerals, with number 1 indicating the topic sentence, number 2 indicating the elements which *directly* support the topic sentence, number 3 indicating the elements which support the number 2's, and so forth.

Three kinds of developmental sequences are possible within a paragraph.

- *Coordinate sequence* of development
- *Subordinate sequence of development*
- *Mixed sequence* of development (both coordinate and subordinate sequences)

Good paragraphs are unified and coherent. A good paragraph is *unified in topic*. In a good paragraph each sentence supports the topic sentence, and the paragraph contains only sentences related to the topic. A good paragraph is also *unified by coherence strategies* which help unify the discourse, such as the following:

- *Repetition* of key terms
- *Transitional* words and phrases
- *Parallel structure*
- *Consistent point of view* (person, tense, number, and tone)
- *Signals of time and place*

LEVELS OF DEVELOPMENT

It is not possible to analyze an discourse without recognizing, as Francis Christensen has suggested, that the development of the sentence and of the paragraph (and of the essay or even book, as well) is made up of various levels of argument. Those levels are determined by the hierarchy of ideas within the argument. Although Christensen calls these levels "levels of generality," that term is not always accurate. Subordinate levels are not always more specific than the levels they support. Therefore, instead of his term "levels of generality," I will call the levels of the argument "levels of development."

On a larger scale, a book might have many levels of development: book, parts of the book (each of which is controlled by a smaller subsidiary thesis of its own), chapters, chapter sections, chapter subsections, paragraphs (each of which is controlled by a topic sentence), mini paragraphs within a paragraph, micro-paragraphs within the mini-paragraphs, and finally the components (each of which is controlled by an assertion of its own). Obviously, some books and essays have many levels of development, and some have only a few. Although we have no standard vocabulary to delineate these various levels, we recognize their existence. Although they differ greatly in size, from hundreds of pages to a few or even a single sentence, at the smallest level—that of the component—they all utilize the same elements in the same ways to develop an argument.

Numbering System for Identifying Levels of Development

Coordinate

It is very difficult to find coordinate paragraphs with just *two* levels of development.

This paragraph comes close, but has some information at level 3 and 4.

1   The picture will run on through supper time with still very little evidence of man's presence on earth.

    2   It will be about 11 o'clock when Neanderthal man appears.

    2   Another half hour will go by before the appearance of Cro-Magnon man

        3   living in caves

        3   and painting crude animal pictures on the walls of his dwelling

    2   Fifteen minutes more will bring Neolithic man,

        3   knowing how to chip stone

            4   and thus produce sharp cutting edges for spears and tools.

    2   In a few minutes more it will appear that man has domesticated the dog, the sheep and possibly, other animals.

    2   He will then begin the use of milk.

    2   He will also learn the arts of basket weaving and the making of pottery and dugout canoes.

Subordinate

(From "The Spider and the Wasp" by Alexander Petrunkevitch)

1   The entire body of a tarantula . . . Is thickly clothed with hair.

    2   especially its legs

    2   Some of it is short and woolly,

    2   some long and stiff.

    2   Touching this body hair produces one of two distinct reactions.

        3   When the spider is hungry, it responds with an immediate and swift attack.

            4   At the touch of a cricket's antennae the tarantula seizes the insect so swiftly that a motion picture taken at the rate of 64 frames per second shows only the result not the process of capture.

        3   But when the spider is not hungry, the stimulation of its hair merely causes it to shake the touched limb.

            4   An insect can walk under its hairy belly unharmed.

Examples of Levels of Development/Coordinate Sequence

Coordinate Sequence: Examples

1   **Joe's little brother chooses rodents for his pets—**

    2   a gerbil

    2   and a hamster.

1   **I don't know how Susan uses all the makeup she owns.**

    2   On the top of her dresser alone, I counted,

        3   ten lipsticks,

        3   three boxes of face powder,

        3   three bottles of liquid makeup,

        3   five containers of blush, 21 colors of eye shadow,

        3   seven eye pencils, and

        3   four differed colors of mascara.

Coordinate Sequence: Examples

1   **It makes sense for me go to college in my hometown.**

    2   I CAN USE PUBLIC TRANSPORTATION,

    2   AND KEEP MY JOB.

    2   IT COSTS ME ALMOST NOTHING TO LIVE AT HOME.

    2   AND I DON'T HAVE TO GO OFF AND LEAVE MY DOG.

Coordinate Sequence: Examples and Reasons

1   **It makes sense for me go to college in my hometown.**

    It is only three miles from my home.

    2   I CAN KEEP MY JOB.

    2   Tuition is $4,000 a year cheaper than anywhere else.

    2   I CAN USE PUBLIC TRANSPORTATION.

    2   IT COSTS ME ALMOST NOTHING TO LIVE AT HOME.

    2   AND I DON'T HAVE TO GO OFF AND LEAVE MY DOG.

Subordinate Sequence

Subordinate Sequence: Examples

1   **Joe's little brother Sam chooses rodents for his pets.**

    2   **He has a gerbil who he keeps in his room,**

        3   **even though he is allergic to it.**

            4   **Now Sam has asthma attacks frequently.**

                5   **Once he had to go to the hospital emergency room,**

                    6   **And they kept him in the hospital for three days.**

Subordinate Sequence: Reasons

1   **It makes sense for me go to college in my hometown.**

    2   I WANT TO SAVE MONEY.

        3   JENNY AND I WANT TO GET MARRIED AS SOON AS I GRADUATE

            4   AND I DON'T WANT TO START OFF MARRIED LIFE IN DEBT,

                5   WHICH RUINS MANY MARRIAGES.

Subordinate Sequence: Examples and Reasons

1 **It makes sense for me go to college in my hometown.**

   2 I WANT TO SAVE MONEY.

      3 I can save $4,000 a year on tuition

         4 because my mother is a professor here,

            5 and professors' children don't pay tuition!

Mixed Sequence

Mixed Sequence: Examples

1 **Joe's little brother Sam loves animals.**

   2 He has a gerbil which he keeps in his room,

      3 even though he is allergic to it.

   2 He keeps a horse at a farm just past the city limits.

      3 and bicycles 16 miles every day to feed and groom it,

         4 even though he only has time to ride it on week ends.

Mixed Sequence: Reasons

1 **It makes sense for me go to college in my hometown.**

   2 I WANT TO SAVE MONEY.

      3 I can save $4,000 a year

   2 I CAN USE PUBLIC TRANSPORTATION,

   2 OR EVEN WALK TO SCHOOL,

      3 which might help me lose some weight!

Mixed Sequence: Mixture of Examples and Reasons

1 **It makes sense for me go to college in my hometown.**

   2 I WANT TO SAVE MONEY.

      3 I can save $4,000 a year on tuition

         4 because my mother is a professor here,

            5 and I would not be charged any tuition!

   2 I CAN USE PUBLIC TRANSPORTATION,

   2 AND KEEP MY JOB.

   2 IT COSTS ME ALMOST NOTHING TO LIVE AT HOME.

Section II: Structure

The structure of any discourse is determined by the organization and order of the whole discourse, including the organization and order within sections and the organization and order within paragraphs of that discourse.

CHAPTER 3

Organization Using Classification

Classification is a "systematic grouping based on shared characteristics (*The American Heritage Dictionary*). And Frank D'Angelo defined **classification** as "the process of grouping similar ideas or objects, the systematic arrangement of things into classes on the basis of shared characteristics" (*Process and Thought in Composition*, page 206, 3rd. Ed.)

The term classification is often used to describe two somewhat different processes, both based on "systematic grouping based on shared characteristics."

First, "to classify" is often used to mean the process of putting an item into a larger **category** (or **class**) of things. One classifies and identifies a person, place, thing, or idea by determining to what larger class of persons, places, things, or ideas it belongs (*x* is a type of *y*). On the basis of this definition of classification, one could classify murder by putting it into any of the following larger classes of actions: crime, act of violence, sin, rite of passage to manhood, patriotic action, act of passion, act of compassion, or even as a Saturday night amusement. Classifying a general topic can greatly help a writer not only in deciding how to narrow and focus his or her own specific topic and in deciding what one wants to say about a topic but also in discovering ideas with which to develop that topic. Obviously, an essay that discussed murder as a sin would have a quite different focus and would develop quite different ideas than an essay that discussed murder as a patriotic action. This kind of classification can help a writer find an interesting focus for his or her paper.

Second, "to classify" is also used to describe the process of taking a group of items and subdividing it into smaller groups of items. One classifies by sorting a group (set) of persons, places, things, or ideas into smaller, subsidiary groups or subsets (types of *x*). Using the second kind of classification, one could classify murders by dividing them into types of murders. One could classify murder into **subsidiary classes** on the basis of legal distinctions: first-degree murder, second-degree murder, third-degree murder, and manslaughter. Or one could classify according to the level of sin: mortal or venal. Or on the basis of the type of murder weapon, or the type of person committing the murder (sane or insane, adult or child, man or woman, etc.). Or the type of person murdered. Or the type of weapon. Or the motive. Or even on the day of the week or the time of the year when murders occur. Or the weather conditions during which murders take place.

Using the first kind of classification, the process of putting an item into a larger class or category, one could classify automobiles as 1) means of transportation, 2) major expenditures in a person's monthly budget, 3) possessions which demonstrate economic status, 4) collectors' items, or 5) sources of frustration in one's day-to-day life. Using the second kind of classification, the process of subdividing a group of items into smaller, subsidiary groups, one could classify cars by body types (sedans, two-doors, convertibles, vans, station wagons, or sports utility vehicles), by brand (Chrysler, Toyota, Mercedes, Ford, or Volkswagen), or by color (red, gray, black, white, or green). This second kind of classification can help one discover subordinate ideas for a topic.

Most textbooks and teachers of writing pay far less attention to the first kind of classification, which involves putting a thing into a larger class, than they do to the second kind of classification, which involves taking a class of things and logically separating that class into subsidiary classes of things.

Scientists find classification essential. Biologists recognize that there is a hierarchy of classes and utilize a classification system called *taxonomy* to identify various levels of classifications. They classify the animal kingdom into phyla, a phylum into subphylums, a subphylum into classes, a class into orders, an order into families, a family into genera, a genus into species, and a species into subspecies.

But in the humanities we do not have standard, convenient hierarchies of terms. Occasionally we utilize terms such as "standard," "average," "miniature," and "microscopic" and prefixes such as "macro-," "micro-," "mega-." "mini-," "super-," and "sub-" to indicate relative differences. For example, we distinguish between "standard," "compact," and "sub-compact" cars and we identify poodles as "standard," "miniature," or "toy." In some cases, exact measurements provide more precise identification: the three standard gauges of electric trains can be precisely identified as "N," "HO," and "O."

Classification not only helps a writer to determine the focus for his or her essay and to narrow the topic for that essay, but to help a writer organize an essay.

Classification can be used at any level within an essay: the whole essay, a section of the essay, a paragraph, or a sentence.

Before classifying a subject, one should consider the following guidelines:

1) Have a context, occasion, or reason for writing. Knowing what you want to accomplish with your classification will help you choose the best classes. Knowing your audience will also help.

2) Choose a basis of classification that suits your purpose. (For example, if you classify voters as male and female, your classification basis is sex.)

3) The classes should be equivalent.

4) In general, you should have more than two classes.

5) Although it is more difficult, a complete classification, one which has a place for all examples, is often superior.

Sentences Using Classification

Example 1

Some books are to be tasted, others to be swallowed, and some few to be chewed and digested.

From "Of Studies," Francis Bacon

Example 2

Reading maketh a full man, conference a ready man, and writing an exact man.

From "Of Studies," Francis Bacon

Example 3

Traditionally, four major types [of schizophrenia] have been recognized: the paranoid, the hebephrenic, the catatonic, and the simple.

From *Interpretations of Schizophrenia*, Silvano Arieti

Example 4

Laboratory experiments prove that tarantulas can distinguish three types of touch: pressure against the body wall, stroking of the body hair, and riffling of certain very fine hairs on the legs called trichoboythraia.

From "The Spider and the Wasp," Alexander Petrunkevitch

Example 5

Parapsychology, UFO's, miracle cures, transcendental meditation and all other paths to instant enlightenment are condemned [by most contemporary Americans].

From "A Few Kind Words for Superstition," Robertson Davies

Example 6

I have earnestly opposed violent tension, but there is a type of constructive, nonviolent tension which is necessary for growth.

Paragraph 10 from "Letter from Birmingham Jail," Martin Luther King, Jr.

Example 7

Everyone seemed to be going to China that year, or else writing rude things about the Arabs, or being frank about Africa. I had other things on my mind. After eleven in London I still had not been much in Britain.

From *Kingdom by the Sea*, Paul Theroux

Example 8

[Let us] inquire into the nature of 'problems.' We know there are solved problems and unsolved problems. The former we may feel, present no issue; but as regards the latter: Are there not problems that are not merely unsolved but insoluble.

From *A Guide for the Perplexed*, E. E. Shoemaker

Example 9

There are four classes of Idols which beset men's minds. To these for distinction's sake I have assigned names—calling the first class Idols of the Tribe; the second, Idols of the Cave; the third, Market-Place; the fourth, Idols of the Theater.

From "Aphorism 39," Francis Bacon

Example 10

In Boston they ask, How much does he know? In New York, How much is he worth? In Philadelphia, Who were his parents?

From *What Paul Bourget Thinks of Us*, Mark Twain

Example 11

There are three types of self-love. In order of increasing intensity, they are: self-love unconcealed, self-love concealed as the love of others, and self-love concealed as self-hate. The first is called "self-esteem" by the subject, "self-assurance" by the lay observer, and "narcissism" by the psychoanalyst. The second is called "love" by the subject, "altruism" by the lay observer, and "maturity" by the psychoanalyst. The third is called "inferiority" by the subject, "stupidity" by the lay observer, and "masochism" by the psychoanalyst.

From *Heresies*, Thomas Szasz

Example 12

Our initial review of the four great Levels of Being can be summed up as follows:

Man can be written	$m + x + y + z$
Animal can be written	$m + x + y$
Plant can be written	$m + x$
Mineral can be written	m

From *A Guide for the Perplexed*, E. E. Shoemaker

Example 13

When the first long-term loans for coffee cultivation were granted in 1953, two types of borrowing privileges were established. The first was designed for small-scale agriculture and allowed the colonist to borrow up to S/.50,000 (about $2,000) over a 4-year period. The second type of borrowing privilege was for large-scale agriculture and set no ceiling on the amount of money that a colonist could receive. Although the latter status was clearly the most favored one, no formal rules were announced to determine which individuals would qualify for such loans. Rather, it became common practice for lending status to be accorded as the result of a deal, usually involving graft or influence peddling of some kind, arranged between the more prominent members of the new group of settlers and bank officials.

From *The Peasants of El Dorado*, Robin Shoemaker

Example 14

[T]here are two types of laws: just and unjust. I would be the first to advocate obeying just laws. One has not only a legal but a moral responsibility to obey just laws. Conversely, one has a moral responsibility to disobey unjust laws. I would agree with St. Augustine that "an unjust law is no law at all."

Paragraph 15 from "Letter from Birmingham Jail," Martin Luther King, Jr.

Paragraphs or Sections Using Classification

Example 1

Kinds of Cakes

There are two basic kinds of cakes: those made with butter or some other kind of shortening and those made without any shortening.

Cakes Made with Shortening.
Many of the cakes with which we are most familiar—standard white, gold, and chocolate cakes, spice cakes, pound cakes, fruit cakes, and gingerbread fall into this category and are frequently referred to as "butter" cakes. These cakes usually use baking powder or baking soda for leavening. More finely grained than those made without shortening, they are easy to fill and frost and make excellent layer cakes.

Sometimes the eggs in butter cakes are added whole; sometimes they are separated and the beaten egg whites are folded in just before baking. Butter cakes made with separately beaten egg whites are lighter and fluffier than cakes made with whole eggs.

Cakes Made Without Shortening.
Sponge cakes and angel food cakes are made without butter or shortening. Sponge cakes use separately beaten egg yolks and whites; angel food cakes are made only with beaten egg whites.

Cakes in this category usually do not use chemical leavening but depend exclusively on the air beaten into eggs or egg whites instead. These cakes are delicate and need to be assembled with special care.

Tortes.
Tortes are European in origin. They are usually light cakes made with separated eggs. Ground nuts or crumbs are often used instead of flour, although many tortes do contain some flour. Tortes are very rich and require no more finishing than a dusting of confectioners' sugar or a little whipped cream. They will stay fresh longer than other cakes.

From *Fannie Farmer Cookbook*

Example 2

There are two kinds of people in the world—those who have a horror of a vacuum and those with a horror of the things that fill it. Translated into domestic interiors, this means people who live with, and without, clutter. (Dictionary definition: jumble, confusion, disorder.) The reasons for clutter, the need to be surrounded by things, goes deep, from security to status. The reasons for banning objects, or living in as selective and austere an environment as possible, range from the esthetic to the neurotic. This is a phenomenon of choice that relates as much to the psychiatrist as to the tastemaker.

Some people clutter compulsively, and others just as compulsively throw things away. Clutter in its highest and most organized form is called collecting. Collecting can be done as the Collyer brothers did it, or it can be done with art and flair. The range is from old newspapers to Faberge.

This provides a third category, or what might be called, calculated clutter, in which the objets d'art, the memorabilia that mark one's milestones and travels, the irresistible and ornamental things that speak to pride, pleasure and temptation, are constrained by decorating devices and hierarchal principles of value. This gives the illusion that one is in control.

From "Modern-Life Battle: Conquering Clutter," Ada Louise Huxtable

Example 3

You did not know that superstition takes four forms? Theologians assure us that it does. First is what they call Vain Observances, such as not walking under a ladder, and that kind of thing. Yet I saw a deeply learned professor of anthropology, who had spilled some salt, throwing a pinch of it over his left shoulder; when I asked him why, he replied, with a wink, that it was "to hit the Devil in the eye." I did not question him further about his belief in the Devil; but I noticed that he did not smile until I asked him what he was doing.

The second form is Divination, or consulting oracles. Another learned professor I know, who would scorn to settle a problem by tossing a coin (which is a humble appeal to Fate to declare itself), told me quite seriously that he had resolved a matter related to university affairs by consulting the I Ching. And why not? There are thousands of people on this continent who appeal to the I Ching, and their general level of education seems to absolve them of superstition. Almost, but not quite. The I Ching, to the embarrassment of rationalists, often gives excellent advice.

The third form is Idolatry, and universities can show plenty of that. If you have ever supervised a large examination room, you know how many jujus, lucky coins and other bringers of luck are placed on the desks of the candidates. Modest idolatry, but what else can you call it?

The fourth form is Improper Worship of the True God. A while ago, I learned that every day, for several days, a $2 bill (in Canada we have $2 bills, regarded by some people as unlucky) had been tucked under a candlestick on the altar of a college chapel. Investigation revealed that an engineering student, worried about a girl, thought that bribery of the Deity might help. When I talked with him, he did not think he was pricing God cheap, because he could afford no more. A reasonable argument, but perhaps God was proud that week, for the scientific oracle went against him.

From "A Few Kind Words for Superstition," Robertson Davies

Example 4

You speak of our activity in Birmingham as extreme. At first I was rather disappointed that fellow clergymen would see my nonviolent efforts as those of an extremist. I began thinking about the fact that I stand in the middle of two opposing forces in the Negro community. One is a force of complacency, made up in part of Negroes who, as a result of long years of oppression, are so drained of self-respect and a sense of "somebodiness" that they have adjusted to segregation; and in part of a few middle-class Negroes who, because of a degree of academic and economic security and because in some ways they profit by segregation, have become insensitive to the problems of the masses. The other force is one of bitterness and hatred, and it comes perilously close to advocating violence. It is expressed in the various black nationalist groups that are springing up across the nation, the largest and best-known being Elijah Muhammad's Muslim movement. Nourished by the Negro's frustration over the continued existence of racial discrimination, this movement is made up of people who have lost faith in America, who have absolutely repudiated Christianity, and who have concluded that the white man is an incorrigible "devil."

I have tried to stand between these two forces, saying that we need emulate neither the "do-nothingism" of the complacent nor the hatred and despair of the black nationalist. For there is a more excellent way of love and nonviolent protest. I am grateful to God that, through the influence of the Negro church, the way of nonviolence became an integral part of our struggle.

If this philosophy had not emerged, by now many streets of the South would, I am convinced, be flowing with blood. And I am further convinced that if our white brothers dismiss as "rabblerousers" and "outside agitators" those of us who employ nonviolent direct action, and if they refuse to support our nonviolent efforts, millions of Negroes will, out of frustration and despair, seek solace and security in black-nationalist ideologies—a development that would inevitably lead to a frightening racial nightmare.

Paragraphs 27-29 from "Letter from Birmingham Jail" Martin Luther King, Jr.

In the following paragraphs, four ways the atomic bomb could have been used in World War II are discussed. Notice that a fifth possibility—that of dropping the bomb on a large, mostly civilian population—is never discussed, probably because the audience for this discourse would know what had happened.

Example 5

One option involved a kind of benign strike: the dropping of a bomb on some built-up area, but only after advance notice had been issued so that residents could evacuate the area and leave an empty slate on which the bomb could write its terrifying signature. . . .

The second option was a tactical strike against a purely military target—an arsenal, railroad yard, depot, factory, harbor-without advance notice. Early in the game, for example, someone had nominated the Japanese fleet concentration at Truk. . . .

The third option was to stage a kind of dress rehearsal by detonating a bomb in some remote corner of the world—a desert or empty island, say—to exhibit to international observers brought in for the purpose what the device could do. . . .

The fourth option involved a kind of warning shot. The thought here was to drop a bomb without notice over a relatively uninhabited stretch of enemy land so the Japanese high command might see at first hand what was in store for them if they failed to surrender soon. . . .

[Erikson does not mention the fifth option, the one selected: bombing a large, heavily populated area.]

From "Of Accidental Judgments and Casual Slaughters," Kai Erikson

Essays Using Classification

"Work, Labor and Play"
W. H. Auden

So far as I know, Miss Hannah Arendt was the first person to define the essential difference between work and labor. To be happy, a man must feel, firstly, free, and secondly, important. He cannot be really happy if he is compelled by society to do what he does not enjoy doing, or if what he enjoys doing is ignored by society as of no value or importance. In a society where slavery in the strict sense has been abolished, the sign that what a man does is of social value is that he is paid money to do it, but a laborer today can rightly be called a wage slave. A man is a laborer if the job society offers him is of no interest to himself but he is compelled to take it by the necessity of earning a living and supporting his family.

The antithesis to labor is play. When we play a game, we enjoy what we are doing, otherwise we should not play it, but it is a purely private activity; society could not care less whether we play it or not.

Between labor and play stands work. A man is a worker if he is personal-   3
ly interested in the job which society pays him to do; what from the point of
view of society is necessary labor is from his point of view voluntary play.
Whether a job is to be classified as labor or work depends, not on the job itself,
but on the tastes of the individual undertakes. The difference does not, for
example coincide with the difference between a manual and a mental job; a gar-
dener or a cobbler may be a worker, a bank clerk a laborer. Which a man is can
be seen from his attitude toward leisure. To a worker, leisure means simply the
hours he needs to relax and rest in order to work efficiently. He is therefore
more likely to take too little leisure than too much; workers die of coronaries
and forget their wives' birthdays. To the laborer, on the other hand, leisure
means freedom from compulsion, so that it is natural for him to imagine that
the fewer hours he has to spend laboring, and the more hours he is free to
play, the better.

"Hoppers"

Garrison Keillor

A hydrant was open on Seventh Avenue above 23rd Street last Friday morning,   1
and I stopped on my way east and watched people hop over the water. It was a
brilliant spring day. The water was a nice clear creek about three feet wide and
ran along the gutter around the northwest corner of the intersection. A gaggle
of pedestrians crossing 23rd went *hop hop hop hop hop* over the creek as a
few soloists jaywalking Seventh performed at right angles to them, and I got
engrossed in the dance. Three feet isn't a long leap for most people, and the
ease of it permits a wide range of expression. Some hoppers went a good deal
higher than necessary.

Long, lanky men don't hop, as a rule. The ones I saw hardly paused at   2
the water's edge, just lengthened one stride and trucked on across—a rather
flatfooted approach that showed no recognition of the space or occasion. Tall
men typically suffer from an excess of cool, but I kept hoping for one of them
to get off the ground. Most of the tall men wore topcoats and carried briefcas-
es, so perhaps their balance was thrown off. One tall man in a brown coat did-
n't notice the water and stepped off the curb into the fast-flowing Hydrant
Creek and made a painful hop, like a wounded heron: a brown heron with a
limp wing attached to a briefcase bulging full of dead fish. He crossed 23rd
looking as though his day had been pretty much shot to pieces.

Short, fat men were superb: I could have watched them all morning. A   3
typical fat man crossing the street would quicken his step when he saw the
creek and, on his approach, do a little shuffle, arms out to the sides, and suddenly and with great concentration *spring*—a nimble step all the more graceful

for the springer's bulk. Three fairly fat men jiggled and shambled across 23rd together, and then one poked another and they saw the water. They stepped forward, studying the angle, and just before the point man jumped for the curb his pals said something, undoubtedly discouraging, and he threw back his head and laughed over his shoulder and threw himself lightly, boyishly, across the water, followed—*boing boing*—by the others.

The women who hopped the water tended to stop and study the creek and find its narrows and measure the distance and then lurch across. They seemed dismayed that the creek was there at all, and one, in a beige suit, put her hands on her hips and glared upstream, as if to say, "Whose water *is* this? This is utterly unacceptable. I am *not* about to jump over this." But then she made a good jump after all. She put her left toe on the edge of the curb, leaned forward with right arm outstretched—for a second, she looked as if she might take off and zoom up toward the Flatiron Building—and pushed off, landing easily on her right toe, her right arm raised. The longest leap was made by a young woman in a blue raincoat carrying a plastic Macy's bag and crossing west on Seventh. She gathered herself up in three long, accelerating strides and sailed, her coat billowing out behind her, over the water and five feet beyond, almost creaming a guy coming out of Radio Shack. He shrank back as she loped past, her long black hair and snow-white hands and face right *there*, then gone, vanished in the crowd.

And then it was my turn. I waited for the green light, crossed 23rd, stopped by the creek flowing around the bend of curb and heard faint voices of old schoolmates ahead in the woods, and jumped heavily across and marched after them.

4

5

CHAPTER 4

Organization Using Analysis

Like classification, *analysis* is a way of organizing information logically and, therefore, another method of organizing ideas for an essay.

The word "analysis" is frequently used—in the media and in ordinary conversation—to have a very general meaning. People use it to mean "summarize," "comment on," "interpret," "evaluate," or "rap about." But for the purposes of this course, it is important that you understand its specific and technical meaning. *Analysis* means "to break a thing down into its component parts." Some people use the word "division" to mean "analysis." One seldom uses analysis merely to divide, but rather to point out the functions, strengths, or weakness of various divisions.

In contrast to classification, which always deals with several items, analysis always deals with a single item. For example, to analyze a fetal pig in a biology laboratory, one cuts the pig up and identifies its component parts. Or, if one analyzes an unknown chemical compound in chemistry lab, one separates out and identifies the elements which make up the compound. If one does *simple analysis*, one simply identifies the elements which make up the unknown compound. If one does *quantitative analysis*, one not only identifies the elements but one also identifies exactly how much of each element is present in the compound. In analyzing an automobile, one identifies its components parts, including the engine, the body, the transmission, and the steering system.

An analysis should be complete: it should include all of the thing or all of the part of a thing which is being analyzed. If one is analyzing the human body, the analysis should include all of the systems of the body. If one is analyzing only the circulatory system or a hand, the analysis should include all the parts of the circulatory system or of the hand. The parts chosen for the analysis should be mutually exclusive. An analysis should be based on some logical of division of parts. Unlike classification, which can sometimes use identical standards for explaining each class, analysis may use different standards for each part being analyzed, because the parts are different. For example, one would use different standards for analyzing the circulatory system than one would for analyzing the skeletal system.

A person, place, or thing can be analyzed by a variety of standards. For example, a textbook could be analyzed on the basis of its contents or on the basis of its its physical make up (spine, cover, glue, paper, dust cover, etc.). A person could be analyzed on the basis of his or her character, body, clothing, or abilities.

One can carry analysis to several levels of development, each one more specific than the previous one. One could do a secondary level of analysis of the engine and a tertiary level of analysis of some component part of the engine. In some cases one can carry analyses to many levels of development. At times one must narrow one's subject and focus one's analysis on only a part of a whole.

In analysis, the paragraphs or sections of the discourse are usually determined by the analytical divisions chosen.

Just as analysis is useful in many academic disciplines and in many practical affairs of everyday life, it is also a useful method of organization for a writer. And just as an awareness of and ability to do categorization and classification are helpful to the writer, analysis is helpful in helping a writer not only in focusing his or her subject and organizing what he or she wants to say about the subject but also in discovering ideas to include in his or her essay.

The two common kinds of analysis are *static analysis* and *dynamic analysis*. *Static analysis* examines the parts of a person, place, thing, or idea. *Dynamic analysis* (*process analysis*) analyses the steps in a process, activity, or procedure. Dynamic analysis may be *informative* or *instructive*. An informative dynamic analysis provides the reader with information about and an understanding of a process. An instructive dynamic process leads the reader through a series of steps to enable him or her to do the process. Instructive analyses must, therefore, be extremely specific and include any warnings that may be necessary to prevent the reader from doing the process wrong.

Sentences Using Analysis

Example 1

For the four years I was in high school, I made the same lunch every day: a sandwich made from two pieces of Mrs. Baird's white bread, goose liver, and two layers of iceberg lettuce (no mayonnaise and no mustard), a package of plain potato chips, a Golden Delicious apple, and four Oreo cookies.

Example 2

[Mangroves] are all short, messy trees, waxy-leaved, laced all over with aerial roots, woody arching buttresses, and weird leathery berry pods. Al this tangles from a black muck soil, a black muck matted like a mud-sopped rag, a muck without any other plants, shaded, cold to the touch, tracked at the water's edge by herons and nosed by sharks.

From "Sojourner," Annie Dillard

Example 3

To this day you may spot me in Manhattan wearing boots and denim jeans with a matching vest and Western-cut hat—topped with a furry cattleman's coat . . . .

From "Playing Cowboy," Larry L. King

Example 4

It [the human liver] is divided into two great lobes, the right and left, and two small lobes, the caudate and the quadrate. . . .

From "Liver," Richard Selzer

Example 5

It is a peculiar sensation, this double-consciousness, this sense of always looking at one's self through the eyes of others. . . .One feels his two-ness— an American, a Negro; two warring ideals in one dark body, whose dogged strength alone keeps it from being torn asunder.

From *John Brown*, Williams Edward Burghardt Du Bois

Example 6

In any nonviolent campaign there are four basic steps: collection of the facts to determine whether injustices exist, negotiation, self purification, and direct action.

From "Letter from Birmingham Jail," Martin Luther King, Jr.

Paragraphs or Sections Using Analysis

Chapter 3 contained a discourse which classified cakes. The following discourse analyzes cakes. Notice that whereas the classification dealt with several kinds of cakes, the analysis is of a single, representative cake. And *Chapter 6* will include a discourse which gives a process analysis of making a cake (a recipe) and a cause and effect discourse presenting the various causes for failures in cake baking.

Example 1

Shortening. Butter, margarine, vegetable shortening, salad oil, or a combination   1
of several of these may be used as shortening in cakes.

    Vegetable shortening is cheaper than butter and somewhat easier to use   2
because of its soft, spreadable consistency. It keeps indefinitely and requires no
refrigeration. We use it in those cakes where the flavor of butter is not important, either because there is very little shortening in the cake or because the flavor of the spices and seasonings in the cake is stronger than the taste of butter.
Because so many people are purists when it comes to using butter in baking,
we've compared carefully the same cake made with butter and with shortening,
but we all found it hard to distinguish a noticeable difference in taste.

    Butter, nevertheless, is generally favored by cooks and bakers. It should   3
be fresh and, preferably, sweet (unsalted). Let it become slightly soft, not
mushy, at room temperature before you use it.

    Salad oil is used most often in chiffon cakes or in "quick" cakes that can   4
be easily beaten without an electric beater.

Sugar. Sugar adds sweetness and tenderness to cakes. If your sugar is lumpy,   5
be sure to sift it before using. Do not use lumpy brown sugar when baking; the
hard lumps will not dissolve in baking. . . .

Eggs. Eggs make a cake rich and give it good taste and texture. As elsewhere   6
in this book use eggs that are officially graded "large." To substitute eggs of a
different size in these recipes, follow the [correct] proportions . . . .

    Some cakes that call for separated eggs depend on beaten egg whites   7
exclusively for leavening, so in these instances it is especially important that the
whites be beaten properly. Always have the eggs at room temperature . . .

    Cutting corners in cakemaking doesn't pay. It would, of course, be easier   8
to beat the egg whites when you first begin to mix a cake, while the beaters are
clean and dry and have not yet been used to combine the other ingredients.
Indeed, many cookbooks do recommend this method for that very reason. But
we have found that egg whites have a tendency to deflate when they stand. And
since their volume is so important to the success of a cake, we recommend that
they be beaten last, just before they are folded into the batter.

Flour. All flour should be stored in airtight containers. The recipes in this   9
chapter call either for all-purpose flour or for cake flour, a soft-wheat flour
that contains more starch and less gluten than hard-wheat bread flour or all-
purpose flour.

Cake flour makes a cake lighter and more crumbly. It can be used in any   10
cake recipe, but since it is more expensive than all-purpose flour, we call for it
only in recipes where we feel it will make a significant difference. It is even a
bit difficult to find in some supermarkets today.

All-purpose flour produces fine cakes, and you can substitute it for cake   11
flour whenever necessary. If you choose to use all-purpose flour in a recipe
calling for cake flour, use two tablespoons less for each cup of cake flour. . . . if
you should wish to substitute cake flour for all-purpose flour, use 2 tablespoons
more per cup.

Quick-mixing all-purpose flour, milled so fine it will pass right through a   12
sifter, is not a substitute for cake flour. Since it will dissolve instantly in cold
(but not hot) liquids, use it, if you wish, in sauces, fillings, and gravies, but not
in cakes.

Do not use self-rising flour in these cake recipes; it is premixed with salt   13
and leavening and requires adjustment of the recipe.

Sifting is a way of lightening flour and thoroughly mixing it with the other   14
dry ingredients. In the past it was considered absolutely essential to sift flour
in any cake recipe, and most cake recipes still call for sifted flour. Flour today,
however, is sifted many times during milling before it is packaged and sent to
the stores. We find that many cakes are just as good when made with unsifted
flour, and this certainly makes them easier to prepare. At least one major flour
company, after extensive research, has arrived at similar conclusions. Thus,
you will find that we have eliminated the direction to sift in many of these
recipes and suggest simply mixing the flour with the other dry ingredients,
blending them well with a fork.

To measure flour without sifting, scoop it up in a dry-measure cup or   15
spoon it lightly into the measuring cup. Level it off with a straight knife. Do
not tap or bang the cup or the flour will settle. Better a little less flour in a cake
than a little more.

We continue to recommend sifting in recipes for refined cakes like sponge   16
or angel food cakes, where the lightness of sifted flour will make it easier to
fold it into the beaten egg whites. When sifting, sift onto wax paper, from
which the dry ingredients can then be added directly to the measuring cup or
mixing bowl. It is better not to wash the sifter, since the flour residue may
cake. Tap out as much of the remaining flour as possible and wrap the sifter in
a plastic bag before putting it away.

Leavening. Use double-acting baking powder in these recipes. For information   17
about baking powder, baking soda, and other leaveners.

Chocolate. Chocolate burns easily. It is best to melt it over simmering water,   18
rather than over a direct flame. For information about kinds of chocolate, storing chocolate, melting chocolate, and substituting cocoa for chocolate.

Dried Fruit and Nuts. Dried fruit and nuts, when added to cake batters, are   19
often floured first to keep them from settling to the bottom.

Dried fruit that is old and hard will not soften during baking. Soften it by   20
boiling it in water for about 10 minutes, then drain it thoroughly and pat it dry
before adding it to the batter. Fruit prepared specifically for use in fruit cakes is
available in stores, especially at holiday time.

Nuts keep best when stored in the refrigerator or freezer. When grinding   21
nuts for tortes, keep them light and fluffy and take care not to overgrind. If
using a blender, do only one cup at a time and turn the motor on and off.
Very finely ground or pulverized nuts will become oily and make a heavy,
sodden cake.

From "Ingredients for a Cake," *Fannie Farmer Cookbook*

Example 2

First	[The human body consists of eight major systems:
Level	(1) the skeletal system, (2) the muscular system,
Analysis	(3) the circulatory system, (4) the nervous system,
	(5) the respiratory system, (6) the digestive system,
	(7) the excretory system, and (8) the reproductive system.]
Second	The skeleton. . .consist[s] of two divisions: the axial skeleton,
Level	a central axis on which is hung. . .[and] the appendicular
Analysis	skeleton.
Third	The axial skeleton consists of the vertebrae (backbone),
Level	the skull, and the ribs and sternum. The appendicular skeleton
Analysis	consists of the appendages (legs and arms), together with the
	pelvic girdle to which the legs are attached, and the pectoral girdle
	to which the arms are fastened.

From *Biology: Its Human Implications*, Garrett Hardin

Example 2

The keyboard is composed of groups of black and white notes, with alternations of two and then three black-note ensembles. Distances between keys
are as follows: from any key to the immediately adjacent key (to the right, of
higher pitch) or lower (to the left, of lower pitch) key is referred to as a *half
step*. Two half steps comprise a *whole step*. Here are some half steps: 1 to 2,
4 to 5, 5 to 6, 12 to 13. Some whole steps: 1 to 3, 5 to 7, 8 to 10, 11 to 13,
12 to 14.

The so-called major scale is a central device in all Western music, a sequence of eight notes constructed according to this formula:

1	2	3	4	5	6	7	8	1
1	1	1/2	1	1	1/2	1	1	

Starting on any key, a major scale is formed by proceeding from the starting point, either one octave higher or one octave lower. Within the scope of one octave range, there are twelve possible starting notes, and thus twelve major scales. In musical nomenclature, alphabet terms are assigned to the notes:

I. The white notes are named by the terms A through G, duplicated through successive octaves.

2. Black notes are named by reference to the adjacent white notes, a black note termed a 'flat' when named by reference to that white note a half step above it, or a 'sharp' relative to that white note a half step below. The black notes thus take either of two names (this may also be true of white notes in minor scales, and harmonic minor scales.)

From "Scales" in *Ways of the Hand*, David Sudnow

Essays Using Analysis

In the following discourse, "Analysis of a Motorcycle" from *Zen and Motorcycle Maintenance*, Robert Pirsig presents a *static analysis*—of a motorcycle. His discourse analyzing the scientific method (See *Chapter 2: Development: Elements and Components*) is a process analysis. Other process analyses will be considered in *Chapter 6: Order* under *"Chronological Order."*

I want flow to turn his analytic approach back upon itself—to analyze analysis itself. I want to do this first of all by giving an extensive example of it and then by dissecting what it is. The motorcycle is a perfect subject for it since the motorcycle itself was invented by classic minds. So listen:

"Analysis of a Motorcycle"
Robert Pirsig

A motorcycle may be divided for purposes of classical rational analysis by means   1
of its component assemblies and by means of its functions.

If divided by means of its component assemblies, its most basic division is   2
into a power assembly and a running assembly.

The power assembly may be divided into the engine and the power-delivery   3
system. The engine will be taken up first.

The engine consists of a housing containing a Power train, a fuel-air sys- 4
tem, an ignition system, a feedback system and a lubrication system.

The power train consists of cylinders, pistons, connecting rods, a crank- 5
shaft and a flywheel.

The fuel-air system components, which are part of the engine, consist of 6
a gas tank and filter, an air cleaner, a carburetor, valves and exhaust pipes.

The ignition system consists of an alternator, a rectifier, a battery, a high- 7
voltage coil and spark plugs.

The feedback system consists of a cam chain, a camshaft, tappets and a 8
distributor.

The lubrication system consists of an oil pump channels throughout the 9
housing for distribution of the oil.

The power-delivery system accompanying the engine consists of a clutch, 10
a transmission and a chain.

The supporting assembly accompanying the power assembly consists of 11
a frame, including foot pegs, seat and fenders; a steering assembly; front and
rear shock absorbers; wheels; control 'levers and cables; lights and horn; and
speed and mileage indicators.

That's a motorcycle divided according to its components. To know what 12
the components are for, a division according to functions is necessary:

A motorcycle may be divided into normal running functions and special, 13
operator-controlled functions.

Normal running functions may be divided into functions during the intake 14
cycle, functions during the compression cycle, functions during the power
cycle and functions during the exhaust cycle.

And so on. I could go on about which functions occur in their proper 15
sequence during, each of the four cycles, then go on to the operator-controlled
functions and that would be a very summary description of the underlying
Corm of a motorcycle. It would be extremely short and rudimentary, as
descriptions of this sort go. Almost any one of the components mentioned can
be expanded on indefinitely. I've read an entire engineering volume on contact
points alone. which are just a small but vital part of the distributor. There are
other types of engines than the single-cylinder Otto engine described here: two-
cycle engines, multiple-cylinder engines, diesel engines, Wankel engines—but
this example is enough.

This description would cover the "what" of the motorcycle in terms of 16
components, and the "how" of the engine in terms of functions. It would badly
need a "where" analysis in the form of an illustration, and also a "why" analysis
in the form of engineering principles that led to this particular conformation of
parts. But the purpose here isn't exhaustively to analyze the motorcycle. It's to
provide a starting point, an example of a mode of understanding of things
which will itself become an object of analysis.

From *Zen and the Art of Motorcycle Maintenance*, Robert Pirsig

Example 2

    Do you find something appealing about the famous tune from Schubert's   1
Unfinished Symphony? If so, then you are responding to one of the most
important elements of music—*melody.*

    Do you find that you feel like tapping your foot during the march move-   2
ment of Tchaikovsky's Pathétique Symphony? If so, then you are responding to
another extremely important element *rhythm.* . . .

    Now [if] melody . . . were buzzed through a tissue-papered comb,
instead of being played by the entire cello section of an orchestra . . .the   3
difference would. . .[be] in the quality of the sound that reached your ears. . .
—*tone color.* . . .

    Now, let us suppose that a pianist is playing one of your favorite songs—
the melody in the right hand, the accompanying chords in the left. Suppose   4
that his finger slips as he plays one of the chords, [and he]play[s] a sour note.
Your. . .awareness of that wrong note comes from your response to another
. . .basic elements—*harmony.* . . .

    Do you have a sense of completeness at the conclusion of a performance
of. . .Beethoven's Ninth Symphony? Are you left with a feeling of satisfaction   5
as well as of elation? If so, part of that sense of satisfaction—of
completion—comes from your feeling for *form,* which is the last of the five
basic elements of music.

    From "Five Basic Elements of Music," David Randolph

CHAPTER 5

Organization by Main Ideas

One can produce an extremely logical and effective discourse by organizing it by *main ideas*. An essay, paragraph, or sentence can be organized by a sequence of problems, of solutions, of reasons, of causes, or effects, of a logical sequence of ideas, or of the writer's assorted ideas about a subject.

The main ideas which control some of the discourses in this section are outlined below. Introductions and conclusions are not included in the outlines.

"The Declaration of Independence" is controlled by three main ideas, which produce a logical sequence, which can be summarized.

a) Whenever x happens, y should happen. (I and II)

b) x has happened. (III)

c) Therefore, y is happening. (IV)

The Declaration of Independence, *Thomas Jefferson, et al.*

Thesis: [The United Colonies are right to separate themselves from British control.]

I. Governments are instituted among Men [to protect human beings] unalienable Rights [including] Life. Liberty and the pursuit of Happiness. (Paragraphs 2 and 3)

II. [W]henever any Form of Government becomes destructive of these ends, it is the Right of the People to alter or to abolish it, and to institute new Government. (Paragraph 4)

III. The history of the present King of Great Britain is a history of repeated injuries and usurpations, all having in direct object the establishment of an absolute Tyranny over these States. (Paragraphs 5-34)

IV. We, therefore . . .do . . . declare, that these United Colonies are, and of Right ought to be FREE AND INDEPENDENT STATES . . . . (Paragraph 35)

The Declaration of Independence
Thomas Jefferson, et al.

In CONGRESS, July 4, 1776.

The Unanimous Declaration of the Thirteen United States of America.

When in the Course of human events, it becomes necessary for one peo- 1
ple to dissolve the political bands which have connected them with another, and
to assume among the powers of the earth, the separate and equal station to
which the Laws of Nature and of Nature's God entitle them, a decent respect to
the opinions of mankind requires that they should declare the causes which
impel them to the separation.

We hold these truths to be self-evident, that all men are created equal, 2
that they are endowed by their Creator with certain unalienable Rights, that
among these are Life, Liberty and the pursuit of Happiness.

That to secure these rights, Governments are instituted among Men, 3
deriving their just powers from the consent of the governed.

That whenever any Form of Government becomes destructive of these 4
ends, it is the Right of the People to alter or to abolish it, and to institute new
Government, laying its foundation on such principles and organizing its powers
in such form, as to them shall seem most likely to effect their Safety and
Happiness. Prudence, indeed, will dictate that Governments long established
should not be changed for light and transient causes; and accordingly all experience hath shewn, that mankind are more disposed to suffer, while evils are
sufferable, than to right themselves by abolishing the forms to which they are
accustomed. But when a long train of abuses and usurpations, pursuing invariably the same Object evinces a design to reduce them under absolute
Despotism, it is their right, it is their duty, to throw off such Government, and
to provide new Guards for their future security. Such has been the patient suf-
ferance of these Colonies; and such is now the necessity which constrains
them to alter their former Systems of Government.

The history of the present King of Great Britain is a history of repeated 5
injuries and usurpations, all having in direct object the establishment of an
absolute Tyranny over these States. To prove this, let Facts be submitted to a
candid world.

He has refused his Assent to Laws, the most wholesome and necessary 6
for the public good.

He has forbidden his Governors to pass Laws of immediate and pressing 7
importance, unless suspended in their operation till his Assent should be
obtained; and when so suspended, he has utterly neglected to attend to them.

He has refused to pass other Laws for the accommodation of large districts 8
of people, unless those people would relinquish the right of Representation in
the Legislature, a right inestimable to them and formidable to tyrants only.

He has called together legislative bodies at places unusual, uncomfortable, and distant from the depository of their public Records, for the sole purpose of fatiguing them into compliance with his measures.   9

He has dissolved Representative Houses repeatedly, for opposing with manly firmness his invasions on the rights of people.   10

He has refused for a long time, after such dissolutions, to cause others to be elected; whereby the Legislative powers, incapable of Annihilation, have returned to the People at large for their exercise; the State remaining in the mean time exposed to all the dangers of invasion from without, and convulsions within.   11

He has endeavored to prevent the population of these States; for that purpose obstructing the Laws for Naturalization of Foreigners; refusing to pass others to encourage their migrations hither, and raising the conditions of new Appropriations of Lands.   12

He has obstructed the Administration of Justice, by refusing his Assent to Laws for establishing Judiciary powers.   13

He has made Judges dependent on his Will alone, for the tenure of their offices, and the amount and payment of their salaries.   14

He has erected a multitude of New Offices, and sent hither swarms of Officers to harass our people, and eat out their substance.   15

He has kept among us, in times of peace, Standing Armies without the Consent of our legislatures.   16

He has affected to render the Military independent of and superior to the Civil power.   17

He has combined with others to subject us to a jurisdiction foreign to our constitution, and unacknowledged by our laws; giving his Assent to their Acts of pretended Legislation: 18

For Quartering large bodies of armed troops among us;   19

For Protecting them, by a mock Trial, from punishment for any Murders which they should commit on the Inhabitants of these States;   20

For cutting off our Trade with all parts of the world;   21

For imposing Taxes on us without our consent;   22

For depriving us in many cases, of the benefits of Trial by Jury;   23

For transporting us beyond Seas to be tried for pretended offences;   24

For abolishing the free System of English Laws in a neighbouring Province, establishing therein an Arbitrary government, and enlarging its Boundaries so as to render it at once an example and fit instrument for introducing the same absolute rule into these Colonies;   25

For taking away our Charters, abolishing our most valuable Laws, and altering fundamentally the Forms of our Governments;   26

For suspending our own Legislatures, and declaring themselves invested with power to legislate for us in all cases whatsoever.   27

He has abdicated Government here, by declaring us out of his Protection and waging War against us.   28

He has plundered our seas, ravaged our Coasts, burnt our towns, and   29
destroyed the lives of our people.

He is at this time transporting large Armies of foreign Mercenaries to   30
compleat the works of death, desolation and tyranny, already begun with circumstances of Cruelty & perfidy scarcely paralleled in the most barbarous
ages, and totally unworthy the Head of a civilized nation.

He has constrained our fellow Citizens taken Captive on the high Seas to   31
bear Arms against their Country, to become the executioners of their friends
and Brethren, or to fall themselves by their Hands.

He has excited domestic insurrections amongst us, and has endeavored   32
to bring on the inhabitants of our frontiers, the merciless Indian Savages,
whose known rule of warfare, is an undistinguished destruction of all ages,
sexes and conditions.

In every stage of these Oppressions We have Petitioned for Redress in the   33
most humble terms: Our repeated Petitions have been answered only by repeated injury. A Prince, whose character is thus marked by every act which may
define a Tyrant, is unfit to be the ruler of a free people.

Nor have We been wanting in attentions to our British brethren. We have   34
warned them from time to time of attempts by their legislature to extend an
unwarrantable jurisdiction over us. We have reminded them of the circumstances of our emigration and settlement here. We have appealed to their
native justice and magnanimity, and we have conjured them by the ties of our
common kindred to disavow these usurpations, which, would inevitably inter-
rupt our connections and correspondence. They too have been deaf to the
voice of justice and of consanguinity. We must, therefore, acquiesce in the
necessity, which denounces our Separation, and hold them, as we hold the rest
of mankind, Enemies in War, in Peace Friends.

We, THEREFORE, the Representatives of the UNITED STATES OF AMERI-   35
CA, in General Congress Assembled, appealing to the Supreme Judge of the
world for the rectitude of our intentions, do, in the Name and by Authority of
the good People of these Colonies, solemnly publish and declare, that these
United Colonies are, and of Right ought to be FREE AND INDEPENDENT
STATES; that they are Absolved from all Allegiance to the British Crown, and
that all political connection between them and the State of Great Britain, is and
ought to be totally dissolved; and that as Free and Independent States, they
have full Power to levy War, conclude Peace, contract Alliances, establish
Commerce, and to do all other Acts and Things which Independent States may
of right do. And for the support of this Declaration, with a firm reliance on the
protection of divine Providence, we mutually pledge to each other our Lives,
our Fortunes and our sacred Honor.

A Few Kind Words for Superstition *by Robertson Davies*

Thesis: Superstition is alive and well today. (end of Paragraph 2)

I. [S]uperstition takes four forms. (Paragraph 3)
[*I. Is developed by classification*]

   A. Vain Observances (Paragraph 3)

   B. Divination (Paragraph 4)

   C. Idolatry (Paragraph 5)

   D. Improper Worship of the True God (Paragraph 6)

II. Superstition seems to run, a submerged river of crude religion, below the surface of human consciousness. (Paragraphs 7-8)

III. Many superstitions are so widespread and so old that they must have risen from a depth of the human mind that is indifferent to race or creed. (Paragraphs 9-10)

IV. Superstition in general is linked to man's yearning to know his fate, and to have some hand in deciding it. (Paragraphs 11-12)

"A Few Kind Words For Superstition"

Robertson Davies

In grave discussions of "the renaissance of the irrational" in our time, superstition does not figure largely as a serious challenge to reason or science. Parapsychology, UFO's, miracle cures, transcendental meditation and all the paths to instant enlightenment are condemned, but superstition is merely deplored. Is it because it has an unacknowledged hold on so many of us? [1]

Few people will admit to being superstitious; it implies naiveté or ignorance. But I live in the middle of a large university, and I see superstition in its four manifestations, alive and flourishing among people who are indisputably rational and learned. [2]

You did not know that superstition takes four forms? Theologians assure us that it does. First is what they call Vain Observances, such as not walking under a ladder, and that kind of thing. Yet I saw a deeply learned professor of anthropology, who had spilled some salt, throwing a pinch of it over his left shoulder; when I asked him why, he replied, with a wink, that it was "to hit the Devil in the eye." I did not question him further about his belief in the Devil: but I noticed that he did not smile until I asked him what he was doing. [3]

The second form is Divination, or consulting oracles. Another learned professor I know, who would scorn to settle a problem by tossing a coin (which is a humble appeal to Fate to declare itself), told me quite seriously that he had resolved a matter related to university affairs by consulting the I Ching. [4]

And why not? There are thousands of people on this continent who appeal to   5
the I Ching, and their general level of education seems to absolve them of
superstition. Almost, but not quite. The I Ching, to the embarrassment of
rationalists, often gives excellent advice.

The third form is Idolatry, and universities can show plenty of that. If you   6
have ever supervised a large examination room, you know how many jujus,
lucky coins and other bringers of luck are placed on the desks of the candidates. Modest idolatry, but what else can you call it?

The fourth form is Improper Worship of the True God. A while ago, I   7
learned that every day, for several days, a $2 bill (in Canada we have $2 bills,
regarded by some people as unlucky) had been tucked under a candlestick on
the altar of a college chapel. Investigation revealed that an engineering student,
worried about a girl, thought that bribery of the Deity might help. When I
talked with him, he did not think he was pricing God cheap, because he could
afford no more. A reasonable argument, but perhaps God was proud that
week, for the scientific oracle went against him.

Superstition seems to run, a submerged river of crude religion, below the   8
surface of human consciousness. It has done so for as long as we have any
chronicle of human behavior, and although I cannot prove it, I doubt if it is
more prevalent today than it has always been. Superstition, the theologians tell
us, comes from the Latin *supersisto* meaning to stand in terror of the Deity.
Most people keep their terror within bounds, but they cannot root it out, nor do
they seem to want to do so.

The more the teaching of formal religion declines, or takes a sociological   9
form, the less God appears to great numbers of people as a God of Love,
resuming his older form of a watchful, minatory power, to be placated and
cajoled. Superstition makes its appearance, apparently unbidden, very early in
life, when children fear that stepping on cracks in the sidewalk will bring ill for-
tune. It may persist even among the greatly learned and devout, as in the case
of Dr. Samuel Johnson, who felt it necessary to touch posts that he passed in
the street. The psychoanalysts have their explanation, but calling a superstition
a compulsion neurosis does not banish it.

Many superstitions are so widespread and so old that they must have   10
risen from a depth of the human mind that is indifferent to race or creed.
Orthodox Jews place a charm on their door-posts; so do (or did) the Chinese.
Some peoples of Middle Europe believe that when a man sneezes, his soul, for
that moment, is absent from his body, and they hasten to bless him, lest the
soul be seized by the Devil. How did the Melanesians come by the same idea?
Superstition seems to have a link with some body of belief that far antedates
the religions we know—religions which have no place for such comforting little
ceremonies and charities.

People who like disagreeable historical comparisons recall that when   11
Rome was in decline, superstition proliferated wildly, and that something of the

same sort is happening in our Western world today. They point to the populari- 12
ty of astrology, and it is true that sober newspapers that would scorn to deal in
love philters carry astrology columns and the fashion magazines count them
among their most popular features. But when has astrology not been popular?
No use saying science discredits it. When has the heart of man given a damn
for science?

Superstition in general is linked to man's yearning to know his fate, and to 13
have some hand in deciding it. When my mother was a child, she innocently
joined her Roman Catholic friends in killing spiders on July 11, until she
learned that this was done to ensure heavy rain the day following, the anniver-
sary of the Battle of Boyne, when the Orangemen would hold their parade. I
knew an Italian, a good scientist, who watched every morning before leaving
his house, so that the first person he met would not be a priest or a nun, as
this would certainly bring bad luck.

I am not one to stand aloof from the rest of humanity in this matter, for 14
when I was a university student, a gypsy woman with a child in her arms used
to appear every year at examination time, and ask a shilling of anyone who
touched the Lucky Baby; that swarthy infant cost me four shillings altogether,
and I never failed an examination. Of course, I did it merely for the joke—or so
I thought then. Now, I am humbler.

1978

"Politics and the English Language"

George Orwell

Most people who bother with the matter at all would admit that the English lan- 1
guage is in a bad way, but it is generally assumed that we cannot by conscious
action do anything about it. Our civilization is decadent and our language—so
the argument runs—must inevitably share in the general collapse. It follows
that any struggle against the abuse of language is a sentimental archaism, like
preferring candles to electric light or hansom cabs to aeroplanes. Underneath
this lies the half-conscious belief that language is a natural growth and not an
instrument which we shape for our own purposes.

Now, it is clear that the decline of a language must ultimately have politi- 2
cal and economic causes: it is not due simply to the bad influence of this or
that individual writer. But an effect can become a cause, reinforcing the original
cause and producing the same effect in an intensified form, and so on indefinitely. A man may take to drink because he feels himself to be a failure, and
then fail all the more completely because he drinks. It is rather the same thing
that is happening to the English language. It becomes ugly and inaccurate
because our thoughts are foolish, but the slovenliness of our language makes it

easier for us to have foolish thoughts. The point is that the process is reversible. Modern English, especially written English, is full of bad habits which spread by imitation and which can be avoided if one is willing to take the necessary trouble. If one gets rid of these habits one can think more clearly, and to think clearly is a necessary first step towards political regeneration: so that the fight against bad English is not frivolous and is not the exclusive concern of professional writers. I will come back to this presently, and I hope that by that time the meaning of what I have said here will have become clearer. Meanwhile, here are five speci- mens of the English language as it is now habitually written.

These five passages have not been picked out because they are especially ³ bad—I could have quoted far worse if I had chosen—but because they illustrate various of the mental vices from which we now suffer. They are a little below the average, but are fairly representative samples. I number them so that I can refer back to them when necessary.

1) I am not, indeed, sure whether it is not true to say that the Milton who once seemed not unlike a seventeenth-century Shelley had not become, out of an experience ever more bitter in each year, more alien [sic] to the founder of that Jesuit sect which nothing could induce him to tolerate.
    Professor Harold Laski (Essay in *Freedom of Expression*)

2) Above all, we cannot play ducks and drakes with a native battery of idioms which prescribes such egregious collocations of vocables as the Basic *put up with* for *tolerate* or *put at a loss* for *bewilder.*
    Professor Lancelot Hogben (*Interglossa*)

3) On the one side we have the free personality: by definition it is not neu- rotic, for it has neither conflict nor dream. Its desires, such as they are, are transparent, for they are just what institutional approval keeps in the forefront of consciousness; another institutional pattern would alter their number and intensity; there is little in them that is natural, irreducible, or culturally dangerous. But on the other side, the social bond itself is noth- ing but the mutual reflection of these self-secure integrities. Recall the definition of love. Is not this the very picture of a small academic? Where is there a place in this hall of mirrors for either personality or fraternity?
    Essay on psychology in Politics (New York)

4) All the "best people" from the gentlemen's clubs, and all the frantic fas- cist captains, united in common hatred of Socialism and bestial horror of the rising tide of the mass revolutionary movement, have turned to acts of provocation, to foul incendiarism, to medieval legends of poisoned wells, to legalize their own destruction of proletarian organizations, and rouse the agitated petty-bourgeoisie to chauvinistic fervour on behalf of the fight against the revolutionary way out of the crisis.
    Communist pamphlet

5) If a new spirit is to be infused into this old country, there is one thorny and contentious reform which must be tackled, and that is the humanization and galvanization of the B.B.C. Timidity here will bespeak canker and atrophy of the soul. The heart of Britain may be sound and of strong beat, for instance, but the British lion's roar at present is like that of Bottom in Shakespeare's *Midsummer Night's Dream*—as gentle as any sucking dove. A virile new Britain cannot continue indefinitely to be traduced in the eyes or rather ears, of the world by the effete languors of Langham Place, brazenly masquerading as "standard English." When the Voice of Britain is heard at nine o'clock, better far and infinitely less ludicrous to hear aitches honestly dropped than the present priggish, inflated, inhibited, schoolma'amish arch braying of blameless bashful mewing maidens!

Letter in *Tribune*

Each of these passages has faults of its own, but, quite apart from avoid- 4
able ugliness, two qualities are common to all of them. The first is staleness of imagery; the other is lack of precision. The writer either has a meaning and cannot express it, or he inadvertently says something else, or he is almost indifferent as to whether his words mean anything or not. This mixture of vagueness and sheer incompetence is the most marked characteristic of modern English prose, and especially of any kind of political writing. As soon as certain topics are raised. the concrete melts into the abstract and no one seems able to think of turns of speech that are not hackneyed: prose consists less and less of *words* chosen for the sake of their meaning, and more and more of *phrases* tacked together like the sections of a prefabricated hen house. I list below, with notes and examples, various of the tricks by means of which the work of prose-construction is habitually dodged:

Dying Metaphors. A newly invented metaphor assists thought by evoking 5
a visual image, while on the other hand a metaphor which is technically "dead" (e.g., *iron resolution*) has in effect reverted to being an ordinary word and can generally be used without loss of vividness. But in between these two classes there is a huge dump of worn-out metaphors which have lost all evocative power and are merely used because they save people the trouble of inventing phrases for themselves. Examples are: *Ring the changes on, take up the cudgels for toe the line, ride roughshod over, stand shoulder to shoulder with, play into the hands of, no axe to grind, grist to the mill, fishing in troubled waters, on the order of the day, Achilles' heel, swan song, hotbed.* Many of these are used without knowledge of their meaning (what is a "rift," for instance?), and incompatible metaphors are frequently mixed, a sure sign that the writer is not interested in what he is saying. Some metaphors now current have been twisted out of their original meaning without those who use them even being aware of the fact. For example, *toe* the line is sometimes written *tow* the line.

Another example is the *hammer and the anvil* now always used with the impli-
cation that the anvil gets the worst of it. In real life it is always the anvil that
breaks the hammer, never the other way about: a writer who stopped to think
what he was saying would be aware of this, and would avoid perverting the
original phrase.

Operators or verbal false limbs. These save the trouble of picking out   6
appropriate verbs and nouns, and at the same time pad each sentence with
extra syllables which give it an appearance of symmetry. Characteristic phrases
are *render inoperative, militate against, make contact with, be subjected to, give
rise to, give grounds for, have the affect of, play a leading part (role) in, making
itself felt, take effect, exhibit a tendency to, serve the purpose of* etc., etc. The
keynote is the elimination of simple verbs. Instead of being a single word, such
as *break, stop, spoil, mend, kill,* a verb becomes a phrase, made up of a noun
or adjective tacked on to some general-purpose verb such as *prove, serve,
form, play, render.* In addition, the passive voice is wherever possible used in
preference to the active, and noun constructions are used instead of gerunds
(*by examination of* instead of *by examining*). The range of verbs is further cut
down by means of the *-ize* and *de-* formations, and the banal statements are
given in appearance of profundity by means of the *not un-* formation. Simple
conjunctions and prepositions are replaced by such phrases as *with respect to,
having regard to, the fact that, by dint of, in view of, in the interests of, on the
hypothesis that;* and the ends of sentences are saved from anticlimax by such
resounding common-places as *greatly to be desired, cannot be left out of
account, a development to be expected in the near future, deserving of serious
consideration, brought to a satisfactory conclusion,* and so on and so forth.

Pretentious diction. Words like *phenomenon, element, individual* (as   7
noun), *objective, categorical, effective, virtual, basic, primary, promote, constitute, exhibit, exploit, utilize, eliminate, liquidate,* are used to dress up simple
statements and give an air of scientific impartiality to biased judgments.
Adjectives like *epoch-making, epic, historic, unforgettable, triumphant, age-old,
inevitable, inexorable, veritable,* are used to dignify the sordid processes of
international politics, while writing that aims at glorifying war usually takes on
an archaic colour, its characteristic words being: *realm, throne, chariot, mailed
fist, trident, sword, shield, buckler, banner, jackboot, clarion.* Foreign words
and expressions such as *cul de sac, ancien régime, deus ex machina, mutatis
mutandis, status quo, gleichshaltung, weltanshauung,* are used to give an air of
culture and elegance. Except for the useful abbreviations *i.e., e.g.,* and *etc.,*
there is no real need for any of the hundreds of foreign phrases now current in
English. Bad writers, and especially scientific, political and sociological writers,
are nearly always haunted by the notion that Latin or Greek words are grander
than Saxon ones, and unnecessary words like *expedite, ameliorate, predict,
extraneous, deracinated, clandestine, subaqueous* and hundreds of others con-

stantly gain ground from their Anglo-Saxon opposite numbers. The Jargon peculiar to Marxist writing (*hyena, hangman, cannibal, petty bourgeois, these gentry, lacquey, flunky, mad dog, White Guard,* etc.) consists largely of words and phrases translated from Russian, German or French; but the normal way of coining a new word is to use a Latin or Greek root with the appropriate affix and, where necessary, the *-ize* formation. It is often easier to make up words of this kind (*deregionalize, impermissible, extramarital, nonfragmentary, and so forth*) than to think up the English words that will cover one's meaning. The result, in general, is an increase in slovenliness and vagueness.

    Meaningless words. In certain kinds of writing, particularly in art criti-   8
cism and literary criticism, it is normal to come across long passages which are almost completely lacking in meaning. Words like *romantic, plastic, values, human, dead, sentimental, natural, vitality,* as used in art criticism, are strictly meaningless, in the sense that they not only do not point to any discoverable object, but are hardly ever expected to do so by the reader. When one critic writes, "The outstanding feature of Mr. X's work is its living quality," while another writes, "The immediately striking thing about Mr. X's work is its peculiar deadness," the reader accepts this as a simple difference of opinion. If words like *black* and *white* were involved, instead of the jargon words *dead* and *living,* he would see at once that language was being used in an improper way. Many political words are similarly abused. The word *Fascism* has now no meaning except in so far as it signifies "something not desirable." The words *democracy, socialism, freedom, patriotic, realistic, justice,* have each of them several different meanings which cannot be reconciled with one another. In the case of a word like *democracy,* not only is there no agreed definition, but the attempt to make one is resisted from all sides. It is almost universally felt that when we call a country democratic we are praising it: consequently the defenders of every kind of regime claim that it is a democracy, and fear that they might have to stop using the word if it were tied down to any one meaning. Words of this kind are often used in a consciously dishonest way. That is, the person who uses them has his own private definition, but allows his hearer to think he means something quite different. Statements like *Marshal Petain was a true patriot, The Soviet Press is the freest in the world, The Catholic Church is opposed to persecution,* are almost always made with intent to deceive. Other words used in variable meanings, in most cases more or less dishonestly, are: *class, totalitarian, science, progressive, reactionary, bourgeois, equality.*

    Now that I have made this catalogue of swindles and perversions, let me   9
give another example of the kind of writing that they lead to. This time it must of its nature be an imaginary one. I am going to translate a passage of good English into modern English of the worst sort. Here is a well-known verse from *Ecclesiastes*:

I returned and saw under the sun, that the race is not to the swift, nor the battle to the strong, neither yet bread to the wise, nor yet riches to men of understanding, nor yet favor to men of skill; but time and chance happeneth to them all.

Here it is in modern English:

Objective consideration of contemporary phenomena compels the conclusion that success or failure in competitive activities exhibits no tendency to be commensurate with innate capacity, but that a considerable element of the unpredictable must invariably be taken into account.

This is a parody, but not a very gross one. Exhibit (3), above, for instance, contains several patches of the same kind of English. It will be seen that I have not made a full translation. The beginning and ending of the sentence follow the original meaning fairly closely, but in the middle the concrete illustrations—race, battle, bread—dissolve into the vague phrase "success or failure in competitive activities." This had to be so, because no modern writer of the kind I am discussing—no one capable of using phrases like "objective consideration of contemporary phenomena"—would ever tabulate his thoughts in that precise and detailed way. The whole tendency of modern prose is away from concreteness. Now analyze these two sentences a little more closely. The first contains forty-nine words but only sixty syllables, and all its words are those of everyday life. The second contains thirty-eight words of ninety syllables: eighteen of its words are from Latin roots, and one from Greek. The first sentence contains six vivid images, and only one phrase ("time and chance") that could be called vague. The second contains not a single fresh, arresting phrase, and in spite of its ninety syllables it gives only a shortened version of the meaning contained in the first. Yet without a doubt it is the second kind of sentence that is gaining ground in modern English. I do not want to exaggerate. This kind of writing is not yet universal, and outcrops of simplicity will occur here and there in the worst-written page. Still, if you or I were told to write a few lines on the uncertainty of human fortunes, we should probably come much nearer to my imaginary sentence than to the one from *Ecclesiastes*.

As I have tried to show, modern writing at its worst does not consist in picking out words for the sake of their meaning and inventing images in order to make the meaning clearer. It consists in gumming together long strips of words which have already been set in order by someone else, and making the results presentable by sheer humbug. The attraction of this way of writing is that it is easy. It is easier—even quicker, once you have the habit—to say *In my opinion it is not an unjustifiable assumption that* than to say *I think*. If you use ready-made phrases, you not only don't have to hunt for words; you also don't have to bother with the rhythms of your sentences, since these phrases

10

11

are generally so arranged as to be more or less euphonious. When you are composing in a hurry—when you are dictating to a stenographer, for instance, or making a public speech—it is natural to fall into a pretentious, Latinized style. Tags like *a consideration which we should do well to bear in mind* or *a conclusion to which all of us would readily assent* will save many a sentence from coming down with a bump. By using stale metaphors, similes and idioms, you save much mental effort, at the cost of leaving your meaning vague, not only for your reader but for yours. This is the significance of mixed metaphors. The sole aim of a metaphor is to call up a visual image. When these images clash—as in *The Fascist octopus has sung its swan song, the jackboot is thrown into the melting pot*—it can be taken as certain that the writer is not seeing a mental image of the objects he is naming; in other words he is not really thinking. Look again at the examples I gave at the beginning of this essay. Professor Laski (1) uses five negatives in fifty-three words. One of these is superfluous, making nonsense of the whole passage, and in addition there is the slip *alien* for *akin*, making further nonsense, and several avoidable pieces of clumsiness which increase the general vagueness. Professor Hogben (2) plays ducks and drakes with a battery which is able to write pre-scriptions and, while disapproving of the every day phrase put up with, is unwilling to look egregious up in the dictionary and see what it means; (3), if one takes an uncharitable attitude towards it, is simply meaningless: probably one could work out its intended meaning by reading the whole of the article in which it occurs. In (4), the writer knows more or less what he wants to say, but an accumulation of stale phrases chokes him like tea leaves blocking a sink. In (5), words and meaning have almost parted company. People who write in this manner usually have a general emotional meaning—they dislike one thing and want to express solidarity with another—but they are not inter-ested in the detail of what they are saying. A scrupulous writer, in every sentence that he writes, will ask himself at least four questions, thus: What am I trying to say? What words will express it? What image or idiom will make it clearer? Is this image fresh enough to have an effect? And he will probably ask himself two more: Could I put it more shortly? Have I said anything that is avoidably ugly? But you are not obliged to go to all this trouble. You can shirk it by simply throwing your mind open and letting the ready—made phrases come crowding in. They will construct your sentences for you—even think your thoughts for you, to a certain extent-and at need they will perform the important service of partially concealing your meaning even from yourself. It is at this point that the special connection between politics and the debase-ment of language becomes clear.

In our time it is broadly true that political writing is bad writing. Where it 12 is not true, it will generally be found that the writer is some kind of rebel, expressing his private opinions and not a "party line." Orthodoxy, of whatever

colour, seems to demand a lifeless, imitative style. The political dialects to be found in pamphlets, leading articles, manifests, White Papers and the speeches of under-secretaries do, of course, vary from party to party, but they are all alike in that one almost never finds in them a fresh, vivid, home-made turn of speech. When one watches some tired hack on the platform mechanically repeating the familiar phrase—*bestial atrocities, iron heel, bloodstained tyranny, free peoples of the world, stand shoulder to shoulder*—one often has a curious feeling that one is not watching a live human being but some kind of dummy: a feeling which suddenly becomes stronger at moments when the light catches the speaker's spectacles and turns them into blank discs which seem to have no eyes behind them. And this is not altogether fanciful. A speaker who uses that kind of phraseology has gone some distance towards turning himself into a machine. The appropriate noises are coming out of his larynx, but his brain is not involved as it would be if he were choosing his words for himself. If the speech he is making is one that he is accustomed to make over and over again, he may be almost unconscious of what he is saying, as one is when one utters the responses in church. And this reduced state of consciousness, if not indispensable, is at any rate favorable to political conformity.

    In our time, political speech and writing are largely the defence of the indefensible. Things like the continuance of British rule in India, the Russian purges and deportations, the dropping of the atom bombs on Japan, can indeed be defended, but only by arguments which are too brutal for most people to face, and which do not square with the professed aims of political parties. Thus political language has to consist largely of euphemism, question begging and sheer cloudy vagueness. Defenseless villages are bombarded from the air, the inhabitants driven out into the countryside, the cattle machine-gunned, the huts set on fire with incendiary bullets: this is called *pacification.* Millions of peasants are robbed of their farms and set trudging along the roads with no more than they can carry: this is called *transfer of population* or *rectification of frontiers.* People are imprisoned for years without trial, or shot in the back of the neck or sent to die of scurvy in Arctic lumber camps: this is called *elimination of unreliable elements.* Such phraseology is needed if one wants to name things without calling up mental pictures of them. Consider for instance some comfortable English professor defending Russian totalitarianism. He cannot say outright, "I believe in killing off your opponents when you can get good results by doing so." Probably, therefore, he will say something like this:

> While freely conceding that the Soviet regime exhibits certain features which the humanitarian may be inclined to deplore, we must, I think, agree that a certain curtailment of the right to political opposition is an unavoidable concomitant of transitional periods, and that the rigours which the Russian people have been called upon to undergo have been amply justified in the sphere of concrete achievement.

13

The inflated style is itself a kind of euphemism. A mass of Latin words 14
falls upon the acts like soft snow, blurring the outlines and covering up all the
details. The great enemy of clear language is insincerity. When there is a gap
between one's real and one's declared aims, one turns as it were instinctively to
long words and exhausted idioms, like a cuttlefish squirting out ink. In our age
there is no such thing as "keeping out of politics." All issues are political
issues, and politics itself is a mass of lies, evasions, folly, hatred and schizophrenia. When the general atmosphere is bad, language must suffer. I should
expect to find—this is a guess which I have not sufficient knowledge to veri-
fy—that the German, Russian and Italian languages have all deteriorated in the
last ten or fifteen years, as a result of dictatorship.

But if thought corrupts language, language can also corrupt thought. 15
A bad usage can spread by tradition and imitation, even among people who
should and do know better. The debased language that I have been discussing
is in some ways very convenient. Phrases like *a not unjustifiable assumption,
leaves much to be desired, would serve no good purpose, a consideration
which we should do well to bear in mind,* are a continuous temptation, a packet
of aspirins always at one's elbow. Look back through this essay, and for certain you will find that I have again and again committed the very faults I am
protesting against. By this morning's post I have received a pamphlet dealing
with conditions in Germany. The author tells me that he "felt impelled" to write
it. I open it at random, and here is almost the first sentence that I see: "[The
Allies] have an opportunity not only of achieving a radical transformation of
Germany's social and political structure in such a way as to avoid a nationalistic
reaction in Germany itself but at the same time of laying the foundations of a
co-operative and unified Europe." You see, he "feels impelled" to write—feels,
presumably, that he has something new to say—and yet his words, like cavalry
horses answering the bugle, group themselves automatically into the familiar
dreary pattern. This invasion of one's mind by ready-made phrases (*lay the
foundations, achieve a radical transformation*) can only be prevented if one is
constantly on guard against them, and every such phrase anesthetizes a portion
of one's brain.

I said earlier that the decadence of our language is probably curable. 16
Those who deny this would argue, if they produced an argument at all, that language merely reflects existing social conditions, and that we cannot influence
its development by any direct tinkering with words and constructions. So far
as the general tone or spirit of a language goes, this may be true, but it is not
true in detail. Silly words and expressions have often disappeared, not through
any evolutionary process but owing to the conscious action of a minority. Two
recent examples were *explore every avenue* and *leave no stone unturned,* which
were killed by the jeers of a few journalists. There is a long list of fly-blown
metaphors which could similarly be got rid of if enough people would interest

themselves in the job; and it should also be possible to laugh the *not un-* for-mation out of existence, to reduce the amount of Latin and Greek in the average sentence, to drive out foreign phrases and strayed scientific words, and, in general, to make pretentiousness unfashionable. But all these are minor points. The defence of the English language implies more than this, and perhaps it is best to start by saying what it does not imply.

To begin with it has nothing to do with archaism, with the salvaging of   17 obsolete words and turns of speech, or with the setting up of a "standard English" which must never be departed from. On the contrary, it is especially concerned with the scrapping of every word or idiom which has outworn its usefulness. It has nothing to do with correct grammar and syntax, which are of no importance so long as one makes one's meaning clear, or with the avoid-ance of Americanisms, or with having what is called a "good prose style." On the other hand it is not concerned with fake simplicity and the attempt to make written English colloquial. Nor does it even imply in every case preferring the Saxon word to the Latin one, though it does imply using the fewest and short-est words that will cover one's meaning. What is above all needed is to let the meaning choose the word, and not the other way about. In prose, the worst thing one can do with words is to surrender to them. When you think of a con-crete object, you think wordlessly, and then, if you want to describe the thing you have been visualizing you probably hunt about till you find the exact words that seem to fit it. When you think of something abstract you are more inclined to use words from the start, and unless you make a conscious effort to prevent it, the existing dialect will come rushing in and do the job for you, at the expense of blurring or even changing your meaning. Probably it is better to put off using words as long as possible and get one's meaning as clear as one can through pictures or sensations. Afterwards one can choose—not simply accept—the phrase that will best cover the meaning, and then switch round and decide what impression one's words are likely to make on another person. This last effort of the mind cuts out all stale or mixed images, all prefabricated phrases, needless repetitions, and humbug and vagueness generally. But one can often be in doubt about the effect of a word or a phrase, and one needs rules that one can rely on when instinct fails. I think the following rules will cover most cases:

(i) Never use a metaphor, simile or other figure of speech which you are used to seeing in print.

(ii) Never use a long word where a short one will do.

(iii) If it is possible to cut a word out, always cut it out.

(iv) Never use the passive when you can use the active.

(v) Never use a foreign phrase, a scientific word or a jargon word if you can think of an everyday English equivalent.

(vi) Break any of these rules sooner than say anything outright barbarous.

These rules sound elementary, and so they are, but they demand a deep   18
change of attitude in anyone who has grown used to writing in the style now fashionable. One could keep all of them and still write bad English, but one could not write the kind of stuff that I quoted in those five specimens at the beginning of this article.

I have not here been considering the literary use of language, but merely   19
language as an instrument for expressing and not for concealing or preventing thought. Stuart Chase and others have come near to claiming that all abstract words are meaningless, and have used this as a pretext for advocating a kind of political quietism. Since you don't know what Fascism is, how can you strug-gle against Fascism? One need not swallow such absurdities as this, but one ought to recognize that the present political chaos is connected with the decay of language, and that one can probably bring about some improvement by starting at the verbal end. If you simplify your English, you are freed from the worst follies of orthodoxy. You cannot speak any of the necessary dialects, and when you make a stupid remark its stupidity will be obvious, even to yourself Political language—and with variations this is true of all political parties, from Conservatives to Anarchists is designed to make lies sound truthful and murder respectable, and to give an appearance of solidity to pure wind. One cannot change this all in a moment, but one can at least change one's own habits, and from time to time one can even, if one jeers loudly enough, send some worn-out and useless phrase—some jackboot, Achilles' heel, hotbed, melting pot, acid test, veritable inferno or other lump of verbal refuse—into the dustbin where it belongs.

1945

CHAPTER 6

Order

In contrast to *organization*, which is the way clusters of material are grouped in a discourse, *order* is the sequence in which information and ideas are presented. Order involves what comes first, second, and so on, to last. A writer can utilize any of the following for determining the order of a discourse, including space, chronology, logic, importance, psychology, or rhetoric.

SPATIAL ORDER

Spatial order is used for describing places, things, or the physical appearance of people. Any of the following orders can be effective: *near-to-far, far-to-near, down-to-up, up-to-down, left-to-right, right-to-left, center-to-periphery, and periphery-to-center.*

Examples of Spatial Order

Example 1

[O]n the outskirts of Kassell, which was the capital of this absurdly unimportant principality [Hesse], there stands a palace large and splendid enough to house a full-blown emperor. And from the main façade of this palace there rises to the very top of the neighboring mountains one of the most magnificent architectural gardens in the world. This garden, which is like a straight wide corridor of formal stone-work driven through the hillside forest, climbs up to a nondescript building in the grandest Roman manner, almost as large as a cathedral and surmounted by a colossal bronze statue of Hercules. Between Hercules at the top and the palace at the bottom lies an immense series of terraces, with fountains and cascades, pools, grottos, spouting tritons, dolphins, nereids and all the other mythological fauna of an eighteenth-century water-garden. The spectacle, when the waters are flowing, is magnificent. There must be the best part of two miles of neoclassic cataract and elegantly canalized foam. The waterworks at Versailles are tame and trivial in comparison.

From "Waterworks and Kings," Aldous Huxley

Example 2

Viewed from the distance of the moon, the astonishing thing about the earth. catching the breath, is that it is alive. The photographs show the dry, pounded surface of the moon in the foreground, dead as an old bone. Aloft, floating free beneath the moist, gleaming membrane of bright blue sky, is the rising earth, the only exuberant thing in this part of the cosmos. If you could look long enough, you would see the swirling of the great drifts of white cloud, covering and uncovering the half-hidden masses of land. If you had been looking for a very long, geologic time, you could have seen the continents themselves in motion, drifting apart on the crustal plates, held afloat by the fire beneath.

From "The World's Biggest Membrane." Lewis Thomas

Example 3

There is a new pond, much smaller than Lake Belleview, on First Avenue between Seventieth and Seventy-first, on the east side of the street. It emerged sometime last year, soon after a row of old flats had been torn down and the hole dug for a new apartment building. By now it is about the average size for Manhattan, a city block long and about forty feet across, maybe eight feet deep at the center, more or less kidney-shaped. rather like an outsized suburban swimming pool except for the things floating, and now the goldfish . . . clearly visible from the sidewalk, hundreds of [goldfish].

From "Ponds." Lewis Thomas

CHRONOLOGICAL ORDER

Chronological order is usually effective for presentation of narrative, process, and some cause and effect discourses. But for other kinds of discourses. chronological order can make it difficult for a reader to perceive the purpose or understand the argument of the discourse. Also, chronological order is frequently not very persuasive. Many writers resort to chronological order because it is often easy to write. The problem with relying on chronological order is that a writer may use it and ignore logical organization when logical organization is preferable.

Chronological order can be used to present *narrative*, *process*, or *cause and effect*, depending on the focus and emphasis of the discourse.

Narrative, Process, and Cause and Effect Discourse

Narrative discourse focuses on the events themselves and the sequence in which they occurred. Narrative answers the question "What?" It is used in expository essays, personal essays, fiction, and occasionally as an extended example in an argumentative essays.

Process discourse focuses on the way something was or should be done. Process answers the question "How?" It is used in expository essays and infrequently in extended examples in argumentative or personal essays.

Cause and effect Discourse focuses on what caused something to occur and what the results of that cause were. Cause and effect discourse addresses and tries to answer the question "Why?" It is used primarily in expository and argumentative discourse.

Narrative Order

Narrative order is usually chronological and stresses the events of what happened to tell a story. It frequently utilizes some of the following transitional words: after, before, during, first, now, once, second, soon, and then.

Examples of Narrative Discourse

Example 1

> I came; I saw; I conquered.
> Julius Caesar

Example 2

> But one way and another we do each year accumulate Christmas savings, a Fruitcake Fund. These moneys we keep hidden in an ancient bead purse under a loose board under the floor under a chamber pot under my friend's county (sixteen rattles). dip snuff (secretly), tame hummingbirds (just try it) till they balance on her finger, tell ghost stories (we both believe in ghosts) so tingling they chill you in July, talk to herself, take walks in the rain, grow the prettiest japonicas in town, know the recipe for every sort of old-time Indian cure, including a magical wart-remover.
>
> Now, with supper finished, we retire to the room in a faraway part of the house where my friend sleeps in a scrap-quilt-covered iron bed painted rose pink, her favorite color. Silently, wallowing in the pleasures of conspiracy, we take the bead purse from its secret place and spill its contents on the scrap quilt. Dollar bills, tightly rolled and green as May buds. Somber fifty-cent pieces, heavy enough to weight a dead man's eyes. Lovely dimes, the liveliest

1

2

coin, the one that really jingles. Nickels and quarters, worn smooth as creek pebbles. But mostly a hateful heap of bitter-odored pennies. Last summer others in the house contracted to pay us a penny for every twenty-five flies we killed. Oh, the carnage of August:

The flies that flew to heaven! Yet it was not work in which we took pride.   3
And, as we sit counting pennies, it is as though we were back tabulating dead flies. Neither of us has a head for figures; we count slowly, lose track, start again. According to her calculations, we have $12.73. According to mine, exactly $15. "I do hope you're wrong, Buddy. We can't mess around with thirteen. The cakes will fall. Or put somebody in the cemetery. Why, I wouldn't dream of getting out of bed on the thirteenth." This is true: she always spends thirteenths in bed. So, to be on the safe side, we subtract a penny and toss it out the window.

Of the ingredients that go into our fruitcakes, whiskey is the most expen-   4
sive, as well as the hardest to obtain: State laws forbid its sale. But everybody knows you can buy a bottle from Mr. Haha Jones. And the next day, having completed our more prosaic shopping, we set out for Mr. Haha's business address, a "sinful" (to quote public opinion) fish-fry and dancing café down by the river. We've been there before, and on the same errand; but in previous years our dealings have been with Haha's wife, an iodine-dark Indian woman with brassy peroxided hair and a dead-tired disposition. Actually, we've never laid eyes on her husband, though we've heard that he's an Indian too. A giant with razor scars across his cheeks. They call him Haha because he's so gloomy, a man who never laughs. As we approach his café (a large log cabin festooned inside and out with chains of garish-gay naked light bulbs and standing by the river's muddy edge under the shade of river trees where moss drifts through the branches like gray mist) our steps slow down. Even Queenie stops prancing and sticks close by. People have been murdered in Haha's café. Cut to pieces. Hit on the head. There's a case coming up in court next month. Naturally these goings-on happen at night when the colored lights cast crazy patterns and the victrola wails. In the daytime Haha's is shabby and deserted. I knock at the door, Queenie barks, my friend calls: "Mrs. Haha, ma'am? Anyone to home?."

Footsteps. The door opens. Our hearts overturn. It's Mr. Haha Jones   5
himself! And he is a giant; he does have scars; he doesn't smile. No, he glowers at us through Satan-tilted eyes and demands to know: "What you want with Haha?"

For a moment we are too paralyzed to tell. Presently my friend half-finds   6
her voice, a whispery voice at best: "If you please, Mr. Haha, we'd like a quart of your finest whiskey."

His eyes tilt more. Would you believe it? Haha is smiling! Laughing,   7
too. "Which one of you is a drinkin' man?"

"It's for making fruitcakes, Mr. Haha. Cooking." This sobers him. He   8
frowns. "That's no way to waste good whiskey." Nevertheless, he retreats into
the shadowed cafe' and seconds later appears carrying a bottle of daisy-yellow
unlabeled liquor. He demonstrates its sparkle in the sunlight and says:
"Two dollars."

We pay him with nickels and dimes and pennies. Suddenly, as he jangles   9
the coins in his hand like a fistful of dice, his face softens. "Tell you what," he
proposes, pouring the money back into our bead purse, "just send me one of
them fruitcakes instead."

"Well," my friend remarks on our way home, "there's a lovely man. We'll   10
put an extra cup of raisins in his cake."

The black stove, stoked with coal and firewood, glows like a lighted   11
pumpkin. Eggbeaters whirl, spoons spin round in bowls of butter and sugar,
vanilla sweetens the air, ginger spices it; melting, nose-tingling odors saturate
the kitchen, suffuse the house, drift out to the world on puffs of chimney
smoke. In four days our work is done. Thirty-one cakes, dampened with
whiskey, bask on window sills and shelves.

Who are they for?   12
Friends.   13

From "A Christmas Memory," Truman Capote

Example 3

If people ask me what Zen is like, I will say that is like learning the art of   1
burglary. The son of a burglar saw his father growing older and thought, "If he
is unable to carry on his profession who will be the breadwinner of the family,
except myself? I must learn the trade." He intimated the idea to his father,
who approved of it.

One night the father took the son to a big house, broke through the fence,   2
entered the house, and, opening one of the large chests, told the son to go in
and pick out the clothing. As soon as the son got into it, the father dropped the
lid and securely applied the lock. The father now came out to the courtyard
and loudly knocked at the door, waking up the whole family; then he quietly
slipped away by the hole in the fence. The residents got excited and lighted
candles, but they found that the burglar had already gone.

The son, who remained all the time securely confined in the chest,   3
thought of his cruel father. He was greatly mortified, then a fine idea flashed
upon him. He made a noise like the gnawing of a rat. The family told the maid
to take a candle and examine the chest. When the lid was unlocked, out came
the prisoner, who blew out the light, pushed away the maid, and fled. The people ran after him. Noticing a well by the road, he picked up a large stone and
threw it into the water. The pursuers all gathered around the well trying to find
the burglar drowning himself in the dark hole.

In the meantime he went safely back to his father's house. He blamed his   4
father deeply for his narrow escape. Said the father. "Be not offended, my son.
Just tell me how you got out of it." When the son told him all about his adventures, the father remarked, "There you are, you have learned the art."

From "Zen and the Art of Burglary," Wu-Tsu Fa-Yen

Example 4

In this place [a university laboratory], already packed, I had assigned to   1
me a small pine table with a rusty tin pan upon it. . . .

When I sat me down before my tin pan, Agassiz brought me a small fish,   2
placing it before me with the rather stern requirement that I should study it, but
should on no account talk to anyone concerning it, nor read anything relating to
fishes, until I had permission to do so. To my inquiry, "What shall I do?" he
said in effect: "Find out what you can without damaging the specimen; when I
think that you have done the work I will question you." In the course of an
hour I thought I had compassed that fish: it was rather an unsavory object,
giving forth the stench of old alcohol, then loathsome to me, though in time I
came to like it. Many of the scales were loosed so that they fell off. It
appeared to me to be a case for a summary report, which I was anxious to
make and get on to the next stage of the business. But Agassiz, though always
within call, concerned himself no further with me that day, or the next, for a
week. At first, this neglect was distressing; but I saw that it was a game, for he
was, as I discerned rather than saw, covertly watching me. So I set my wits to
work upon the thing, and in the course of a hundred hours or so thought I had
done much—a hundred times as much as seemed possible at the start. I got
interested in finding out how the scales went in series, their shape, the form
and placement of the teeth, etc. Finally, I felt full of the subject, and probably
expressed it in my bearing; as for words about it then, there were none from
my master except his cheery "Good Morning." At length, on the seventh day,
came the question, "Well?" and my disgorge of learning to him as he sat on the
edge of my table puffing his cigar. At the end of the hour's telling, he swung
off and away, saying: "That is not right." Here I began to think that, after all,
perhaps the rules for scanning Latin verse were not the worst infliction in the
world. Moreover, it was clear that he was playing a game with me to find if I
were capable of doing hard, continuous work without the support of a teacher,
and this stimulated me to labor. I went at the task anew, discarded my notes,
and in another week of ten hours a day labor I had results which astonished
myself and satisfied him. Still there was no trace of praise in words or manner.
He signified that it would do by placing before me a half a peck of bones, telling
me to see what I could make of them, with no further directions to guide me. I
soon found that they were skeletons of half a dozen fishes of different species;
the jaws told me so much at a first inspection. The task evidently was to fit the

separate bones together in their proper order. Two months or more went to this task with no other help than an occasional looking over my groupings with the stereotyped remark: "That is not right." Finally, the task was done, and I was again set upon alcoholic specimens—this time a remarkable lot of specimens representing, perhaps, twenty species of the side-swimmers or Pleuronectidae.

"How Agassiz Taught Shaler," Nathaniel Southgate Shaler

Process Discourse

Chronological order is used to explain a process. It stresses the events of what happened to tell a story. It frequently utilizes some of the following transitional words: after, before, following, next, prior to, and step. A writer of a *process discourse* may find it useful a sequence of numbers or letters or bullets to indicate each step in the process.

Process essays have two separate purposes. *Informational process essays* attempt to provide the reader with an understanding of the process. *Instructional essays* give the reader directions to enable the reader to carry out the process. Consequently, instructional essays must be much more specific.

Often, instructions are clearer and easier to follow if the steps are numbered and even, in some cases, if the numbered steps are presented as a list rather than in normal paragraph form.

Examples of Process Discourse

Example 1

The Game of Hearts [Three to six players using a standard pack of 52 playing cards].

The Deal: The whole pack is dealt, one at a time in rotation to the left.

The Play: The player at the left of the dealer leads first. A player must follow suit to a lead if able; if unable to follow suit, he may play any card. A trick is won by the highest card played of the suit led. The winner of a trick leads to the next.

Scoring: All players are provided at the outset with equal numbers of chips. Before each deal, equal antes are put into a pool. After the play, if one player alone is clear (has taken no heart), he wins the whole pool. If two are clear, they divide the pool. If all four are painted (win hearts) or if all the hearts are taken by one player, the pool is a jack, that is, it remains on the table to be won later, increased by subsequent antes.

"How to Play the Game of Hearts," Hoyle's Rules of Games

Example 2

Jones is now ready for casketing (this is the present participle of the verb "to casket"). In this operation, his right shoulder should be depressed slightly "to turn the body a bit to the right and soften the appearance of lying flat on the back." Positioning the hands is a matter of importance, and special rubber positioning blocks may be used. The hands should be cupped slightly for a more lifelike, relaxed appearance. Proper placement of the body requires a delicate sense of balance. It should lie as high as possible in the casket, yet not so high that the lid, when lowered, will hit the nose. On the other hand, we are cautioned, placing the body too low "creates the impression that the body is in a box."

The American Way of Dying, Jessica Mitford

Example 3

Dig a pit 3 ft. deep. Line bottom with 6 ins. of ashes, put roots in, and cover with 6 ins. of sand. Pack down litter, such as leaves, straw, etc., and cover pit with burlap bags, old rugs, etc.

[Canna Roots], *10,000 Garden Questions*, F. F. Rockwell, ed.

The following discourse is an instructional process analysis, explaining how to make a cake. Notice the differences in this discourse and in the classification of cakes (*Chapter 3*), the analysis of a cake (*Chapter 4*), and the causes of cake-baking failures (in the Cause and Effect section of this chapter).

Example 4

Mexican Chocolate Cake
(Two 8-inch round layers)

4 tablespoons cocoa	1 teaspoon vanilla
1 cup (200 g) plus 3 tablespoons sugar	2 eggs
1/2 cup (1 dL) milk	1 cup (140 g) flour
I/4 pound (115 g) butter, or margarine	1/2 teaspoon cinnamon
1/2 teaspoon baking soda	1/2 teaspoon salt

Preheat oven to 350°F (180°C). Grease and lightly flour two 8-inch round cake pans. Put the cocoa, butter, and 3 tablespoons water in a small bowl and heat in the microwave until all are melted. Add the sugar, vanilla, salt, baking soda and cinnamon and mix well. Alternately add the flour and

milk, beginning and ending with flour. Beat in the eggs, beating well. Spread
in the pans and bake for 30-35 minutes; test with a toothpick until it comes
out clean. Cool in the pans for 5 minutes before turning out onto racks.
Frost when completely cool.

From *Fannie Farmer Cookbook*

Example 5

Unlike the stones of the first course [layer], which were moved into
place fairly easily, the stones of the other 123 courses had to be raised to the
top of the preceding course before they could be pushed into place. Mahnud
Hotep solved this problem by building ramps of rubble held together with Nile
mud. One ramp began at each corner of the pyramid and rose gradually
along the west side resting on the unfinished steps of the casing. Logs,
embedded in the top of the ramp, helped reduce deterioration under the run-
ner of the sleds. As each course was finished, the ramps were extended by
workmen whose job it was to build and maintain them.

As soon as the ramps were ready, work gangs began hauling the blocks
for the second course into place. Usually twenty men pulled the sled while
the others either pushed from behind with levers or poured liquid on the road-
way to reduce friction under the runners.

[How to construct a pyramid], *Pyramid*, David Macaulay

Example 6

Put a generous puddle of oil on the [sharpening] stone—this will soon
disappear into the surface of a new stone, and you will need to keep adding
more oil. Press the knife blade flat against the stone in the puddle of oil,
using your index finger. Whichever way the cutting edge of the knife faces is
the side of the blade that should get a little more pressure. Move the blade
around three or four times in a narrow oval about the size of your fingernail,
going counterclockwise when the sharp edge is facing right. Now turn the
blade over in the same spot on the stone, press hard, and move it around the
small oval clockwise, with more pressure on the cutting edge that faces left.
Repeat the ovals, flipping the knife blade over six or seven times, and apply-
ing lighter pressure to the blade the last two times. Wipe the blade clean with
a piece of rag or tissue and rub it flat on the piece of leather strop at least
twice on each side. Stroke away from the cutting edge to remove the little
burr of metal that may be left on the blade.

How to Sharpen Your Knife, Florence H. Pettit

"The World's Biggest Membrane"

Lewis Thomas

Viewed from the distance of the moon, the astonishing thing about the earth,   1
catching the breath, is that it Is alive. The photographs show the dry, pounded
surface of the moon in the foreground, dead as an old bone. Aloft, floating free
beneath the moist, gleaming membrane of bright blue sky, is the rising earth,
the only exuberant thing in this part of the cosmos. If you could look long
enough, you would see the swirling of the great drifts of white cloud, covering
and uncovering the half-hidden masses of land. If you had been looking for a
very long, geologic time, you could have seen the continents themselves in
motion, drifting apart on their crustal plates, held afloat by the fire beneath. It
has the organized, self-contained look of a live creature, full of information,
marvelously skilled in handling the sun.

It takes a membrane to make sense out of disorder in biology. You have   2
to be able to catch energy and hold it, storing precisely the needed amount and
releasing it in measured shares. A cell does this, and so do the organelles
inside. Each assemblage is poised in the flow of solar energy, tapping off energy from metabolic surrogates of the sun. To stay alive, you have to be able to
hold out against equilibrium, maintain imbalance, bank against entropy, and
you can only transact this business with membranes in our kind of world.

When the earth came alive it began constructing its own membrane, for   3
the general purpose of editing the sun. Originally, in the time of prebiotic elab-
oration of peptides and nucleotides from inorganic ingredients in the water on
the earth, there was nothing to shield out ultraviolet radiation except the water
itself. The first thin atmosphere came entirely from the degassing of the earth
as it cooled, and there was only a vanishingly small trace of oxygen in it.
Theoretically, there could have been some production of oxygen by photo-dis-
sociation of water vapor in ultraviolet light, but not much. This process would
have been self-limiting, as Urey showed, since the wave lengths needed for
photolysis are the very ones screened out selectively by oxygen; the production
of oxygen would have been cut off almost as soon as it occurred.

The formation of oxygen had to await the emergence of photosynthetic   4
cells, and these were required to live in an environment with sufficient visible
light for photosynthesis but shielded at the same time against lethal ultraviolet.
Berkner and Marshall calculate that the green cells must therefore have been
about ten meters below the surface of water, probably in pools and ponds shallow enough to lack strong convection currents (the ocean could not have been
the starting place. You could say that the breathing of oxygen into atmosphere
was the result of evolution, or you could turn it around and say that evolution
was the result of oxygen. You can have it either way. Once the photosynthetic
cells had appeared, very probably counterparts of today's blue-green algae, the

future respiratory mechanism of the earth was set in place. Early on, when the level of oxygen had built up to around 1 per cent of today's atmospheric concentration, the anaerobic life of the earth was placed in jeopardy, and the inevitable next stage was the emergence of mutants with oxidative systems and ATP. With this, we were off to an explosive developmental stage in which great varieties of respiring life, including the multicellular forms, became feasible.

Berkner has suggested that there were two such explosions of new life, like vast embryological transformations, both dependent on threshold levels of oxygen. The first, at 1 per cent of the present level, shielded out enough ultraviolet radiation to permit cells to move into the surface layers of lakes, rivers, and oceans. This happened around 600 million years ago, at the beginning of the Paleozoic era, and accounts for the sudden abundance of marine fossils of all kinds in the record of this Period. The second burst occurred when oxygen rose to 10 per cent of the present level. At this time, around 400 million years ago, there was a sufficient canopy to allow life out of the water and onto the land. From here on it was clear going, with nothing to restrain the variety of life except the limits of biologic inventiveness. 5

It is another illustration of our fantastic luck that oxygen filters out the very bands of ultraviolet light that are most devastating for nucleic adds and proteins, while allowing full penetration of the visible light needed for photosynthesis. If It had not been for this semipermeability, we could never have come along. 6

The earth breathes, in a certain sense. Berkner suggests that there may have been cycles of oxygen production and carbon dioxide consumption, depending on relative abundances of plant and animal life, with the ice ages representing periods of apnea. An overwhelming richness of vegetation may have caused the level of oxygen to rise above today's concentration, with a corresponding depletion of carbon dioxide. Such a drop in carbon-dioxide may have impaired the "greenhouse" property of the atmosphere, which holds in the solar heat otherwise lost by radiation from the earth's surface. The fall in temperature would in turn have shut off much of living, and, in a long sigh, the level of oxygen may have dropped by 90 per cent. Berkner speculates that this is what happened to the great reptiles; their size may have been all right for a richly oxygenated atmosphere, but they had the bad luck to run out of air. 7

Now we are protected against lethal ultraviolet rays by a narrow rim of ozone, thirty miles out. We are safe, well ventilated, and incubated, provided we can avoid technologies that might fiddle with that ozone, or shift the levels of carbon dioxide. Oxygen is not a major worry for us, unless we let fly with enough nuclear explosives to kill off the green cells in the sea; if we do that, of course, we are in for strangling. 8

It is hard to feel affection for something as totally impersonal as the   9
atmosphere, and yet there it is, as much a part and product of life as wine or
bread. Taken all in all, the sky is a miraculous achievement. It works, and for
what it is designed to accomplish it is as infallible as anything in nature. I
doubt whether any of us could think of a way to improve on it, beyond maybe
shifting a local cloud from here to there on occasion. The word "chance" does
not serve to account well for structures of such magnificence. There may
have been elements of luck in the emergence of chloroplasts, but once these
things were on the scene, the evolution of the sky became absolutely ordained.
Chance suggests alternatives, other possibilities; different solutions. This may
be true for gills and swim-bladders and forebrains, matters of detail, but not
for the sky. There was simply no other way to go.

We should credit it for what it is: for sheer size and perfection of func-   10
tion, it is far and away the grandest product of collaboration in all of nature. It
breathes for us, and it does another thing for our pleasure. Each day, millions
of meteorites fall against the outer limits of the membrane and are burned to
nothing by the friction. Without this shelter, our surface would long since
have become the pounded powder of the moon. Even though our receptors
are not sensitive enough to hear it; there is comfort in knowing that the sound
is there overhead, like the random noise of rain on the roof at night.

Cause and Effect Discourse

Cause and *effect* frequently use chronological order to explain the
relationship between the causes and effects in a sequence of events. It
stresses why events happened in order to explain the causal relationship among them. It frequently utilizes some of the following transitional words: cause, effect, consequently, due to, if, result(s), so, then,
thus, and therefore.

A *cause* is a force or influence that produces an effect. It is the
situation or event responsible for bringing about an action, event,
condition, or result. An *effect* is anything that has been caused. It is
the result of an action or a force, something produced. One cause
may produce only one or many effects. Likewise one effect may be
produced by a single cause or by a combination of causes. Some
events may produce a causal chain in which effect becomes a cause
which produces its own effect. Sometimes causes may be reciprocal,
as Orwell explains in "Politics and the English Language."

Examples of Cause and Effect Discourse

Example 1

The individual who has learned how to make the correlation between threshold pains and their cause doesn't panic when they occur; he or she does something about relieving the stress and tension. Then if the pain persists despite the absence of apparent cause, the individual will telephone the doctor.

"Pain is Not the Ultimate Enemy," Norman Cousins

Example 2

Many things can cause cake failures.

Too much leavening, not enough liquid, insufficient creaming or insufficient mixing, or two slow an oven produces a course texture.

Too much shortening, too much sugar, too slow an oven, or overbaking can produce a heavy, compact texture.

Too much flour or too much leavening, not enough sugar or shortening, overbeaten egg whites, or overbaking can produce a dry cake.

Too much flour, baking too long, too hot an oven, too little sugar, or too little shortening can produce a thick, heavy crust.

Too much flour or baking in too hot an oven produces a hump or cracks on the top of a cake.

Undermixing the ingredients, or adding too much sugar produces a soggy layer or a streak at the bottom.

Too much sugar produces a moist, sticky crust.

Too much leavening, shortening, or sugar, baking in too slow an oven, or underbaking, or moving the cake during baking makes a cake fall.

Too large a pan, too hot an oven, or too little leavening produces an under-sized cake.

Too small a pan, too slow an oven, or too much shortening, sugar, or leavening can make a cake run over the edge of the pan.

Causes of Failures in Cake Baking. Adapted from a chart in *Better Homes and Gardens Cookbook.*

The writers of "The Declaration of Independence" the actions of the King of Great Britain which "caused" the American colonies severing "all political connection between them and the State of Great Britain" are a list of the King of Great Britain's "repeated injuries and usurpations" tactics intended to establish "Tyranny over these States." The following are a few of those causes:

Example 3

He has refused his Assent to Laws, the most wholesome and necessary for the public good.

He Has forbidden his Government to pass laws of immediate and pressing importance, unless suspended in their operation till his Assent should be obtained; and when so suspended, he has utterly neglected to attend to them.

He has refused to pass other Laws for the accommodation of large districts of people, unless those people would relinquish the right of Representation in the Legislature, a right inestimable to them and formidable to tyrants only.

"The Declaration of Independence," Thomas Jefferson, et al.

Example 4

In public, the best way to avoid attack is to present yourself in a manner that discourages would-be assailants. It's as though we send out messages telling others that their attack is either likely or unlikely to be resisted.

Through body language and general attitude, the victim sends a subtle yet unmistakable message to the mugger. It says something like "Please don't attack me! I'm so afraid." To a mugger, the most impulsive of criminals, this communication is tantamount to an engraved invitation. Expecting no opposition, he moves in immediately.

The conclusion is inescapable: *you must show yourself as someone with self-worth, someone who cares what happens and will mount a vigorous defense if attacked* [italics Dobson's].

From "Not Looking Like a Victim," *SAFE and Alive*, Terry Dobson

Example 5

But that still doesn't explain the throngs who came pell-mell to stare and conjecture at the dead whale that washed up at Corporation Beach and dominated it for a day like some extravagant momento mori. Surely we were not flattering ourselves, consciously or unconsciously, with any human comparisons to that rotting hulk. Nor was there much, in its degenerate state, that it had to teach us. And yet we came—why?

The answer may be so obvious that we have ceased to recognize it. Man, I believe, has a crying need to confront otherness in the universe. Call it nature, wilderness, the "great outdoors," or what you will—we crave to look out and behold something other than our own human faces staring back at us, expectantly and increasingly frustrated. What the human spirit wants, as Robert Frost said, "Is not its own love back in copy-speech, / But counter-love, original response."

"Very Like a Whale," Robert Finch

In Petrunkevitch's essay that follows, "The Spider and the Wasp,"

Paragraphs 1-2   function as introduction

Paragraphs 4-7   are present a classification of the spider's tactile
                  responses. They explain the causes and effects
                  of the spider's tactile response, first, to pressure
                  on the body wall, second, to touching of the
                  common hair, and, third, to air movement.

Paragraphs 13-16 present speculations about more general
                  causes and effects.

Essays Using Cause and Effect Discourse

"The Spider and the Wasp"

Alexander Petrunkevitch

To hold its own in the struggle for existence, every species of animal must have   1
a regular source of food, and if it happens to live on other animals, its survival
may be very delicately balanced. The hunter cannot exist without the hunted; if
the latter should perish from the earth, the former would, too. When the hunted
also prey on some of the hunters, the matter may become complicated.

This is nowhere better illustrated than in the insect world. Think of the   2
complexity of a situation such as the following: There is a certain wasp, Pimpla
inquisilor, whose larvae feed on several years in succession. In a Paris museum
is a tropical specimen which is said to have been living in captivity for 25 years.

A fertilized female tarantula lays from 200 to 400 eggs at a time; thus it is   3
possible for a single tarantula to produce several thousand young. She takes no
care of them beyond weaving a cocoon of silk to enclose the eggs. After they
hatch, the young walk away, find convenient places, in which to dig their bur-
rows and spend the rest of their lives in solitude. Tarantulas feed mostly on
insects and millipedes. Once their appetite is appeased, they digest the food for
several days before eating again. Their sight is poor, being limited to sensing a
change in the intensity of light and to the perception of moving objects. They
apparently have little or no sense of hearing, for a hungry tarantula will pay no
attention to a loudly chirping cricket placed in its cage unless the insect happens
to touch one of its legs.

But all spiders, and especially hairy ones, have an extremely delicate sense   4
of touch. Laboratory experiments prove that tarantulas can distinguish three

types of touch: pressure against the body wall, stroking of the body hair, and riffling of certain very fine hairs on the legs called trichobothria: Pressure against
the body, by a finger or the end of a pencil, causes the tarantula to move off
slowly for a short distance. The touch excites no defensive response unless the
approach is from above, where the spider can see the motion, in which case it
rises on its hind legs, lifts its front legs, opens its fangs and holds this threat-
ening posture as long as the object continues to move. When the motion stops,
the spider drops back to the ground, remains quiet for a few seconds, and then
moves slowly away.

The entire body of a tarantula, especially its legs, is thickly clothed with   5
hair. Some of it is short and woolly, some long and stiff. Touching this body
hair produces one of two distinct reactions. When the spider is hungry, it
responds with an immediate and swift attack. At the touch of a cricket's antennae the tarantula seizes the insect so swiftly that a motion picture taken at the
rate of 64 frames per second shows only the result not the process of capture.
But when the spider is not hungry, the stimulation of its hair merely causes it to
shake the touched limb. An insect can walk under its hairy belly unharmed.

The trichobothria, very fine hairs growing from disk-like membranes of the   6
legs, were once thought to be the spider's hearing organs, but we now know
that they have nothing to do with sound. They are sensitive only to air movement. A light breeze makes them vibrate slowly without disturbing the common
hair. When one blows gently on the trichobothria, the tarantula reacts with a
quick jerk of its four front legs. If the front and hind legs are stimulated at the
same time, the spider makes a sudden jump. This reaction is quite independent
of the state of its appetite.

These three tactile responses—to pressure on the body wall, to moving of   7
the common hair, and to flexing of the trichobothria—are so different from one
another that there is no possibility of confusing them. They serve the tarantula
adequately for most of its needs and enable it to avoid most annoyances and
dangers. But they fail the spider completely when it meets its deadly enemy, the
digger wasp Pepsis.

These solitary wasps are beautiful and formidable creatures. Most species   8
are either a deep shiny blue all over, or deep blue with rusty wings. The largest
have a wing span of about four inches. They live on nectar. When excited, they
give off a pungent odor—a warning that they are ready to attack. The sting is
much worse than that of a bee or common wasp, and the pain and swelling last
longer. In the adult stage the wasp lives only a few months. The female produces but a few eggs, one at a time at intervals of two or three days. For each
egg the mother must provide one adult tarantula, alive but paralyzed. The tarantula must be of the correct species to nourish the larva. The mother wasp
attaches the egg to the paralyzed spider's abdomen. Upon hatching from the
egg, the larva is many hundreds of times smaller than its living but helpless

victim. It eats no other food and drinks no water. By the time it has finished its single gargantuan meal and becomes ready for wasphood, nothing remains of the tarantula but its indigestible chitinous skeleton.

The mother wasp goes tarantula-hunting when the egg in her ovary is almost ready to be laid. Flying low over the ground late on a sunny afternoon, the wasp looks for its victim or for the mouth of a tarantula burrow, a round hole edged by a bit of silk. The sex of the spider makes no difference, but the mother is highly discriminating as to species. Each species of Pepsis requires a certain species of tarantula, and the wasp will not attack the wrong species. In a cage with a tarantula which is not its normal prey the wasp avoids the spider, and is usually killed by it in the night.

9

Yet when a wasp finds the correct species, it is the other way about. To identify the species the wasp apparently must explore the spider with her antennae. The tarantula shows an amazing tolerance to this exploration. The wasp crawls under it and walks over it without evoking any hostile response. The molestation is so great and so persistent that the tarantula often rises on all eight legs, as if it were on stilts. It may stand this way for several minutes. Meanwhile the wasp, having satisfied itself that the victim is of the right species, moves off a few inches to dig the spider's grave. Working vigorously with legs and jaws, it excavates a hole 8 to 10 inches deep with a diameter slightly larger than the spider's girth. Now and again the wasp pops out of the hole to make sure that the spider is still there.

10

When the grave is finished, the wasp returns to the tarantula to complete her ghastly enterprise. First she feels it all over once more with her antennae. Then her behavior becomes more aggressive. She bends her abdomen, protruding her sting, and searches for the soft membrane at the point where the spider's leg joins its body—the only spot where she can penetrate the horny skeleton. From time to time, as the exasperated spider slowly shifts ground, the wasp turns on her back and slides along with the aid of her wings, trying to get under the tarantula for a shot at the vital spot. During all this maneuvering. which can last for several minutes, the tarantula makes no move to save itself. Finally the wasp corners it against some obstruction and grasps one of its legs in her powerful jaws. Now at last the harassed spider tries a desperate but vain defense. The two contestants roll over and over on the ground. It is a terrifying sight and the outcome is always the same. The wasp finally manages to thrust her sting into the soft spot and holds it there for a few seconds while she pumps in the poison. Almost immediately the tarantula falls paralyzed on its back. Its legs stop twitching; its heart stops beating. Yet it is not dead, as is shown by the fact that if taken from the wasp it can be restored to some sensitivity by being kept in a moist chamber for several months.

11

After paralyzing the tarantula, the wasp cleans herself by dragging her body along the ground and rubbing her feet, sucks the drop of blood oozing

12

from the wound in the spider's abdomen, then grabs a leg of the flabby, helpless animal in her jaws and drags it down to the bottom of the grave. She stays there for many minutes, sometimes for several hours, and what she does all that time in the dark we do not know. Eventually she lays her egg and attaches it to the side of the spider's abdomen with a sticky secretion. Then she emerges, fills the grave with soil carried bit by bit in her jaws, and finally tramples the ground all around to hide any trace of the grave from prowlers. Then she flies away, leaving her descendant safely started in life.

In all this the behavior of the wasp evidently is qualitatively different from that of the spider. The wasp acts like an intelligent animal. This is not to say that instinct plays no part or that she reasons as man does. But her actions are to the point; they are not automatic and can be modified to fit the situation. We do not know for certain how she identifies the tarantula—probably it is by some olfactory or chemotactile sense—but she does it purposefully and does not blindly tackle a wrong species.   13

On the other hand, the tarantula's behavior shows only confusion. Evidently the wasp's pawing gives it no pleasure, for it tries to move away. That the wasp is not simulating sexual stimulation is certain, because male and female tarantulas react in the same way to its advances. That the spider is not anesthetized by some odorless secretion is easily shown by blowing lightly at the tarantula and making it jump suddenly. What, then, makes the tarantula behave as stupidly as it does?   14

No clear, simple answer is available. Possibly the stimulation by the wasp's antennae is masked by a heavier pressure on the spider's body, so that it reacts as when prodded by a pencil. But the explanation may be much more complex. Initiative in attack is not in the nature of tarantulas; most species fight only when cornered so that escape is impossible. Their inherited patterns of behavior apparently prompt them to avoid problems rather than attack them. For example, spiders always weave their webs in three dimensions, and when a spider finds that there is insufficient space to attach certain threads in the third dimension, it leaves the place and seeks another, instead of finishing the web in a single plane. This urge to escape seems to arise under all circumstances, in all phases of life, and to take the place of reasoning. For a spider to change the pattern of its web is as impossible as for an inexperienced man to build a bridge across a chasm obstructing his way.   15

In a way the instinctive urge to escape is not only easier but more efficient than reasoning. The tarantula does exactly what is most efficient in all cases except in an encounter with a ruthless and determined attacker dependent for the existence of her own species on killing as many tarantulas as she can lay eggs. Perhaps in this case the spider follows its usual pattern of trying to escape, instead of seizing and killing the wasp, because it is not aware of its danger. In any case, the survival of the tarantula species as a whole is protected by the fact that the spider is much more fertile than the wasp.   16

"Pain Is Not the Ultimate Enemy"

Norman Cousins

Americans are probably the most pain-conscious people on the face of the
earth. For years we have had it drummed into us in print, on radio, over television, in everyday conversation that any hint of pain is to be banished as
though it were the ultimate evil. As a result, we are becoming a nation of
pill-grabbers and hypochondriacs, escalating the slightest ache into a searing
ordeal.

We know very little about pain and what we don't know makes it hurt all
the more. Indeed, no form of illiteracy in the United States is so widespread
or costly as ignorance about pain—what it is, what causes it, how to deal with
it without panic. Almost everyone can rattle off the names of at least a dozen
drugs that can deaden pain from every conceivable cause—all the way from
headaches to hemorrhoids. There is far less knowledge about the fact that
about 90 percent of pain is self-limiting, that it is not always an indication of
poor health, and that, most frequently, it is the result of tension, stress, worry,
idleness, boredom, frustration, suppressed rage, insufficient sleep, overeat-
ing, poorly balanced diet, smoking, excessive drinking, inadequate exercise,
stale air, or any of the other abuses encountered by the human body in modern society.

The most ignored fact of all about pain is that the best way to eliminate
it is to eliminate the abuse. Instead, many people reach almost instinctively
for the painkillers—aspirins, barbiturates, codeines, tranquilizers, sleeping
pills, and dozens of other analgesics or desensitizing drugs.

Most doctors are profoundly troubled over the extent to which the medical profession today is taking on the trappings of a pain-killing industry.
Their offices are overloaded with people who are morbidly but mistakenly
convinced that something dreadful is about to happen to them. It is all too
evident that the campaign to get people to run to a doctor at the first sign of
pain has boomeranged. Physicians find it difficult to give adequate attention
to patients genuinely in need of expert diagnosis and treatment because their
time is soaked up by people who have nothing wrong with them except a temporary indisposition or a psychogenic ache.

Patients tend to feel indignant and insulted if the physician tells them he
can find no organic cause for the pain. They tend to interpret the term "psychogenic" to mean that they are complaining of nonexistent symptoms. They
need to be educated about the fact that many forms of pain have no underlying physical cause but are the result, as mentioned earlier, of tension, stress,
or hostile factors in the general environment. Sometimes a pain may be a
manifestation of "conversion hysteria". . .the name given by Jean Charcot to
physical symptoms that have their origins in emotional disturbances.

Obviously, it is folly for an individual to ignore symptoms that could be a   6
warning of a potentially serious illness. Some people are so terrified of getting bad news from a doctor that they allow their malaise to worsen, sometimes past the point of no return. Total neglect is not the answer to
hypochondria. The only answer has to be increased education about the way
the human body works, so that more people will be able to steer an intelligent
course between promiscuous pill-popping and irresponsible disregard of genuine symptoms.

Of all forms of pain, none is more important for the individual to under-   7
stand than the "threshold" variety. Almost everyone has a telltale ache that is
triggered whenever tension or fatigue reaches a certain point. It can take the
form of a migraine-type headache or a squeezing pain deep in the abdomen or
cramps or a pain in the lower back or even pain in the joints. The individual
who has learned how to make the correlation between such threshold pains
and their cause doesn't panic when they occur; he or she does something
about relieving the stress and tension. Then, if the pain persists despite the
absence of apparent cause, the individual will telephone the doctor.

If ignorance about the nature of pain is widespread, ignorance about the   8
way pain-killing drugs work is even more so. What is not generally under-
stood is that many of the vaunted pain-killing drugs conceal the pain without
correcting the underlying condition. They deaden the mechanism in the body
that alerts the brain to the fact that something may be wrong. The body can
pay a high price for suppression of pain without regard to its basic cause.

Professional athletes are sometimes severely disadvantaged by trainers   9
whose job it is to keep them in action. The more famous the athlete, the
greater the risk that he or she may be subjected to extreme medical measures
when injury strikes. The star baseball pitcher whose arm is sore because of a
torn muscle or tissue damage may need sustained rest more than anything
else. But his team is battling for a place in the World Series; so the trainer or
team doctor, called upon to work his magic, reaches for a strong dose of
Butazolidine or other powerful pain suppressants. Presto, the pain disap-
pears! The pitcher takes his place on the mound and does superbly. That
could be the last game, however, in which he is able to throw a ball with full
strength. The drugs didn't repair the torn muscle or cause the damaged tissue
to heal. What they did was to mask the pain, enabling the pitcher to throw
hard, further damaging the torn muscle. Little wonder that so many star athletes are cut down in their prime, more the victims of overzealous treatment of
their injuries than of the injuries themselves.

The king of all painkillers, of course, is aspirin. The U.S. Food and Drug   10
Administration permits aspirin to be sold without prescription, but the drug,
contrary to popular belief, can be dangerous and, in sustained doses, potentially lethal. Aspirin is self-administered by more people than any other drug

in the world. Some people are aspirin-poppers, taking ten or more a day.
What they don't know is that the smallest dose can cause internal bleeding.
Even more serious perhaps is the fact that aspirin is antagonistic to collagen,
which has a key role in the formation of connective tissue. Since many forms
of arthritis involve disintegration of the connective tissue, the steady use of
aspirin can actually intensify the underlying arthritic condition.

Aspirin is not the only pain-killing drug, of course, that is known to have   11
dangerous side effects. Dr. Daphne A. Roe, of Cornell University, at a medical
meeting in New York City in 1974, presented startling evidence of a wide
range of hazards associated with sedatives and other pain suppressants.
Some of these drugs seriously interfere with the ability of the body to metab-
olize food properly, producing malnutrition. In some instances, there is also
the danger of bone-marrow depression, interfering with the ability of the body
to replenish its blood supply.

Pain-killing drugs are among the greatest advances in the history of   12
medicine. Properly used, they can be a boon in alleviating suffering and in
treating disease. But their indiscriminate and promiscuous use is making
psychological cripples and chronic ailers out of millions of people. The
unremitting barrage of advertising for pain-killing drugs, especially over television, has set the stage for a mass anxiety neurosis. Almost from the moment
children are old enough to sit upright in front of a television screen, they are
being indoctrinated into the hypochondriac's clamorous and morbid world.
Little wonder so many people fear pain more than death itself.

It might be a good idea if concerned physicians and educators could get   13
together to make knowledge about pain an important part of the regular
school curriculum. As for the populace at large, perhaps some of the same
techniques used by public-service agencies to make people cancer-conscious
can be used to counteract the growing terror of pain and illness in general.
People ought to know that nothing is more remarkable about the human body
than its recuperative drive, given a modicum of respect. If our broadcasting
stations cannot provide equal time for responses to the pain-killing advertise-
ments, they might at least set aside a few minutes each day for common-
sense remarks on the subject of pain. As for the Food and Drug
Administration, it might be interesting to know why an agency that has ener-
getically warned the American people against taking vitamins without pre-
scriptions is doing so little to control over-the-counter sales each year of billions of painkilling pills, some of which can do more harm than the pain they
are supposed to suppress.

1979

Logical Order

Logical order is determined by the steps an argument. Logical order may be *deductive* or *inductive*, or it may follow the major steps of any other sequence of argument.

Deductive Order

In the development of a paragraph or essay *deductive order* presents materials in an order that makes the reader's encounter with those materials a deductive experience. Using an order similar to that of a syllogism, the writer wound present first a major premise, then a minor premise, and then a conclusion. Because such a process would limit the writer's persuasive tactics and because the presentation of all of the steps of a syllogism would get tedious for the reader, writer's usually use enthymemes (modified versions of syllogisms which are more effective in exposition and argument than are syllogisms).

Formal deduction is the process of reaching conclusions by beginning with a major premise, adding a minor premise, and from the major and minor premises reaching a conclusion. Formal deduction utilize various processes for using syllogisms, either-or propositions, if-then propositions, and other patterns of formal logic.

Writers seldom use all of the steps of formal logic in ordinary exposition, argument or expression. Rather than presenting all the steps of a formal syllogism, they use an *enthymeme*, which is similar to a syllogism, but which 1) is presented for its persuasive effect rather than its logical irrefutability, 2) has fewer steps than a formal syllogism (often with the more persuasive steps included and the less persuasive steps omitted), and 3) may or may not presents its steps in the same order in which they would be presented in a syllogism. Although the enthymeme is usually only thought of as being a rhetorical analogy to the formal syllogism,. writers also use enthymemic adaptations of either-or arguments, if-then propositions, and other formal arguments.

If a discourse were controlled by a syllogistic argument, the first part of the essay would develop the major premise, the second part the minor premise, and the third (final) part by the conclusion of the argument.

Inductive Order

In logic, *induction* involves the process of gathering specific evidence and data and then drawing conclusions from that evidence and data. A writer might use induction to determine ideas for a paper, but might or might not present that evidence and ideas in an inductive order.

In the development of a paragraphs or an entire essay, *inductive order* presents ideas and information in an order that makes the reader's encounter with those materials an inductive experience. The paragraph or essay presents evidence before generalizations, assertions, or opinions. The reader then encounters the writer's evidence before he or she encounters the writer's ideas about those ideas.

Other Logical Orders

One could use the steps of any logical argument to determine the order of a discourse. For example, "The Declaration of Independence" is not only organized by but is also ordered by the three main steps of its argument.

Order of Importance

In *least-to-most order*, a writer begins with the least important or persuasive idea, example, or reason, and presents materials in a sequence of increasing importance or persuasiveness.

In *most-to-least order*, a writer begins with the most important or persuasive idea, example, or reason, and presents materials in a sequence of diminishing importance or persuasiveness.

Psychological Order

Writers, especially of persuasive discourse, usually try to present their materials in whatever sequence will be the most persuasive to the reader. Obviously, the most effect *psychological order* would vary from audience to audience and from topic to topic.

Classical Order

In *classical order* a writer follows the sequence prescribed by classical rhetoricians—a sequence that writers and speakers have employed for thousands of years because it is so effective in persuading readers and listeners. Classical order is comprised of five steps:

Classical Order

exordium	introduction
narratio	statement of essential facts
confirmatio	proof of one's case
refutio	discrediting of opposing arguments
peroratio	conclusion

Sometimes the order of the confirmatio and refutio are reversed. And other variations of these five main parts are occasionally used.

Combinations of Orders

There are many other effective ways of ordering a discourse, including various combinations of the orders presented above. A great number of discourses use a combination of orders.

Ineffective Orders

Often inexperience writers or writers insensitive to the rhetorical demands of a writing situation will present their materials in ways that prevent their writing from being effective—even if it contains good ideas and good developmental material. Sometimes a writer may simply present ideas in the order in which those ideas occurred to him or her. Such an order is rarely the most effective order. If the order of in which ideas are presented is too chaotic, the discourse can become incomprehensible.

Section III: Secondary Discourse

Secondary discourse is made up of parts of an essay which may help to clarify part of the primary discourse or to persuade the reader to accept the arguments of the primary discourse, but it is never logical support for the ideas of the primary discourse. Secondary discourse includes definitions, comparisons, analogies, parenthetical insertions, namings, and non-verbal communications.

CHAPTER 7

Secondary Discourse

Definition, Comparison, Analogy
and Other Parenthetical Insertions

Many things can contribute to the effectiveness of an essay—to clarifying the facts in an expository essay, to enhancing the persuasive effect of an argumentative essay, and to enriching the emotion, personality, and interest of the personal essay. But it is possible to distinguish between those elements in an essay which directly develop the main ideas of the essay and other things which only indirectly enhance that development.

A discourse is all of the words, sentences, paragraphs, and punctuation which make up any written document. That discourse can be analyzed as *primary discourse* and *secondary discourse*. *Primary discourse* consists of 1) *ideas* (the thesis, the main ideas, and the subsidiary ideas) and 2) *evidence* (facts) which support any of those ideas, and 3) *reasons* which support those ideas or which explain any of the evidence.

Because in contemporary Western culture the only things we accept as proof of an idea are evidence and logical reasons, the only reasonable support for an idea in the primary discourse are subsidiary ideas, evidence, and/or reasons. Essays are made up of a sequence of main ideas, each of which advances the thesis—controlling idea of the essay. But sometimes other approaches are necessary or useful to enable the reader to better understand an idea. *Secondary discourse* enhances the primary discourse, but secondary discourse is never logical proof of any ideas in the primary discourse.

Just as primary discourse is composed of elements and components and is structured on the basis of certain organizational and ordering principles, secondary discourse is made up of the same elements and structures. The difference is in the function the discourse serves within an essay.

Secondary discourse includes *definitions, comparisons, analogies* and other tactics which enhance but do not prove an idea.

Stipulative definitions are essential when a writer is stipulating his or her own meaning of a word. *Lexical definitions* are the standard meanings of a word—meanings which can be found in a dictionary. Definitions are essential if the writer is using terms with which the reader is unfamiliar; such definitions are lexical (they state the commonly-accepted or dictionary meaning of a word). Lexical definitions are also useful in reminding readers of the meaning of an uncommon word or in specifying which of the traditional, lexical definitions of a word the writer intends.

Because secondary discourse can clarify and enhance an essay you should practice writing various kinds of definitions, comparisons, and analogies.

Definitions

Definitions can function as primary discourse or as secondary discourse. They function most frequently as *secondary discourse*.

All secondary discourses are miniature discourses which have been inserted into a larger discourse to clarify or enhance the larger discourse. Consequently, when a definition sentence or definition paragraph is separated from the complete discourse in which it occurs, it is not possible to know if it functioned in that essay as primary or secondary courses. (This first set of examples all functioned as secondary discourse. Following them will be an explanation of how definitions can function as primary discourse and examples of such discourse.)

Definitions often function merely as definitions, as secondary discourse which helps to explain what the writer means by word(s) in the primary discourse.

Definitions function as primary discourse when they function both as definitions and as assertions, in which the writer asserts that a particular word should have a certain meaning—the meaning the writer is arguing for. In the following examples, the paragraph "Espalier Fruit Trees," happens to be a complete discourse in itself and functions therefore as primary discourse. But the paragraph "The Intrapsychic Self" is just a small portion of Arieti's discussion of depression; this paragraph functions as secondary discourse. Arieti thought it was necessary to provide a definition of "depression" before discussing it further.

Paragraphs Using Definition

Example 1

As a subjective experience, depression is difficult to define or even describe. It is a pervading feeling of unpleasantness, often accompanied by bodily symptoms such as numbness, parethesias of the skin, changes in the muscular tone, and decreases in respiration, pulsation, and perspiration. The head of a depressed person has a tendency to bend, the legs to flex, the trunk to be tilted forward. In severe depression the face has a special expression, with more wrinkles than usual and slightly swollen eyelids. Movements and thoughts are retarded, and the person has a general feeling of weakness.

From *The Intrapsychic Self*, Silvano Arieti

Example 2

[An espalier fruit tree] is a tree trained in formal shape to a given number of branches, usually in a vertical plane. The tree is planted against a wall, building, or trellis, where it takes up little space and provides decoration as well as fruit. It may be trained to a single shoot or to 2 shoots opposite each other, or in a fan or other shapes. The training is begun when the tree is very young. Espalier fruit trees have always been popular in Europe, where the protection afforded by wall training makes it possible to grow orchard fruits in climates less favorable than those in this country.

[Espalier Fruit Trees], *10,000 Garden Questions*, F. F. Rockwell

Common Methods of Defining Words

■ Definition by *classification* (also called *formal definition*, *logical definition*, *Aristotelian definition* and *classical definition*) consists of two steps. First one puts the word to be defined in its class (preferably in the smallest class possible). Second, one differentiates that word from other members of that class. One might define a "sloop" as a sailboat which has only one mast and a single foresail.

■ Definition by *synonym* involves giving providing another word which has the same meaning as the word being defined. To be useful to a reader, the synonym should be an easier, more familiar word. One might define "hydrophobia" as either "fear of water" or "rabies," depending on which meaning of the word "hydrophobia" one intended.

■ Definition by *example* involves giving an example of the word being defined. One might define "sport utility vehicle" by citing a Ford Explorer or a "sloop" as the America's Cup contender "Intrepid."

■ Definition by *analysis* or *description* involves dividing the thing being defined into its subordinate parts. When using analysis, one must give a complete analysis or description of the thing.

■ Definition by *comparison* is often used to define a thing of like kind with which the reader my be unfamiliar and involves naming or describing a similar thing with which the reader probably is familiar. One might define British football by explaining how it is like (and unlike) American football.

■ Definition by *analogy* or *metaphor* uses the same process as definition by comparison, but names or describes a similar thing of *unlike kind*. One might define, as Martin Luther King, Jr. does, the "tension" produced by segregation by comparing it to a boil which must be lanced.

■ Definition by *contrast* or *negation* involves naming or describing a thing or thing(s) which are the opposite of the thing being defined. One might define "love" by stating that it is not hatred, not jealousy, not bitterness, and not selfish.

■ An *operational* definition involves describing the steps of the process or procedure which is being defined. One could define "photosynthesis" by describing the process by which plants transform light and water into food or define "internal combustion engine" by describing how an internal combustion engine works.

■ Definition by *enumeration* of the words of things which belong in the class of things which the word being defined describes. One might define "spices" by enumerating cinnamon, ginger, nutmeg, cloves, and cardamom.

■ An *etymological* definition involves naming and defining the words from earlier language(s) from which the word being defined. One might define "prestidigitation" by explaining that it comes, as *The American Heritage Dictionary* explains, from the French word "prestidigitateur," which means "juggler" and from the Latin words "presto" which means "fast" and the word "digit," which means finger.

Sentences Using Definition and Functioning as Secondary Discourse

Example 1

Stress, the noun, is a shortening of distress, rooted in the Latin *disringere*, 'to hinder, molest.' Stress, the verb, has another root as well: the Latin *stringere*, 'to draw tight, press together,' which is related to *strain*. Here is a stringent lesson: The result of stress is strain.

From "Emphasis on Stress," William Safire

Example 2

Psychological stress refers to all processes, whether originating in the external environment or within the person, which impose a demand or requirement upon the organism, the resolution or handling of which requires . . . activity of the mental apparatus before any other system is involved or activated. Stress, in its psychiatric sense, is what happens when unconscious impulses call for action that conflicts with ordinary behavior.

From "Emphasis on Stress," William Safire

Example 3

. . . amoeba-like foulard blobs.

From "Neckties and Class," Paul Fussell

Example 4

Wacky Wafers [are]. . .eight absurd-tasting coins in as many flavors.

From "Matters of Taste," Alexander Theroux

Example 5

'[E]rotica' is rooted in eros or passionate love, and thus in the idea of positive choice, free will, the yearning for a particular person.

From "Erotica and Pornography," Gloria Steinem

Example 6

'Pornography' begins with a root meaning 'prostitution' or 'female captives,' thus letting us know that the subject is not mutual love, or love at all, but domination and violence against women.

From "Erotica and Pornography," Gloria Steinem

Example 7

[M]angrove[s] . . . . are all short, messy trees, waxy-leaved, laced all over with aerial roots, woody arching buttresses, and weird leathery berry pods. All this tangles from a black much soil . . . .

From "Sojourner," Annie Dillard

Example 8

A 'thermal pulse [is] a wave of blinding light and intense heat'

From "Nothing to Report," Jonathan Schell

Example 9

A lethal dose, by convention, is considered to be the amount of radiation that, if delivered over a short period of time, would kill half the able-bodied young adult population.

From "Nothing to Report," Jonathan Schell

Example 10

An induction furnace [is] a device that produces a magnetic field and can heat up to high temperatures anything within it that is resistant to electricity.

From "How to Make a Nuclear Bomb," John McPhee

Example 11

A spore is the kind of reproductive cell made by every flowering plant.

From "Let's Get Botanical," Sara B. Stein

Example 12

. . .'demand-pull,' which means that demands for good and services during a specified period are exceeding the available supplies of those goods and services.

From *The Harvest Reader*, William A. Hefferman and Mark Johnson, Eds.

Example 13

Facts are the world's data.

From *The Harvest Reader*, William A. Hefferman and Mark Johnson, Eds.

Example 14

Theories are structures of ideas that explain and interpret facts.

From *The Harvest Reader*, William A. Hefferman and Mark Johnson, Eds.

Example 15

Aristotle defined rhetoric as 'the faculty of discovering . . . what are the available means of persuasion.

From *The Harvest Reader*, William A. Hefferman and Mark Johnson, Eds.

Example 16

Superstition comes from the Latin *supersisto*, meaning to stand in terror of the Deity.

From "A Few Kind Words for Superstition," Robertson Davies

Example 17

In any nonviolent campaign there are four basic steps: collection of the facts to determine whether injustices exist, negotiation; self purification; and direct action.

From "Letter from Birmingham Jail," Martin Luther King, Jr.

Paragraphs Using Definition and Functioning as Secondary Discourse

Example 1

A just law is a man-made code that squares with the moral law or the law of God. An unjust law is a code that is out of harmony with the moral law. To put it in the terms of St. Thomas Aquinas: An unjust law is a human law that is not rooted in eternal law and natural law. Any law that uplifts human personality is just. Any law that degrades human personality is unjust. All segregation statutes are unjust because segregation distorts the soul and damages the personality. It gives the segregator a false sense of superiority and the segregated a false sense of inferiority.

Paragraph 16 from "Letter from Birmingham Jail," Martin Luther King, Jr.

Example 2

Let us consider a more concrete example of just and unjust laws. An unjust law is a code that a numerical or power majority group compels a minority group to obey but does not make binding on itself. This is difference made legal. By the same token, a just law is a code that a majority compels a minority to follow and that is willing to follow itself.

Paragraph 17 from "Letter from Birmingham Jail," Martin Luther King, Jr.

Example 3

Sometimes a law is just on its face and unjust in its application. For instance, I have been arrested on a charge of parading without a permit. Now, there is nothing wrong in having an ordinance which requires a permit for a parade. But such an ordinance becomes unjust when it is used to maintain segregation and to deny citizens the First-Amendment privilege of peaceful assembly and protest.

Paragraph 19 from "Letter from Birmingham Jail," Martin Luther King, Jr.

Example 4

We received a letter from the Writer's War Board the other day asking for a statement on 'The Meaning of Democracy.' It presumably is our duty to comply with such a request, and it is certainly our pleasure.

Surely the Board knows what democracy is. It is the line that forms on the right. It is the "don't" in "don't shove." It is the hole in the stuffed shirt through which the sawdust slowly trickles; it is the dent in the high hat. Democracy is the recurrent suspicion that more than half of the people are right more than half of the time. It is the feeling of privacy in the voting booths, the feeling of communion in the libraries, the feeling of vitality everywhere. Democracy is a letter to the editor. Democracy is the score at the beginning of the ninth. It is an idea which hasn't been disproved yet, a song the words of which have not gone bad. It's the mustard on the hot dog and the cream in the rationed coffee. Democracy is a request from a War Board, in the middle of a morning in the middle of a war, wanting to know what democracy is.

From "Democracy," E. B. White

Example 5

But there is of culture another view, in which not solely the scientific passion, the sheer desire to see things as they are, natural and proper in an intelligent being, appears as the ground of it. There is a view in which all the love of our neighbor, the impulses towards action, help, and beneficence, the desire for removing human error, clearing human confusion, and diminishing human misery, the noble aspiration to leave the world better and happier than we found it—motives eminently such as are called social—come in part of the grounds of culture, and the main and pre-eminent part. Culture is then properly described not as having origin in curiosity, but as having its origin in the love of perfection; it is a study of perfection. It moves by the force, not merely or primarily of the scientific passion for pure knowledge, but also of the moral and social passion for doing good. As, in the first view of it, we took for its worthy motto Montesquieu's words: "To render an intelligent being more intelligent!" so, in the second view of it, there is no better motto which it can have than these words of Bishop Wilson: "To make reason and the will of God prevail!"

Only, whereas the passion for doing good is apt to be overhasty in determining what reason and the will of God say, because its turn is for acting rather than thinking, and it wants to be beginning to act; and whereas it is apt to take its own conceptions, which proceed from its own state of development and share in all the imperfections and immaturities of this, for a basis of action; what distinguishes culture is, that it is possessed by the scientific passion as well as by the passion of doing good; that it demands worthy notations of reason and the will of God, and does not readily suffer its own crude conceptions to substitute themselves for them. And knowing that no action or institution can be salutary and stable which is not based on reason and the will of God, it is not so bent on acting and instituting, even with the great aim of diminishing human error and misery every before its thoughts, but that it can remember that acting and instituting are of little use, unless we know how and what we ought to act and to institute.

From "Culture," Matthew Arnold

In the following example, "Imagination in Orbit" Isaac Asimov presents his definition of "science-fiction"—a definition which explains what he means when he uses the term "science-fiction." He may be asserting this definition or he may be simply taking this definition for granted. Then, on the basis of that definition, he asserts and presents a full argument in favor of what kinds of material science-fiction will consist. One would have to read his definition in the context of his entire essay to determine if he is using the definition as assertion (primary discourse) or as definition (secondary discourse). In that essay he is using the definition as secondary discourse. It is indicated by italics.

True s-f [science fiction] is not to be confused with weird stories or horror stories or tales of the supernatural. It is not the sheer catalog of destruction, designed in Hollywood to appease the rebellious appetites of the teen-ager and to display the tricks and special effects of the camera. The best definition of s-f that I know of is, indeed, almost sociological in its gravity. It goes as follows: *Science-fiction is that branch of literature which is concerned with the impact of scientific and technological advance upon human beings.*

From "Imagination in Orbit," Isaac Asimov

Definition Essays

In his "Of Revenge," Francis Bacon discusses "revenge." He seems to assume that everyone knows what "revenge" means. His purpose does not seem to be to assert (i.e. not to argue in favor of) what the word "revenge" should mean. He is rather arguing against people taking revenge (except in special cases). His definition of "revenge" functions, therefore, as definition (secondary discourse).

"Of Revenge"

Francis Bacon

Revenge is a kind of wild justice; which the more man's nature runs to, the more ought law to weed it out. For as the first wrong, it doth but offend the law; but the revenge of that wrong putteth the law out of office. Certainly, in taking revenge, a man is but even with his enemy; but in passing it over, he is superior; for it is a prince's part to pardon. And Solomon, I am sure, saith, *It is the glory of a man to pass by an offence.* That which is past is gone, and irrevocable; and wise men have enough to do with things present and to come: therefore they do but trifle with themselves, that labour in past matters. There is no man doth a wrong for the wrong's sake, but thereby to purchase himself profit, or pleasure, or honour, or the like. Therefore why should I be angry with a man for loving himself better than me? And if any man should do wrong merely out of ill nature, why, yet it is but like the thorn or briar, which prick and scratch, because they can do no other. The most tolerable sort of revenge is for those wrongs which there is no law to remedy; but then let a man take heed the revenge be such as there is no law to punish; else a man's enemy is still before-hand, and it is two for one. Some, when they take revenge, are desirous the party should know whence it cometh: this is the most generous. For the delight seemeth to be not so much in doing the hurt as in making the party repent: but base and crafty cowards are like the arrow that flieth in the dark. Cosmus, Duke of Florence, had a desperate saying against perfidious or neglecting friends, as if those wrongs were unpardonable: *You shall read* (saith he) *that we are commanded to forgive our enemies; but you never read that we are commanded to forgive our friends.* But yet the spirit of Job was in a better tune: *Shall we (*saith he) *take good at God's hands, and not be content to take evil also?* And so of friends in a proportion. This is certain, that a man that studieth revenge keeps his own wounds green, which otherwise would heal and do well. Public revenges are for the most part fortunate; as that for the death of Caesar; for the death of Pertinax; for the death of Henry the third of France; and many more. But in private revenges it is not so. Nay rather vindictive persons live the life of witches; who as they are mischievous, so end they unfortunate.

Outline of Bacon's "Of Revenge"

In his logical definition Bacon first decides in what class an item belongs and, then enumerates its features which distinguish it from other members of that class:

> Item   =   Class + Distinguishing features
>
> Revenge   =   A kind of wild justice + done arbitrarily by a person without legal authority

  I. Private [which Bacon asserts is intolerable]

     A. For deeds which the law would punish

        1. Makes the revenger also a criminal

        2. Makes the revenger equal to the culprit; to forego revenge makes the revenger superior

        3. To be angry with the either of the following is a waste of energy

      a. The person who commits a crime for profit

      b. The person who commits crime out of ill nature

   B. For deeds which the law would not punish [which Bacon asserts is tolerable]

II. For deeds which the law would not punish

   A. Better to be open about revenge than crafty

   B. Be careful not to break the law yourself

   C. Should be able to tolerate evil from a friend

III. Revenge makes a person vindictive, witch-like, and absorbed with the past.

COMPARISONS

Comparisons are often used to explain the unfamiliar (by comparing it with something familiar), to suggest a value or size or strength of something (by comparing it to something else) to strengthen the persuasive or emotional power of an argument (by comparing the object, person, or idea to something which has greater persuasive or emotional power), and for other purposes. Comparisons involve things of like kind. Comparisons are frequently useful as definitions.

Examples of Comparisons

Example 1

Rice Krispie hearts that taste like budgie food.

From "Matters of Taste," Alexander Theroux

Example 2

No school day was complete but that we sang "The Eyes of Texas," "Texas, Our Texas," "Beautiful Texas." I mean, try substituting "Rhode Island" or "North Dakota," and it sounds about half-silly even to a Texan.

From "Playing Cowboy," Larry L. King

Example 3

In no sense do I advocate evading or defying the law, as would the rabid segregationist.

Paragraph 20 from "Letter from Birmingham Jail," Martin Luther King, Jr.

Example 4

It was never in my program to believe in 'bad seeds,' to think that not every Ted Bundy has a terrible childhood to account for his serial murders, or that it isn't simply political mendacity that motivates people like Henry Kissinger to instigate bombing raids and population destabilizations.

From "On Rediscovering Evil," Mark Jacobson

Example 5

Just as the prophets of the eighth century B.C. left their villages and their home towns, and, just as the Apostle Paul left his village of Tarsus and carried the gospel of Jesus Christ to the far corners of the Greco-Roman world, . . . Macedonian call for aid.

Paragraph 3 from "Letter from Birmingham Jail'" Martin Luther King, Jr.

Example 6

But more basically, I am in Birmingham because injustice is here. Just as the prophets of the eighth century B.C. left their villages and carried their "thus saith the Lord" far beyond the boundaries of their home towns, and just as the Apostle Paul left his village of Tarsus and carried the gospel of Jesus Christ to the far corners of the Greco-Roman world, so am I compelled to carry the gospel of freedom beyond my own home town.

Paragraph 3 from "Letter from Birmingham Jail'" Martin Luther King, Jr.

Example 7

Like Paul, I must constantly respond to the Macedonian call for aid.

Paragraph 3 from "Letter from Birmingham Jail," Martin Luther King, Jr.

Example 8

Oppressed people cannot remain oppressed forever. The yearning for freedom eventually manifests itself, and that is what has happened to the American Negro. Something within him has reminded him of his birthright of freedom, and something without has reminded him that it can be gained. Consciously or unconsciously, he has been caught up by the Zeitgeist, and with his black brothers of Africa and his brown and yellow brothers of Asia, South America, and the Caribbean, the United States Negro is moving with a sense of great urgency toward the promised land of racial justice. If one recognizes this vital urge that has engulfed the Negro community, one should readily understand why public demonstrations are taking place.

Paragraph 30 "Letter from Birmingham Jail," Martin Luther King, Jr.

Essays Using Comparison

"Denmark and the Jews"

Hannah Arendt

At the Wannsee Conference, Martin Luther, of the Foreign Office, warned of   1
great difficulties in the Scandinavian countries, notably in Norway and
Denmark. (Sweden was never occupied, and Finland, though in the war on the
side of the Axis, was one country the Nazis never even approached on the
Jewish question. This surprising exception of Finland, with some two thousand
Jews, may have been due to Hitler's great esteem for the Finns, whom perhaps
he did not want to subject to threats and humiliating blackmail.) Luther proposed postponing evacuations from Scandinavia for the time being, and as far
as Denmark was concerned, this really went without saying, since the country
retained its independent government, and was respected as a neutral state,
until the fall of 1943, although it, along with Norway, had been invaded by the
German Army in April, 1940. There existed no Fascist or Nazi movement in
Denmark worth mentioning, and therefore no collaborators. In Norway, however, the Germans had been able to find enthusiastic supporters; indeed, Vidkun
Quisling, leader of the pro-Nazi and anti-Semitic Norwegian party, gave his
name to what later became known as a "quisling government." The bulk of
Norway's seventeen hundred Jews were stateless, refugees from Germany; they
were seized and interned in a few lightning operations in October and
November, 1942. When Eichmann's office ordered their deportation to
Auschwitz, some of Quisling's own men resigned their government posts. This
may not have come as a surprise to Mr. Luther and the Foreign Office, but what
was much more serious, and certainly totally unexpected, was that Sweden
immediately offered asylum, and even Swedish nationality, to all who were per-
secuted. Dr. Ernst von Weizsäcker, Undersecretary of State of the Foreign
Office, who received the proposal, refused to discuss it, but the offer helped
nevertheless. It is always relatively easy to get out of a country illegally, whereas it is nearly impossible to enter the place of refuge without permission and
to dodge the immigration authorities. Hence, about nine hundred people,
slightly more than half of the small Norwegian community, could be smuggled
into Sweden.

It was in Denmark, however, that the Germans found out how fully justi-   2
fied the Foreign Offices's apprehensions had been. The story of the Danish
Jews is *sui generis,* and the behavior of the Danish people and their government was unique among all the countries in Europe—whether occupied, or a
partner of the Axis, or neutral and truly independent. One is tempted to recommend the story as required reading in political science for all students who
wish to learn something about the enormous power potential inherent in non-

violent action and in resistance to an' opponent possessing vastly superior
means of violence. To be sure, a few other countries in Europe lacked proper
"understanding of the Jewish question," and actually a majority of them were
opposed to "radical" and "final" solutions. Like Denmark, Sweden, Italy, and
Bulgaria proved to be nearly immune to anti-Semitism, but of the three that
were in the German sphere of influence, only the Danes dared speak out on the
subject to their German masters. Italy and Bulgaria sabotaged German orders
and indulged in a complicated game of double-dealing and double-crossing,
saving their Jews by a tour de force of sheer ingenuity, but they never contest-
ed the policy as such. That was totally different from what the Danes did.
When the Germans approached them rather cautiously about introducing the
yellow badge, they were simply told that the King would be the first to wear it,
and the Danish government officials were careful to point out that anti-Jewish
measures of any sort would cause their own immediate resignation. It was
decisive in this whole matter that the Germans did not even succeed in introducing the vitally important distinction between native Danes of Jewish origin,
of whom there were about sixty-four hundred, and the fourteen hundred
German Jewish refugees who had found asylum in the country prior to the war
and who now had been declared stateless by the German government. This
refusal must have surprised the Germans no end, since it appeared so "illogical" for a government to protect people to whom it had categorically denied
naturalization and even permission to work. (Legally, the prewar situation of
refugees in Denmark was not unlike that in France, except that the general cor-
ruption in the Third Republic's civil services enabled a few of them to obtain
naturalization papers, through bribes or "connections," and most refugees in
France could work illegally, without a permit. But Denmark, like Switzerland,
was no country *pour se debrouiller*) The Danes, however, explained to the
German officials that because the stateless refugees were no longer German
citizens, the Nazis could not claim them without Danish assent. This was one
of the few cases in which statelessness turned out to be an asset, although it
was of course not statelessness per se that saved the Jews but, on the contrary, the fact that the Danish government had decided to protect them. Thus,
none of the preparatory moves, so important for the bureaucracy of murder,
could be carried out, and operations were postponed until the fall of 1943.

What happened then was truly amazing; compared with what took place in   3
other European countries, everything went topsy-turvy. In August, 1943—
after the German offensive in Russia had failed, the Afrika Korps had surren-
dered in Tunisia, and the Allies had invaded Italy—the Swedish government
canceled its 1940 agreement with Germany which had permitted German
troops the right to pass through the country. Thereupon, the Danish workers
decided that they could help a bit in hurrying things up; riots broke out in
Danish shipyards, where the dock workers refused to repair German ships and

then went on strike. The German military commander proclaimed a state of emergency and imposed martial law, and Himmler thought this was the right moment to tackle the Jewish question, whose "solution" was long overdue. What he did not reckon with was that—quite apart from Danish resistance— the German officials who had been living in the country for years were no longer the same. Not only did General von Hannecken, the military commander, refuse to put troops at the disposal of the Reich plenipotentiary, Dr. Werner Best; the special S.S. units (*Einsatz-kommandos*) employed in Denmark very frequently objected to "the measures they were ordered to carry out by the central agencies"—according to Best's testimony of Nuremberg. And Best himself, an old Gestapo man and former legal adviser to Heydrich, author of a then famous book on the police, who had worked for the military government in Paris to the entire satisfaction of his superiors, could not longer be trusted, although it is doubtful that Berlin ever learned the extent of his unreliability. Still, it was clear from the beginning that things were not going well, and Eichmann's office sent one of its best men to Denmark—Rolf Gunther, whom no one had ever accused of not possessing the required "ruthless toughness." Gunther made no impression on his colleagues in Copenhagen, and now von Hannecken refused even to issue a decree requiring all Jews to report for work.

Best went to Berlin and obtained a promise that all Jews from Denmark would be sent to Theresienstadt regardless of their category—a very important concession, from the Nazis' point of view. The night of October 1 was set for their seizure and immediate departure—ships were ready in the harbor—and since neither the Danes nor the Jews nor the German troops stationed in Denmark could be relied on to help, police units arrived from Germany for a door-to-door search. At the last moment, Best told them that they were not permitted to break into apartments, because the Danish police might then interfere, and they were not supposed to fight it out with the Danes. Hence they could seize only those Jews who voluntarily opened their doors. They found exactly 477 people, out of a total of more then 7,800, at home and willing to let them in. A few days before the date of doom, a German shipping agent, Georg F. Duckwitz, having probably been tipped off by Best himself, had revealed the whole plan to Danish government officials, who, in turn, had hurriedly informed the heads of the Jewish community. They, in marked contrast to Jewish leaders in other countries, had then communicated the news openly in the synagogues on the occasion of the New Year services. The Jews had just time enough to leave their apartments and go into hiding, which was very easy in Denmark, because, in the words of the judgment, "all sections of the Danish people, from the King down to simple citizens," stood ready to receive them.

They might have remained in hiding until the end of the war if the Danes had not been blessed with Sweden as a neighbor. It seemed reasonable to ship the Jews to Sweden, and this was done with the help of the Danish fishing

4

5

fleet. The cost of transportation for people without means—about a hundred dollars per person—was paid largely by wealthy Danish citizens, and that was perhaps the most astounding feat of all, since this was a time when Jews were paying for their own deportation, when the rich among them were paying fortunes for exit permits (in Holland, Slovakia, and, later, in Hungary) either by bribing the local authorities or by negotiating "legally" with the S.S., who accepted only hard currency and sold exit permits, in Holland, to the tune of five or ten thousand dollars per person. Even in places where Jews met with genuine sympathy and a sincere willingness to help, they had to pay for it, and the chances poor people had of escaping were nil.

It took the better part of October to ferry all the Jews across the five to fifteen miles of water that separates Denmark from Sweden. The Swedes received 5,919 refugees, of whom at least 1,000 were of German origin, 1,310 were half-Jews, and 686 were non-Jews married to Jews. (Almost half the Danish Jews seem to have remained in the country and survived the war in hiding.) The non-Danish Jews were better off than ever before; they all received permission to work. The few hundred Jews whom the German police had been able to arrest were shipped to Theresienstadt. They were old or poor people, who either had not received the news in time or had not been able to comprehend its meaning. In the ghetto, they enjoyed greater privileges than any other group because of the never-ending "fuss" made about them by Danish institutions and private persons. Forty-eight persons died, a figure that was not particularly high, in view of the average age of the group. When everything was over, it was the considered opinion of Eichmann that "for various reasons the action against the Jews in Denmark has been a failure," whereas the curious Dr. Best declared that "the objective of the operation was not to seize a great number of Jews but to clean Denmark of Jews, and this objective has now been achieved."

Politically and psychologically, the most interesting aspect of this incident is perhaps the role played by the German authorities in Denmark, their obvious sabotage of orders from Berlin. It is the only case we know of in which the Nazis met with open native resistance, and the result seems to have been that those exposed to it changed their minds. They themselves apparently no longer looked upon the extermination of a whole people as a matter of course. They had met resistance based on principle, and their "toughness" had melted like butter its the sun, they had even been able to show a few timid beginnings of genuine courage. That the ideal of "toughness," except, perhaps, for a few half-demented brutes, was nothing but a myth of self-deception, concealing a ruthless desire for conformity at any price, was clearly revealed at the Nuremberg Trials, where the defendants accused and betrayed each other and assured the world that they "had always been against it" or claimed, as Eichmann was to do, that their best qualities had been "abused" by their superiors. (In Jerusalem, he accused "those in power" of having abused his "obedience." "The subject of a good government is lucky, the subject of a bad government is unlucky. I had no luck.") The atmosphere had changed, and although most of them must have known that they were doomed, not a single one of them had the guts to defend the Nazi ideology. Werner Best claimed at Nuremberg that he had played a complicated double role and that it was thanks to him that the Danish officials had been warned of the impending catastrophe; documentary evidence showed, on the contrary, that he himself had proposed the Danish operation in Berlin, but he explained that this was all part of the game. He was extradited to Denmark and there condemned to death, but he appealed the sentence, with surprising results; because of "new evidence," his sentence was commuted to five years in prison, from which he was released soon afterward. He must have been able to prove to the satisfaction of the Danish court that he really had done his best.

1963

ANALOGIES

Analogies are used in the same way and for the same purposes as comparisons. But analogies involve things of unlike kind. Analogies are frequently useful as definitions.

Examples of Analogies

Example 1

Most often, it [the term 'stress'] is used by people who feel tired, wornout, and are making an analogy to metallurgy—stressed metal is more brittle, more liable to be fractured.

From "Emphasis on Stress," William Safire

Example 2

We use our parents like recurring dreams, to be entered into when needed, they are always there for love or for hate.

From "My Father," Doris Lessing

Example 3

As the least drop of wine tinges the whole goblet, so the least particle of truth colors our whole life. It is never isolated, or simply added as treasure to our stock. When any real progress is made, we unlearn and learn anew what we thought we knew before.

From *Journal*, Henry David Thoreau

Example 4

But again I am thankful to God that some noble souls from the ranks of organized religion have broken loose from the paralyzing chains of conformity and joined us as active partners in the struggle for freedom. They have left their secure congregations and walked the streets of Albany, Georgia, with us. They have gone down the highways of the South on tortuous rides for freedom. Yes they have gone to jail with us. Some have been dismissed from their churches, have lost the support of their bishops and fellow ministers. But they have acted in the faith that right defeated is stronger than evil triumphant. Their witness has been *the spiritual salt that has preserved* the true meaning of the gospel in troubled times. They have *carved a tunnel of hope* through the *dark mountain of disappointment.*

Paragraph 43 of "Letter from Birmingham Jail," Martin Luther King, Jr.

Example 5

American cities—unlike those in countries such as Italy, Sweden, and Japan, which have kept a balance of authority and responsibility [comparison]—are *zoos and jungles, in which not the animals but the citizens are locked up* [analogy].

From "We Must Excise Savage Behavior, Not Excuse It," Georgie Anne Geyer

Example 6

Analogy is a conceptual instrument constructed by means of the proper arrangement of words, *just as the microscope and the telescope are optical instruments constructed by means of the proper arrangement of lenses. If an object is too small or too far to be perceptible with the naked eye*, we can often see it by viewing it through an optical instrument. In the same way, if an idea is emotionally too close or too far for us to perceive, we can often see it by viewing it through an analogy.

From *Heresies*, Thomas Szasz

Example 7

There is no more reason or justification to restrict the sale of drugs to state-licensed pharmacists *than there is to restrict the sale of foods to state-licensed nutritionists.*

From *Heresies*, Thomas Szasz

Example 8

Describing a helicopter's landing at a ski resort, William F. Jr. says that he hears "a great whirring . . . ; it appeared as though a cyclone had suddenly focused on the snow courtyard between the shop and the ski lift."

From "Why We Don't Complain," William F. Buckley, Jr.

Essays Using Analogy

"The Perfect House"

Farley Mowat

As I grew to know the People, so my respect for their intelligence and ingenuity   1
increased. Yet I could not reconcile my feelings of respect with the poor, shod-
dy dwelling places that they constructed. As with most Eskimos, the winter
homes of the Ihalmiut are the snow-built domes we call *igloos*. (*Igloo* in
Eskimo means simply "house" and thus an igloo can be built of wood or stone,
as well as of snow.) But unlike most other Innuit, the Ihalmiut make snow
houses which are cramped, miserable shelters. I think the People acquired the
art of igloo construction quite recently in their history and from the coast
Eskimos. Certainly they have no love for their igloos, and prefer the skin tents.
This preference is related to the problem of fuel.

   Any home in the arctic, in winter, requires some fuel if only for cooking.   2
The coast peoples make use of fat lamps, for they have an abundance of fat
from the sea mammals they kill, and so they are able to cook in the igloo, and
to heat it as well. But the Ihalmiut can ill afford to squander the precious fat of
the deer, and they dare to burn only one tiny lamp for light. Willow must serve
as fuel, and while willow burns well enough in a tent open at the peak to allow
the smoke to escape, when it is burned in a snow igloo, the choking smoke
leaves no place for human occupants. So snow houses replace the skin tents
of the Ihalmiut only when winter has already grown old and the cold has
reached the seemingly unbearable extremes of sixty or even seventy degrees
below zero. Then the tents are grudgingly abandoned and snow huts built.
From that time until spring no fires may burn inside the homes of the People,
and such cooking as is attempted must be done outside, in the face of the bliz-
zards and gales.

   Yet though tents are preferred to igloos, it is still rather hard to under-   3
stand why. . . . Great, gaping slits outline each hide on the frame of a tent.
Such a home offers hardly more shelter than a thicket of trees, for on the
unbroken sweep of the plains the winds blow with such violence that they drive
the hard snow through the tents as if the skin walls did not really exist. But the
People spend many days and dark nights in these feeble excuses for houses,
while the wind rises like a demon of hatred and the cold comes as if it meant to
destroy all life in the land. In these tents there may be a fire; but consider this
fire, this smoldering handful of green twigs, dug with infinite labor from under
the drifts. It gives heat only for a few inches out from its sullen coals so that it
barely suffices to boil a pot of water in an hour or two. The eternal winds pour
into the tent and dissipate what little heat the fire can spare from the cook-pots.
The fire gives comfort to the Ihalmiut only through its appeal to the eyes.

However, the tent with its wan little fire is a more desirable place than the   4
snow house with no fire at all. At least the man in the tent can have a hot bowl
of soup once in a while, but after life in the igloos begins, almost all food must
be eaten while it is frozen to the hardness of rocks. Men sometimes take skin
bags full of ice into the beds so that they can have water to drink, melted by the
heat of their bodies. It is true that some of the People build cook shelters outside the igloos but these snow hearths burn very badly, and then only when it is
calm. For the most part the winds prevent any outside cooking at all, and anyway by late winter the willow supply is so deeply buried under the drifts, it is
almost impossible for men to procure it.

So you see that the homes of the Ihalmiut in winter are hardly models of   5
comfort. Even when spring comes to the land the improvement in housing conditions is not great. After the tents go up in the spring, the rains begin. During
daylight it rains with gray fury and the tents soak up the chill water until the
hides hang slackly on their poles while rivulets pour through the tent to drench
everything inside. At night, very likely, there will be frost and by dawn everything not under the robes with the sleepers will be frozen stiff.

With the end of the spring rains, the hot sun dries and shrinks the hides   6
until they are drum-taut, but the ordeal is not yet over. Out of the steaming
muskegs come the hordes of bloodsucking and flesh-eating flies and these find
that the Ihalmiut tents offer no barrier to their invasion. The tents belong equally to the People and to the flies, until midsummer brings an end to the plague,
and the hordes vanish.

My high opinion of the People was often clouded when I looked at their   7
homes. I sometimes wondered if the Ihalmiut were as clever and as resourceful
as I thought them to be. I had been too long conditioned to think of home as
four walls and a roof, and so the obvious solution of the Ihaimiut housing problem escaped me for nearly a year. It took me that long to realize that the People
not only have good homes, but that they have devised the one perfect house.

The tent and the igloo are really only auxiliary shelters. The real home of   8
the Ihalmiut is much like that of the turtle, for it is what he carries about on his
back. In truth it is the only house that can enable men to survive on the merciless plains of the Barrens. It has central heating from the fat furnace of the
body, its walls are insulated to a degree of perfection that we white men have
not been able to surpass, or even emulate. It is complete, light in weight, easy
to make and easy to keep in repair. It costs nothing, for it is a gift of the land,
through the deer. When I consider that house, my opinion of the astuteness of
the Ihalmiut is no longer clouded.

Primarily the house consists of two suits of fur, worn one over the other,   9
and each carefully tailored to the owner's dimensions. The inner suit is worn
with the hair of the hides facing in-ward and touching the skin while the outer
suit has its hair turned out to the weather. Each suit consists of a pullover

parka with a hood, a pair of fur trousers, fur gloves and fur boots. The double motif is extended to the tips of the fingers, to the top of the head, and to the soles of the feet where soft slippers of harehide are worn next to the skin.

The high winter boots may be tied just above the knee so that they leave   10 no entry for the cold blasts of the wind. But full ventilation is provided by the design of the parka. Both inner and outer parkas hang slackly to at least the knees of the wearer, and they are not belted in winter. Cold air does not rise, so that no drafts can move up under the parkas to reach the bare flesh, but the heavy, moisture-laden air from close to the body sinks through the gap between parka and trousers and is carried away. Even in times of great physical exertion, when the Ihalmiut sweats freely, he is never in any danger of soaking his clothing and so inviting quick death from frost afterwards. The hides are not in contact with the body at all but are held away from the flesh by the soft resiliency of the deer hairs that line them, and in the space between the tips of the hair and the hide of the parka there is a constantly moving layer of warm air which absorbs all the sweat and carries it off.

Dressed for a day in the winter, the Ihalmiut has this protection over all   11 parts of his body, except for a narrow oval in front of his face and even this is well protected by a long silken fringe of wolverine fur, the one fur to which the moisture of breathing will not adhere and freeze.

In the summer rain, the hide may grow wet, but the layer of air between   12 deerhide and skin does not conduct the water, and so it runs off and is lost while the body stays dry. Then there is the question of weight. Most white men trying to live in the winter arctic load their bodies with at least twenty-five pounds of clothing, while the complete deerskin home of the Innuit weighs about seven pounds. This of course, makes a great difference in the mobility of the wearers. A man wearing tight-fitting and too bulky clothes is almost as helpless as a man in a diver's suit. But besides their light weight, the Ihalmiut clothes are tailored so that they are slack wherever muscles must work freely beneath them. There is ample space in this house for the occupant to move and to breathe, for there are no partitions and walls to limit his motions, and the man is almost as free in his movements as if he were naked. If he must sleep out, without shelter, and it is fifty below, he has but to draw his arms into his parka, and he sleeps nearly as well as he would in a double-weight eiderdown bag.

This is in winter, but what about summer? I have explained how the   13 porous hide nevertheless acts as a raincoat. Well, it does much more than that. In summer the outer suit is discarded and all clothing pared down to one layer. The house then offers effective insulation against heat entry. It remains surprisingly cool, for it is efficiently ventilated. Also, and not least of its many advantages, it offers the nearest thing to perfect protection against the flies. The hood is pulled up so that it covers the neck and the ears, and the flies find it nearly impossible to get at the skin underneath. But of course the Ihalmiut have long since learned to live with the flies, and they feel none of the hysterical and frustrating rage against them so common with us.

In the case of women's clothing, home has two rooms. The back of the parka has an enlargement, as if it were made to fit a hunchback, and in this space, called the *amaul*, lives the unweaned child of the family. A bundle of remarkably absorbent sphagnum moss goes under his backside and the child sits stark naked, in unrestricted delight, where he can look out on the world and very early in life become familiar with the sights and the moods of his land. He needs no clothing of his own, and as for the moss—in that land there is an unlimited supply of soft sphagnum and it can be replaced in an instant. 14

When the child is at length forced to vacate this pleasant apartment, proba- bly by the arrival of competition, he is equipped with a one-piece suit of hides which looks not unlike the snow suits our children wear in the winter. Only it is much lighter, more efficient, and much less restricting. This first home of his own is a fine home for the Ihalmiut child, and one that his white relatives would envy if they could appreciate its real worth. 15

"The Allegory of the Cave"
Plato

And now, I said, let me show in a figure how far our nature is enlightened or unenlightened: Behold! human beings living in an underground den, which has a mouth open towards the light and reaching all along the den; here they have been from their childhood, and have their legs and necks chained so that they cannot move, and can only see before them, being prevented by the chains from turning round their heads. Above and behind them a fire is blazing at a distance, and between the fire and the prisoners there is a raised way; and you will see, if you look, a low wall built along the way, like the screen which marionette players have in front of them, over which they show the puppets. 1

I see. 2

And do you see, I said, men passing along the wall carrying all sorts of vessels, and statues and figures of animals made of wood and stone and various materials, which appear over the wall? Some of them are talking, others silent. 3

You have shown me a strange image, and they are strange prisoners. 4

Like ourselves, I replied; and they see only their own shadows, or the shadows of one another, which the fire throws on the opposite wall of the cave? 5

True, he said; how could they see anything but the shadows if they were never allowed to move their heads? 6

And of the objects which are being carried in like manner they would only see the shadows? 7

Yes, he said. 8

And if they were able to converse with one another, would they not sup- 9
pose that they were naming what was actually before them?

Very true. 10

And suppose further that the prison had an echo which came from the 11
other side, would they not be sure to fancy when one of the passers-by spoke
that the voice which they heard came from the passing shadow?

No question, he replied. 12

To them, I said, the truth would be literally nothing but the shadows of 13
the images.

That is certain. 14

And now look again, and see what will naturally follow if the prisoners 15
are released and disabused of their error. At first, when any of them is liberat-
ed and compelled suddenly to stand up and turn his neck round and walk and
look look towards the light. he will suffer sharp pains; the glare will distress
him and he will be unable to see the realities of which in his former state he
had seen the shadows; and then conceive someone saying to him, that what
he saw before was an illusion. but that now, when he is approaching nearer to
being and his eye is turned towards more real existence, he has a clearer
vision—what will be his reply? And you may further imagine that his instruc-
tor is pointing to the objects as they pass and requiring him to name them—
will he not be perplexed? Will he not fancy that the shadows which he formerly saw are truer than the objects which are now shown to him?

Far truer. 16

And if he is compelled to look straight at the light, will he not have a pain 17
in his eyes which will make him turn away to take refuge in the objects of
vision which he can see. and which he will conceive to be in reality clearer
than the things which are now being shown to him?

True, he said. 18

And suppose once more, that he is reluctantly dragged up a steep and 19
rugged ascent, and held fast until he is forced into the presence of the sun
himself, is he not likely to be pained and irritated? When he approaches the
light his eyes will be dazzled and he will not be able to see anything at all of
what are now called realities.

Not all in a moment, he said. 20

He will require to grow accustomed to the sight of the upper world. And 21
first he will see the shadows best, next the reflections of men and other
objects in the water, and then the objects themselves; then he will gaze upon
the light of the moon and the stars and the spangled heaven; and he will see
the sky and the stars by night better than the sun or the light of the sun
by day?

Certainly. 22

Last of all he will be able to seé the sun, and not mere reflections of him   23
in the water, but he will see him in his own proper place, and not in another;
and he will contemplate him as he is.

Certainly.   24

He will then proceed to argue that this is he who gives the season and   25
the years, and is the guardian of all that is in the visible world, and in a certain
way the cause of all things which he and his fellows have been accustomed to
behold?

Clearly, he said, he would first see the sun and then reason about him.   26

And when he remembered his old habitation, and the wisdom of the den
and his fellow-prisoners, do you not suppose that he would felicitate himself
on the change, and pity them?

Certainly, he would.   27

And if they were in the habit of conferring honors among themselves   28
selves on those who were quickest to observe the passing shadows and to
remark which of them went before, and which followed after, and which were
together; and who were therefore best able to draw conclusions as to the
future, do you think that he would care for such honors and glories, or envy
the possessors of them? Would he not say with Homer,

> Better to be the poor servant of a poor master,

and to endure anything, rather than think as they do and live after their
manner?

Yes, he said, I think that he would rather suffer anything than entertain   29
these false notions and live in this miserable manner.

Imagine once more, I said, such an one coming suddenly out of the sun   30
to be replaced in his old situation; would he not be certain to have his eyes
full of darkness?

To be sure, he said.   31

And if there were a contest, and he had to compete in measuring the   32
shadows with the prisoners who had never moved out of the den, while his
sight was still weak, and before his eyes had become steady (and the time
which would be needed to acquire this new habit of sight might be very considerable) would he not be ridiculous? Men would say of him that up he went
and down he came without his eyes; and that it was better not even to think
of ascending; and if any one tried to loose another and lead him up to the
light, let them only catch the offender, and they would put him to death.

No question, he said.   33

This entire allegory, I said, you may now append, dear Glaucon, to the   34
previous argument, the prison-house is the world of sight, the light of the fire
is the sun, and you will not misapprehend me if you interpret the journey

upwards to be the ascent of the soul into the intellectual world according to my poor belief, which, at your desire, I have expressed—whether rightly or wrongly God knows. But, whether true or false, my opinion is that in the world of knowledge the idea of good appears last of all, and is seen only with an effort; and, when seen, is also inferred to be the universal author of all things beautiful and right, parent of light and of the lord of light in this visible world, and the immediate source of reason and truth in the intellectual; and that this is the power upon which he who would act rationally either in public or private life must have his eye fixed.

I agree, he said, as far as I am able to understand you. 35

Moreover, I said, you must not wonder that those who attain to this 36
beatific vision are unwilling to descend to human affairs; for their souls are ever hastening into the upper world where they desire to dwell; which desire of theirs is very natural, if our allegory may be trusted.

Yes, very natural. 37

And is there anything surprising in one who passes from divine contem- 38
plations to the evil state of man, misbehaving himself in a ridiculous manner; if, while his eyes are blinking and before he has become accustomed to the surrounding darkness, he is compelled to fight in courts of law, or in other places, about the images or the shadows of images of justice, and is endeavoring to meet the conceptions of those who have never yet seen absolute justice?

Anything but surprising, he replied. 39

Any one who has common sense will remember that the bewilderments 40
of the eyes are of two kinds, and arise from two causes, either from coming out of the light or from going into the light, which is true of the mind's eye, quite as much as of the bodily eye; and he who remembers this when he sees any one whose vision is perplexed and weak, will not be too ready to laugh; he will first ask whether that soul of man has come out of the brighter life, and is unable to see because unaccustomed to the dark, or having turned from darkness to the day is dazzled by excess of light. And he will count the one happy in his condition and state of being, and he will pity the other; or, if he have a mind to laugh at the soul which comes from below into the light, there will be more reason in this than in the laugh which greets him who returns from above out of the light into the den.

That, he said, is a very just distinction. 41

4th century B.C.

PARENTHETICAL INSERTIONS

*Parenthetical insertion*s are brief comments—asides—in which the writer leaves the discussion of the primary subject and makes some kind of comment about something else—often an expression of personal opinion or a direct comment to the reader.

In "Why I Want a Wife," an essay which begins with a brief narrative about a recently divorced man who said he wanted a wife, and which then defines all of a wife's traditional duties by describing all of the things which she, a wife, does, Judy Syfers concludes by saying—in a personal opinion directed to the reader—"My God, who wouldn't want a wife?" And in "Politics and the English Language, before George Orwell says "These five passages have not been picked out because they are especially bad—I could have quoted far worse if I had chosen—but because they illustrate various of the mental vices from which we now suffer." Here, the clause, "I could have quoted far worse if I had chosen" is a *parenthetical insertion*.

In the introductory portion of "Of Accidental Judgments and Casual Slaughters," Kai Erikson makes two assertions, of which the second is "together they constitute the only occasion in history was made to employ [atomic weapons] in that way" then says "I want to reflect here on the second of those points. The 'decision to drop'— I will explain in a minute why quotation marks are useful here—is a fascinating historical episode." Here, the clause within the dashes is a parenthetical comment.

Parenthetical comments may or not be set off by parentheses. Sometimes they are separated from the primary text by a pair of commas or by a pair of dashes. And sometimes they are not identified by punctuation in any way, which is the case in this passage from Larry L King's "Playing Cowboy": "I donned my Cowboy Outfit to greet the selection committee and aw-shucked and consarned 'em half to death; Easterners just can't resist a John Wayne quoting Shakespeare. I've got to admit there's satisfaction in it for every good ol' boy who country-slicks the city dudes." In this passage, the last sentence is a parenthetical comment.

Parenthetical comments can be used without distracting the reader only if they are very brief. Also, they are less likely to confuse a reader of they are set off within parentheses or within a pair of dashes.

Examples of Parenthetical Insertions

Example 1

The socialization of stress, and its voguish selection as the root of all modem health evil, has not hitherto been subjected to linguistic examination. (How you doin', reader? Most people your age and social class are about three paragraphs further on. You're sure you grasped the full import of the academese in the sentence before this parenthetical aside? Your peer group is looking over your shoulder.)

From "Emphasis on Stress," William Safire

Example 2

(Significantly, there is no milieu tie pattern for dentists.)

From "Neckties and Class," Paul Fussell

Example 3

I will explain in a minute why quotation marks are useful here.

From "Of Accidental Judgements and Casual Slaughters," Kai Erikson

NAMING

In the middle of a paragraph whose purpose is to describe the morning scene near a cabin, in which the writer includes the description of a carp leaping from the water, the following two types of secondary discourse are inserted. The first is a *naming*. Naming is the opposite of defining. In a definition the word is part of the *primary discourse* and the definition is the secondary discourse. In naming, something is described as part of the primary discourse, and the naming is *secondary discourse*. The secondary discourse in the following example is a parenthetical comment about the old man.

Examples of Naming

Example 1

The old man next door said these leaping fish were carp. Himself, he preferred muskie, for he was a real fisherman and muskie gave him a fight.

From "Where the World Began," Margaret Laurence

Example 2

Early in August the seas will be teeming with fish. This will be what geologists call the Devonian period.

From "But a Watch in the Night," James C. Rettie

CHARTS, GRAPHS, FORMULAS, EQUATIONS AND REPRESENTATIONS IN OTHER LANGUAGE SYSTEMS

Charts, *graphs*, *formulas*, *equations*, and other representations of ideas and facts in language systems other than traditional English prose can also provide useful explanations.

Example 1

It should be no surprise that . . . large firms tend to be simply less profitable than small ones. . . . [As was pointed out by] the Temporary National Economic Committee in 1940 ("Those with an investment under $500,000 enjoyed a higher return than those with more than $5,000,000 and twice as high a return as those with more than $50,000,000"); again by California economist H. O. Stekler, examining profits of manufacturing firms in 1949 and 1955-57 ("For the profitable firm, there is a declining relationship between profitability and size"); and yet again by the U. S. Senate Antitrust Subcommittee in 1963 ("In twenty-three out of thirty basic industries, profit rates either decreased consistently as firm size increased or else had no connection with increased size"). The most graphic demonstration of small firm profitability is probably this table compiled by Stekler:

SIZE AND PROFITABILITY

Assets	Rate of Return	Assets	Rate of Return
$ 0-50,000	137	1-5,000,000	113
50-100,000	130	5-10,000,000	108
100-250,000	120	10-50,000,000	105
250-500,000	118	50-100,000,000	107
500-1,000,000	119	100,000,000+	100

From "The Myth of Bigness," Kirkpatrick Sale

Example 2

The large scale coffee growers were being placed by the state bank at a distinct advantage over the small farmers of the region. The figures presented in Table 5 reveal the nature of this advantage. The large-scale farmers were granted nearly 80 percent of the total supply of bank credit even though they represented only one-third of the borrowing population.

Loan characteristics	Small-scale agriculture	Large-scale agriculture
A. Number of loans	309	173
B. Number of hectares worked with loans	S/1,522	2,984
C. Total value of loans	S/. 8,411,400	S/.28,006,640
D. Average amount allotted per loan (C/A)	S/.27,221	S/.161,888
E. Average amount allotted per hectare (C/B)	S/.5,527	S/.9,386

The Peasants of El Dorado, Robin Shoemaker

Example 3

If *a, b,* and *c* are the lengths of the side of a right triangle and *c* is the length of the hypotenuse (longest side), then the sums of the squares of *a* and *b* equals the square of *c*.

$$a^2 + b^2 = c^2$$

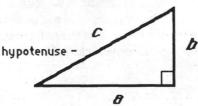

The Pythagorean Theorem

Example 4

The keyboard is composed of groups of black and white notes, with alternations of two and then three black-note ensembles. Distances between keys are as follows: from any key to the immediately adjacent key (to the right, of higher pitch) or lower (to the left, of lower pitch) key is referred to as a half step. Two half steps comprise a whole step. Here are some half steps: 1 to 2, 4 to 5, 5 to 6, 12 to 13. Some whole steps: 1 to 3, 5 to 7, 8 to 10, 11 to 13, 12 to 14:

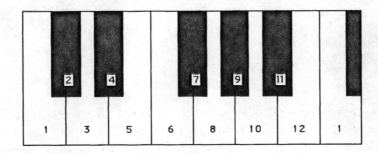

The so-called major scale is a central device in all Western music, a sequence of eight notes constructed according to this formula:

1	2	3	4	5	6	7	8
	1	1	1/2	1	1	1	1/2

Starting on any key, a major scale is formed by proceeding from the starting point, either one octave higher or one octave lower. Within the scope of one octave range, there are twelve possible starting notes, and thus twelve major scales.

In musical nomenclature, alphabet terms are assigned the notes on the piano.

1. White notes are named by the terms A through G, duplicated through successive octaves.

2. Black notes are named by reference to the adjacent white ones, a black note termed a 'flat' when named by reference to that white note a half step above it, or a 'sharp' relative to that white note a half step below. The black notes thus take either of two names (this may also be true of white notes in certain circumstances).

From "Scales," *Ways of the Hand*, David Sudnow

Section IV:
Unity and
Coherence

If a discourse has unity and coherence, it is much more
readable and convincing to a reader. Unity and coherence
are achieved by the inclusion of unity devices and coherence devices.

CHAPTER 8

Unity & Coherence

A well-written discourse is unified and coherent. A unified discourse has a central subject and is controlled by its thesis sentence. All of its parts support the thesis sentence. It contains no irrelevant or contradictory material. A *coherent discourse* is logical and readable. Its parts are logically related, organized, and ordered, and they are adequately connected to each other with coherence devices which help to guide the reader through the discourse. Whether or not a discourse is unified and coherent is determined primarily by the elements and components of which it is comprised. But unity can be enhanced by the appropriate use of unity indicators.

UNITY

A *unified discourse* has a central subject and is controlled by a central thesis and when its parts all contribute to the understanding of that subject and the development of that thesis.

Unity indicators are integral arts of the discourse's ideas, evidence, and reasons, and a discourse which is unified in subject, thesis, and parts nearly always inevitably contains unity indicators. Unity indicators cannot be deleted from the discourse. Unity indicators, include *controlling ideas* (thesis and topic sentences), *recurring elements* (ideas, evidence, and reasons), and what Robin Bell Markels (in *A New Perspective on Cohesion in Expository Paragraphs*) calls *"recurrences."* Recurrences include the following: identical repetitions of key terms, of synonyms for those terms, and of pronouns which refer to those terms, members of the same class as the key terms, and definite articles that refer to the key term. Recurrences can also be implied by parallel structure. Unlike coherence devices, which are not a part of the essential elements of a discourse, unity indicators always coincide with and are inseparable from those essential elements. (They include the nouns, adjectives, and verbs which make up the discourse.)

COHERENCE

Coherence is achieved in a discourse when the writer makes clear the connection between the parts of the discourse and how those parts contribute to the overall discourse

Coherence devices are connectors which indicate the relationships between the various elements and components of the discourse and which help to provide signals to guide the reader. Coherence devices indicate the relationship between a part of and the whole discourse and between parts of the discourse. They indicate the beginning of a new part or the conclusion of a previous part. The provide signals which help the reader anticipate what will appear next. They make it easier for the reader to comprehend the discourse.

Coherence devices have traditionally been called "transition devices," but that phrase that oversimplifies by suggesting that all such devices do is connect one part of a discourse with the following parts. But coherence devices can function *cohesively* by indicating the relationship between a part of the discourse and the whole discourse, or they may function *adhesively* by indicating the relationship between one part of a discourse an another. Or they may simultaneously function cohesively and adhesively.

Cohesive devices indicate the relationship of a part of a discourse and the whole discourse and provide *cohesion* between a part of the discourse and either to the discourse as a whole or to a section of the discourse of which the part belongs.

■ *Titles* and *subtitles*

■ *Headings, outline form, font, numbering*, and other indicators of relationships within the discourse indicate the hierarchy of main and subordinate parts within a discourse and the relationship of any part of a discourse to the whole.

■ *Introductions* function cohesively to introduce major subjects and ideas and to initiate the whole discourse.

■ *Conclusions* function cohesively to conclude major subjects and ideas and to resolve the whole discourse.

■ *Transitions* can indicate the relationships between a part of the discourse and the whole discourse.

Adhesive devices enhance coherence by indicating the relationship of one part of a discourse to another part of that discourse.

■ *Introductions* function adhesively to lead into the first part of the body of the discourse.

■ *Conclusions* function adhesively (to provide adhesion to the last part of the body of the discourse) and provide links between either contiguous or non-contiguous parts of a discourse.

■ *Transitions* usually function adhesively to connect two contiguous or non-contiguous parts of a discourse adhesively.

■ *Intratextual references* or *cross-references* indicate the relationship of one part of a discourse to another part which appears somewhere else in the discourse.

■ *Intertextual references* (*bridges*) appear only in a discourse that is responding to, expanding on, or arguing with another discourse. Because Martin Luther King, Jr., is responding to the statement by the Alabama clergymen, his "Letter" contains several bridges.

The most commonly employed coherence devices are *introductions, conclusions,* and *transitions*, any of which may be as brief as a single word (for a sentence or short paragraph) or several paragraphs long (for an extended discourse).

Introductions

Introductions signal the beginning of any discourse. Within a discourse smaller sections and paragraphs may also have their own introductions. Such internal introductions signal that a new section of the discourse is about to begin.

The primary purposes of introductions to essays are to lead a reader into an essay, suggest the essay's main subject, thesis, and perhaps primary subdivisions, and to, if possible, whet the reader's interest in the subject. Among the tasks which can be achieved by the introduction, according to Randall E. Dekker,[1] are 1) "To identify the subject and set its limitations. . . . 2) To interest the reader. . . . 3) To set the tone [of the discourse]. . . . [and] 4) Frequently . . . to indicate the plan of organization."[2] But more basic than any of these purposes and rhetorical tactics of an introduction within a particular discourse is the basic function of an introduction of any discourse—to provide coherence. Depending on the length of the discourse, an introduction can be a short as a single sentence or many paragraphs long.

Introductions which are generally acceptable and frequently used in our culture can be divided into four categories: *efficient introductions, classical introductions, commonly used introductions*, and *commonly recommended introductions*.

Efficient Introductions

Very short, efficient introductions are being used more and more frequently. Efficient introductions may do any of the following:

- They present the thesis sentence alone.

- They indicate the main organization of the essay.

- They give a summary of the main ideas of the essay.

Classical Introductions

In classical rhetoric it was traditional to begin with an *introduction* (a "leading into"), *proemium* ("before the song"), or *exordium* ("beginning or web") to prepare an audience rather to have "an abrupt, immediate entry into the body of our discourse."[3] This preparation was supposed to a) "inform the audience of the end or object of our discourse [the thesis or conclusion] and b) "dispose the audience to be receptive to what we say" (Corbett, p. 303). Quoting Richard Whately's *Elements of Rhetoric*, Edward P. J. Corbett lists the following traditional ways of arousing interest in the subject:

- *Introduction inquisitive*—to show that our subject is important, curious, or interesting.

- *Introduction paradoxical*—to show that although the points we are trying to establish seem improbable, they must after all be admitted.

- *Introduction corrective*—to show that our subject has been neglected, misunderstood, or misrepresented.

- *Introduction preparatory*—to explain an unusual mode of developing our subject; or to forestall some misconception of our purpose; or to apologize for some deficiencies.

- *Introduction narrative*—to rouse interest in our subject by using an anecdote.[4]

Commonly Used Introductions

Narrative Introduction

The ***narrative introduction***, an extended example demonstrating the problem or situation the essay will discuss, is often written to produce a strong emotional reaction in the reader, has become the most frequently utilized introduction in popular articles in contemporary magazines with large circulations.

Narrative introductions—one traditional classical introduction—are often very representative, extended examples of contemporary social problems (such as drunk driving, drug addiction, or teenage pregnancy) and have great emotional power. Sometimes these narrative introductions also provide evidence which is utilized later in the primary discourse of the essay or as a touchstone against which much of the primary discourse is compared.

Funnel Introduction

One method for developing "the introductory paragraph" that has received extremely widespread endorsement by secondary school and college writing teachers is the ***funnel introduction***, which was named and explained by Sheridan Baker in *The Practical Stylist* and *The Complete Stylist*. Baker suggests that the writer think of the beginning paragraph as a "funnel" and suggests that "The inevitable psychology of interest, as you move your reader through your first paragraph and into your essay, urges you to put your thesis last—in the last sentence of your beginning paragraph," because "The clearest and most emphatic place for your thesis sentence is at the end . . . of the beginning paragraph."[5]

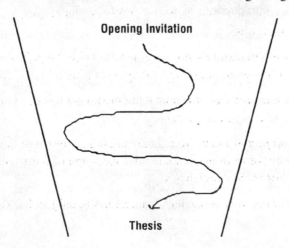

Opening Invitation

Thesis

Occasional Introduction

Another type of introduction, which is related to the writer's experience, but which has a particular focus, is the **occasional introduction**, an introduction that describes the particular event or experience which prompted the writer to think and write about his or her subject.

Opposing Opinion Introduction

Also fairly common is an introduction that omits the *exordium* and begins with the second step of the classical argument, the presentation of an opposing opinion that the writer intends to refute.

Definition Introduction

Frequently a writer will begin a discourse by *defining* one or more terms that are central to the discourse.

Framing Introduction

Some introductions are frames into which their discourses are inserted. In Martin Luther King's "Letter From Birmingham Jail," the introduction (paragraph 1) and the complementary close (paragraphs 48-50) form the frame for his letter.

Commonly Recommended Introductions

Other common types of introductions which are frequently recommended in textbooks are the following. Randall E. Dekker, who provides a more extensive list of introductions in his *Patterns of Exposition* than many textbook writers, recommends some of the above types of introductions as well as the following:

- Showing the *significance* of the subject or stressing its importance,

- Giving the *background* on the subject,

- Using a pertinent *rhetorical device*, such as *analogy, allusion, quotation*, or *paradox* that will attract the reader's interest,

- Using a short but vivid *comparison* or *contrast*,

- Posing a *challenging* or *controversial question*,

- Referring to the *writer's experience* on the subject or *qualifications* for dealing with the subject (This differs from the occasional introduction which specifies what event served as the catalyst for the writer to write the essay.),

- Presenting a *startling statistic* or other *facts*,

- Making an *unusual statement*, or

- Making a *commonplace remark*.[6]

Other types of introductions that are frequently recommended in writing textbooks include the following:

- *Relating* the subject to a *topical event* or *current controversy*,

- Making a statement that takes a *new look* at a familiar situation,

- *Attacking* a currently accepted assumption, or

- Recounting an *amusing anecdote*.

Sample Introductions

Example 1

Every species has its niche, its place in the grand scheme of things.

From "Every Species Has Its Niche." Paul Colvinaux

Example 2

Altruism is the performance of an unselfish act. As a pattern of behavior this act must have two properties: it must benefit someone else, and it must do so to the disadvantage of the benefactor. It is not merely a matter of being helpful, it is helpfulness at a cost to yourself.

From "Altruistic Behavior." Desmond Morris

Example 3

I belong to that classification of people known as wives. I am A Wife. And, not altogether incidentally, I am a mother.

From "I Want a Wife," Judy Syfers

Example 4

It is a melancholy object to those who walk through this great town or travel in the country, when they see the streets, the roads, and cabin doors, crowded with beggars of the female sex, followed by three, four, or six children, all in rags and importuning every passenger for alms. These mothers, instead of being able to work for their honest livelihood, are forced to employ all their time in strolling to beg sustenance for their helpless infants: who as they grow up either turn thieves for want of work, or leave their dear native country to fight for the pretender in Spain, or sell themselves in the Barbados.

I think it is agreed by all parties that this prodigious number of children in the arms, or on the backs, or at the heels of their mothers, and frequently of

their fathers, is in the present deplorable state of the kingdom a very great additional grievance; and, therefore, whoever could find out a fair, cheap, and easy
method of making these children sound, useful members of the commonwealth,
would deserve so well of the public as to have his statue set up for a preserver of
the nation.

> From "A Modest Proposal," Jonathan Swift

Example 5

In spite of over two thousand years of contact, Westerners and Arabs still
do not understand each other. Proxemic research reveals some insights into this
difficulty.

> From "Proxemics and the Arab World," Edward T. Hall

Example 6

I am on the advisory committee concerned with Canadian radio and television, and so I have been trying to do some reading in communication theory.
I find it an exciting subject to read about, because so much of the writing is in
the future tense, with so many sentences beginning: "We shall soon be able to
. . . " But I have also become aware of a more negative side to it, as to most
technology. The future that is technically feasible may not be the future that
society can absorb. There is a great gap now between what we are doing and
what we have the means to do, and many writers regard this as a disease peculiar to our time that we shall get over when we feel less threatened by novelty.
But I doubt that the gap can be so soon or so easily closed. When I read sym-
posia by technical experts telling me what the world could be like 100 years from
now, I feel a dissolving of identity, with all the familiar social landmarks disappearing, as though I were in Noah's flood climbing a tree. As I imagine that this
is what most people feel, I suspect that the world 100 years from now will be
much more like the world today than the experts suggest.

> From "Communications," Northrop Frye

Transitions

Transitions can function both *adhesively* or *cohesively* to contribute to
the coherence of a discourse.

Transitions provide coherence by showing the relationship of one
part of an essay to the whole and or to another part which precedes or
follows it. Often words or phrases function primarily as transition
devices and suggest certain types of temporal relationships that stress
narration (for example, *before, after, once, now, yearly, then, soon, last
week, on that day, often, late*), other types of temporal relationships that

stress process (*first, second, next, before, after*), and still others that
stress causal relationships (*because, therefore, if, then, so, as a result,
consequently, so, accordingly*). Transitions may help to maintain the
focus and to stress the main purposes and ideas of a discourse.

Transitions usually indicate one of the following things or ideas is
about to appear.

■ That the *first member of a series* is about to appear,

■ That an *additional number of a series* is about to appear,

■ That the *last member of a series* is about to appear,

■ That *something similar* will follow,

■ That *something different* will follow,

■ That *something both similar and different* will follow (usually
introduced by a word like "nevertheless").

■ That a *new assertion* is about to appear,

■ That a *subordinate assertion* is about to appear,

■ That *evidence supporting an assertion* is about to appear,

■ That *reasons supporting an assertion* are about to appear,

■ That *more specific evidence explaining the evidence* just cited is
about to appear,

■ That a *corollary* or *more specific reasons* that follow from the most
recently cited reason are about to appear,

■ That *other related*—even, sometimes, *more general reasons supporting the reason* just given—is about to appear.

■ That *reasons (interpretations) explaining the just-cited evidence* are
about to appear,

■ That *evidence supporting the just-cited reason* will appear,

■ That some kind of *secondary discourse* is about to appear.
Sometimes this transition may be nothing more than punctuation
marks, (a pair of commas, dashes, or parentheses).

Conclusions

Conclusions signal the ending of any discourse. Within a discourse smaller sections and paragraphs may also have their own conclusions. Such internal conclusions signal that a new section of the discourse is about to begin or that a section of the discourse is ending.

Conclusions can also be categorized as efficient, classical, commonly used, and commonly recommended. Conclusions often utilize many of the same tactics as do introductions. They may be very short or quite long. There are five general categories of conclusions: *efficient conclusions, classical conclusions, commonly used conclusions, commonly recommended conclusions*, and what can be called *organic conclusions*.

Efficient Conclusions

Efficient conclusions are frequently employed by contemporary writers. Among the most straight-forward and efficient conclusions are the following:

- The simplest conclusion is the restatement of the thesis sentence.

- Restating the main ideas or reviewing the organizational plan of the essay.

- Giving a summary of the essay.

Classical Conclusions

Certain traditional types of conclusions were accepted by classical rhetoricians. Corbett specifies the following standard types of *classical conclusions*: *epilogue* (something said in addition to what had gone before); *anakephalaiosis* or *recapitulation*; *peroratio* (literally "a finishing off of one's plea"); *enumeratio* (an enumeration or summing up); and/or *affectus* (producing the appropriate emotion in the reader).

Relying on Aristotle, Corbett cites four things that writers generally strive to do in the conclusion:

1) *to inspire* the audience with a favorable opinion of ourselves and an unfavorable opinion of our opponents;

2) *to amplify* the force of the points we have made in the previous section and to extenuate the force of the points made by the opposition;

3) *to rouse* the appropriate emotions in the audience;

4) *to restate* in a summary way our facts and arguments.[7]

Corbett explains that "Aristotle is suggesting that these are the things that we may do in the conclusion, that we must do all of them in every discourse."[8] Of those four, Aristotle considered the *recapitulation* to be the most common and useful. Corbett explains that in a recapitulation rhetoricians frequently utilize *amplification* "the process by which we highlight, ... [or] make as 'big as possible' the points we have made" and *extenuation*, which "insists that the points made by the opposition are insignificant, weak, or inferior."[9] Corbett also points out that some speakers like to rely heavily on emotional appeals[10] and ethical appeals[11] in their conclusions.

Commonly Used Contemporary Conclusions

Nearly all of the tactics listed among common introductions have also been used as conclusions. But the *funnel conclusion* is an inverted funnel. Just as popular as the funnel introduction is what Sheridan Baker has called the *"inverted funnel" conclusion*. According to Baker, in such a conclusion "the thoughts starts moderately narrow— it is more or less the thesis you have had all the time—and then pours out broader and broader implications and finer emphases."[12]

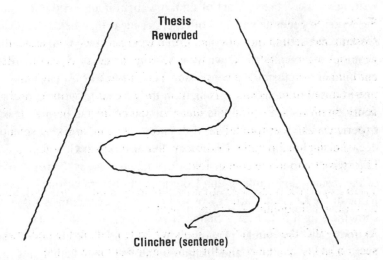

Thesis Reworded

Clincher (sentence)

Commonly Recommended Conclusions

In *Patterns of Exposition*, Randall E. Decker provides a representative sample of the kinds of conclusions frequently recommended in writing textbooks. They include the following:

- Using word signals, such as "finally," and "in conclusion;"

- Changing the tempo, perhaps by changing the sentence length;

- Restating the central idea of the discourse;

- Reaching the climax of the essay;

- Making suggestions, perhaps offering solutions to a problem;

- Explaining the importance of the subject of the discourse;

- Echoing the introduction; and

- Using some rhetorical device. [13]

Organic Conclusions

Organic conclusions are conclusions which evolve out of the discourse or are generated by the discourse).

All of the above conclusions tell the reader that the essay has achieved pretty much what the writer initially set out to do. But, as anyone who has done much writing probably knows, sometimes, while writing an essay, the very act of thinking about it and writing it leads the writer to generate new and often better ideas than he or she possessed when setting out to write. Often emerging out of an essay that develops organically as the writer is writing the essay is a quite different kind of conclusion—a conclusion I often think of as magical, inspired, and miraculous. It is as if, in the process of writing, one suddenly discovers a new and fine idea that one never had before. It is an experience like that which Pascal describes the hard-working scientist occasionally having in the laboratory, like that which George Livingstone Lowe's describes Coleridge having had as the result of all of the reading and thinking that Coleridge did before writing "The Rime of the Ancient Mariner," or like that which cartoonists suggest by showing a light bulb over a character's head, or like what Isaac Asimov calls "the eureka phenomenon." It is as if, as a result of planning, thinking, working, and all those other little mundane things that go into the 99% that can be summarized as "perspiration," one is blessed with the gift or grace of the 1% of inspiration. If this happens when one is writing an essay, one is able to carry one's idea not only beyond but also into higher realms than one had previously thought or even imagined possible. Such writing may have been best described by my colleague Marjorie McCorquodale, who when I asked her how she achieved the particularly well-written prose in one of her essays, replied, "Oh, my dear, I call that my *magical* style!"

Such a thing that is generated by one's writing can be considered a *conclusion* (either of a part or a whole essay) because it inevitably *follows* one's previous deliberations. But such a thing must also be considered another *main division* or even a more elevated and significant thesis than one had previously planned.

Perhaps, if one were to outline an essay, such a thing might appear as just one more additional Roman numeral (for an entire essay) or another number (for the conclusion to a subsidiary part of an essay). But, since it emerges at or toward the end of one's deliberations and since it differs in origin and in kind from other divisions of the paper, it seems appropriate to discuss it in this section on conclusions.

For it is also, to a greater or lesser degree, a conclusion, and for any writer, the most exhilarating kind of conclusion. Unfortunately, unlike the creation of all other kinds of conclusions, a writer can never make it happen. But when it does happen, it provides the writer with great joy and the reader with the pleasure of encountering fresh, original, and often quite creative or significant insights.

[Unfortunately and somewhat ironically, I have no such "magical" conclusion to offer here. Hence I must make do with a conclusion that recapitulates my argument and offers some suggestions for the applications of the theories of analysis of the essay which I have developed here.]

Sample Conclusions

Example 1

In seeking substitutes for the primeval hunt there are many pitfalls, and cultures which make poor choices, or play the game badly, do so at their peril. The nature of the sporting behavior of mankind clearly deserves greater attention than it has received in the past.

From "Sporting Behavior," Desmond Morris

Example 2

Political language—and with variations this is true of all political parties, from Conservatives to Anarchists—is designed to make lies sound truthful and murder respectable, and to give an appearance of solidity to pure wind. One cannot change this all in a moment, but one can at least change one's own habits, and from time to time one can even, if one jeers loudly enough, send some worn-out and useless phrase—some *jackboot, Achilles' heel, hotbed, melting pot, acid test, veritable inferno* or other lump of verbal refuse—into the dustbin where it belongs.

From "Politics and the English Language," George Orwell

Example 3

Fatherhood can be, if not conquered, at least "turned down" in this generation—by the combined efforts of all of us together. [Italics Barthelme's].

From *The Dead Father*, Don Barthelme

Example 4

The rising violence of crowds, routinely blamed on the violence of modern sports and the habit of taking them too seriously, arises . . . out of a failure to take them seriously enough—to abide by the conventions that should bind spectators and players.

From "Spectatorship," Christopher Lasch

Example 5

It has often been pointed out that the electronic media revive many of the primitive and tribal conditions of a pre-literate culture, but there is no fate in such matters, no necessity to go around the circle of history again. Democracy and book culture are interdependent, and the rise of oral and visual media represents, not a new order to adjust to, but a subordinate order to be contained.

From "Communications," Northrop Frye

Chapter Notes

1. *Patterns of Exposition.* Boston: Little, Brown, 1978.

2. Dekker, VI (Boston: Little, Brown, 1978), pp. 350-51.

3. Edward P. J. Corbett, *Classical Rhetoric for the Modern Student* (New York: Oxford, 1965), p. 303.

4. Whatley, *Elements of Rhetoric* (Carbondale, Ill.: 1828), summarized by Corbett, pp. 304-305.

5. Sheridan Baker, *The Practical Stylist*, 5th Ed. (New York: Harper and Row, 1981), p. 24.

6. Dekker, pp. 150-52.

7. Corbett, p. 329.

8. Corbett, p. 329.

9. Corbett, p. 334.

10. Corbett, p. 334.

11. Corbett, p. 337.

12. Baker, p. 30.

13. Dekker, pp. 341-42.

Section V: Compound Discourse

CHAPTER 9

Compound Discourse

B oth a *compound discourse* and a *comparative discourse* bring two or more subjects together. In a compound discourse, the primary discourse has two or more subjects, which are sometimes brought together for evaluation. In a compound essay, both parts of the essay are primary discourse.

Compound ideas (*generalizations*, *assertions*, or *opinions*) are equally important parts of a discourse. For example, one might develop an essay evaluating two comparable mid-sized automobiles. Both automobiles are central and of equal importance to the primary discourse, regardless of how the discourses are organized and ordered. (One might discuss Automobile A completely and then discuss Automobile B. Or one might discuss the engines of A and B, and then discuss their transmissions, and so on.) Both subjects are of importance in the primary discourse in which they occur. A compound discourse might be charted in the following manner (Figure A).

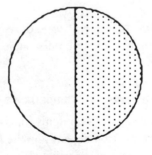

Figure A

If one part of the compound discourse occupied more space in the essay than the other, one might divide the circle proportionately.

COMPARISON

In a *comparative discourse*, the writer's purpose is to learn about the less familiar or make assertions about the less familiar by comparing it with the more familiar. In a *comparison essay*, the primary subject is primary discourse, the explanation of or assertions about which constitute the purpose of the essay. The secondary discourse is developed not for its own sake but for the purpose of explaining or strengthening assertions about the primary subject.

Since the comparison is always secondary or external to a primary discourse, a discourse which incorporated a comparison might be charted in the following manner:

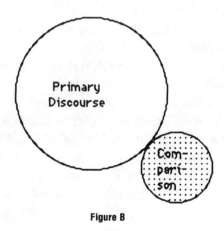

Primary
Discourse

Com-
pari-
son

Figure B

Compound elements (*ideas*, *evidence*, or *reasons*) or *compound components* can occur at any level of a discourse. They can also occur in secondary discourse.

The Functions of Compounds and Comparisons

Whether the bringing together of two items for comparison is a compound discourse or a comparison depends on the focus and purpose of the overall discourse. If the writer's purpose is to examine and study and discuss both items, then it is compound discourse. If the second item is used merely to explain (or to strengthen or enhance) the argument about another item in the primary discourse, then the second item is comparative discourse (secondary discourse).

A comparison does not advance or develop the primary discourse.

Methods of Organizing Compound (or Comparison) Essays

Method I: Subject by subject

Thesis: A and B can be compared on several standards.

    I (Paragraph 1): Subject A
        Standard 1
        Standard 2
        Standard 3
        Standard 4
        Standard 5

   II (Paragraph 2): Subject B
        Standard 1
        Standard 2
        Standard 3
        Standard 4
        Standard 5

Method II: Similarities and Differences

Thesis: A and B can be compared on several points.

    I (Paragraph 1): Similarities
        Subject A
        Subject B

   II (Paragraph 2): Differences
        Subject A
        Subject B

Method III: Standard by Standard

Thesis: A and B can be compared on several points.

    I (Paragraph 1): Standard 1
        Subject A
        Subject B

   II (Paragraph 2): Standard 2
        Subject A
        Subject B

   II (Paragraph 3): Standard 3
        Subject A
        Subject B   *etc.*

Although discourses containing extended comparisons may appear to be very much like compound discourses, they have different purposes.

In the following example, a comparison (secondary discourse which is used to enhance the writer's point about Roosevelt) is indicated by italics.

Roosevelt played the game of politics with virtuosity, and both his successes and his failures were carried off in splendid style; his performance seemed to flow with effortless skill. Churchill is acquainted with darkness as well as light. *Like all inhabitants and even transient visitors of inner worlds, he gives evidence of seasons of agonized brooding and slow recovery. Roosevelt might have spoken of sweat and blood, but when Churchill offered his people tears, he spoke a word* which might have been uttered by Lincoln or Mazzini or Cromwell [This underlined portion is actually a tertiary discourse; it is a comparison used to enhance Berlin's discussion of Churchill, which is itself a secondary discourse being used to enhance Berlin's discussion of Roosevelt.] but not Roosevelt, greathearted, generous, and perceptive as he was.

From "Mr. Churchill," Isaiah Berlin

But in the following paragraph, King has two subjects: first, his disappointment with the white moderate's failure to support the civil rights movement, and, second, his praise of those who have supported it.

I had hoped that the white moderate would see this need. Perhaps I was too optimistic; perhaps I expected too much. I suppose I should have realized that few members of the oppressor race can understand the deep groans and passionate yearnings of the oppressed race, and still fewer have the vision to see that injustice must be rooted out by strong, persistent, and determined action. I am thankful, however, that some of our white brothers in the South have grasped the meaning of this social revolution and committed themselves to it. They are still all too few in quantity, but they are big in quality. Some— such as Ralph McGill, Lillian Smith, Harry Golden, James McBridge Dabbs, Ann Braden, and Sarah Patton Boyle—have written about our struggle in eloquent and prophetic terms. Others have marched with us down nameless streets of the South. They have languished in filthy, roach-infested jails, suffering the abuse and brutality of policemen who view them as "dirty nigger-lovers." Unlike so many of their moderate brothers and sisters, they have recognized the urgency of the moment and sensed the need for powerful "action" antidotes to combat the disease of segregation.

Paragraph 32 from "Letter from Birmingham Jail," Martin Luther King, Jr.

In the following passage, King is concerned with the state of the contemporary church. He discusses the early church only in order to point out the differences.

There was a time when the church was very powerful—in the time when the early Christians rejoiced at being deemed worthy to suffer for what they believed. In those days the church was not merely a thermometer that recorded the ideas and principles of popular opinion; it was a thermostat that transformed the mores of society. Whenever the early Christians entered a town, the people in power became disturbed and immediately sought to convict the Christians for being "disturbers of the peace" and "outside agitators." But the Christians pressed on, in the conviction that they were "a colony of heaven," called to obey God rather than man. Small in number, they were big in commitment. They were too God-intoxicated to be "astronomically intimidated." By their effort and example they brought an end to such ancient evils as infanticide and gladiatorial contests.

Things are different now. So often the contemporary church is a weak, ineffectual voice with an uncertain sound. So often it is an archdefender of the status quo. Far from being disturbed by the presence of the church, the power structure of the average community is consoled by the church's silent—and often even vocal—sanction of things as they are.

But the judgment of God is upon the church as never before. If today's church does not recapture the sacrificial spirit of the early church, it will lose its authenticity, forfeit the loyalty of millions, and be dismissed as an irrelevant social club with no meaning for the twentieth century. Every day I meet young people whose disappointment with the church has turned into outright disgust.

Paragraphs 40-42 from "Letter from Birmingham Jail," Martin Luther King, Jr.

In the following paragraphs, Arendt's subject is concentration camps. She discusses slavery only in order to show how much worse concentration camps were.

Forced labor as a punishment is limited as to time and intensity. The convict retains his rights over his body; he is not absolutely tortured and he is not absolutely dominated. Banishment banishes only from one part of the world to another part of the world, also inhabited by human beings; it does not exclude the human world altogether. Throughout history slavery has been an institution within a social order; slaves were not, like concentration camp inmates, withdrawn from the sight and hence the protection of their fellow-men; as instruments of labor they had a definite price and as property a definite value. The concentration-camp inmate has no price, because he can always be replaced; nobody knows to whom he belongs, because he is never seen. From the point of view of normal society he is absolutely superfluous, although in times of acute labor shortage, as in Russia and in Germany during the war, he is used for work.

From *The Origins of Totalitarianism*, Hannah Arendt

Essays Using Compound and Comparison Discourse

"Two Views of the Mississippi"
Mark Twain

Now when I had mastered the language of this water, and had come to know   1
every trifling feature that bordered the great river as familiarly as I knew the letters of the alphabet, I had made a valuable acquisition. But I had lost something, too. I had lost something which could never be restored to me while I
lived. All the grace, the beauty, the poetry, had gone out of the majestic river!
I still keep in mind a certain wonderful sunset which I witnessed when steam-
boating was new to me. A broad expanse of the river was turned to blood; in
the middle distance the red hue brightened into gold, through which a solitary
log came floating black and conspicuous; in one place a long, slanting mark lay
sparkling upon the water; in another the surface was broken by boiling, tumbling rings, that were as many-tinted as an opal; where the ruddy flush was
faintest, was a smooth spot that was covered with graceful circles and radiating
lines, ever so delicately traced; the shore on our left was densely wooded, and
the somber shadow that fell from this forest was broken in one place by a long,
ruffled trail that shone like silver; and high above the forest wall a clean-
stemmed dead tree waved a single leafy bough that glowed like a flame in the
unobstructed splendor that was flowing from the sun. There were graceful
curves, reflected images, woody heights, soft distances; and over the whole
scene, far and near, the dissolving lights drifted steadily, enriching it every
passing moment with new marvels of coloring.

I stood like one bewitched. I drank it in, in a speechless rapture. The   2
world was new to me, and I had never seen anything like this at home. But as I
have said, a day came when I began to cease from noting the glories and the
charms which the moon and the sun and the twilight wrought upon the river's
face; another day came when I ceased altogether to note them. Then, if that
sunset scene had been repeated, I should have looked upon it without rapture,
and should have commented upon it, inwardly, after this fashion: "This sun
means that we are going to have wind tomorrow; that floating log means that
the river is rising, small thanks to it; that slanting mark on the water refers to a
bluff reef which is going to kill somebody's steamboat one of these nights, if it
keeps on stretching out like that; those tumbling 'boils' show a dissolving bar
and a changing channel there; the lines and circles in the slick water over yon-
der are a warning that that troublesome place is shoaling up dangerously; that
silver streak in the shadow of the forest is the 'break' from a new snag, and he
has located himself in the very best place he could have found to fish for
steamboats; that tall dead tree, with a single living branch, is not going to last

long, and then how is a body ever going to get through this blind place at night without the friendly old landmark?"

No, the romance and beauty were all gone from the river. All the value   3 any feature of it had for me now was the amount of usefulness it could furnish toward compassing the safe piloting of a steamboat. Since those days, I have pitied doctors from my heart. What does the lovely flush in a beauty's cheek mean to a doctor but a "break" that ripples above some deadly disease? Are not all her visible charms sown thick with what are to him the signs and symbols of hidden decay? Does he ever see her beauty at all, or doesn't he simply view her professionally, and comment upon her unwholesome condition all to himself? And doesn't he sometimes wonder whether he has gained most or lost most by learning his trade?

1883

"Grant and Lee: A Study in Contrasts"
Bruce Catton

When Ulysses S. Grant and Robert E. Lee met in the parlor of a modest house   1 at Appomattox Court House, Virginia, on April 9, 1865, to work out the terms for the surrender of Lee's Army of Northern Virginia, a great chapter in American life came to a close, and a great new chapter began.

These men were bringing the Civil War to its virtual finish. To be sure,   2 other armies had yet to surrender, and for a few days the fugitive Confederate government would struggle desperately and vainly, trying to find some way to go on living now that its chief support was gone. But in effect it was all over when Grant and Lee signed the papers. And the little room where they wrote out the terms was the scene of one of the poignant, dramatic contrasts in American history.

They were two strong men, these oddly different generals, and they repre-   3 sented the strengths of two conflicting currents that, through them, had come into final collision.

Back of Robert E. Lee was the notion that the old aristocratic concept   4 might somehow survive and be dominant in American life.

Lee was tidewater Virginia, and in his background were family, culture,   5 and tradition. . . the age of chivalry transplanted to a New World which was making its own legends and its own myths. He embodied a way of life that had come down through the age of knighthood and the English country squire. America was a land that was beginning all over again, dedicated to nothing much more complicated than the rather hazy belief that all men had equal rights, and should have an equal chance in the world. In such a land Lee stood for the feeling that it was somehow of advantage to human society to have a pronounced inequality in the social structure. There should be a leisure class, backed by ownership of land; in turn, society itself should be keyed to the land as the chief source of wealth and influence. It would bring forth (according to this ideal) a class of men with a strong sense of obligation to the community; men who lived not to gain advantage for themselves, but to meet the solemn obligations which had been laid on them by the very fact that they were privileged. From them the country would get its leadership; to them it could look for the higher values—of thought, of conduct, of personal deportment—to give it strength and virtue.

Lee embodied the noblest elements of this aristocratic ideal. Through him, the landed nobility justified itself. For four years, the Southern states had fought a desperate war to uphold the ideals for which Lee stood. In the end, it almost seemed as if the Confederacy fought for Lee; as if he himself was the Confederacy. . . the best thing that the way of life for which the Confederacy stood could ever have to offer. He had passed into legend before Appomattox. Thousands of tired, underfed, poorly clothed Confederate soldiers, long-since past the simple enthusiasm of the early days of the struggle, somehow considered Lee the symbol of everything for which they had been willing to die. But they could not quite put this feeling into words. If the Lost Cause, sanctified by so much heroism and so many deaths, had a living justification, its justification was General Lee.   6

Grant, the son of a tanner on the Western frontier, was everything Lee was not. He had come up the hard way, and embodied nothing in particular except the eternal toughness and sinewy fiber of the men who grew up beyond the mountains. He was one of a body of men who owed reverence and obeisance to no one, who were self-reliant to a fault, who cared hardly anything for the past but who had a sharp eye for the future.   7

These frontier men were the precise opposites of the tidewater aristocrats. Back of them, in the great surge that had taken people over the Alleghenies and into the opening Western country, there was a deep. implicit dissatisfaction with a past that had settled into grooves. They stood for democracy, not from any reasoned conclusion about the proper ordering of human society, but simply because they had grown up in the middle of democracy and knew how it worked. Their society might have privileges, but they would be privileges each man had won for himself. Forms and patterns meant nothing. No man was born to anything, except perhaps to a chance to show how far he could rise. Life was competition.   8

Yet along with this feeling had come a deep sense of belonging to a national community. The Westerner who developed a farm, opened a shop or set up in business as a trader, could hope to prosper only as his own community prospered—and his community ran from the Atlantic to the Pacific and from Canada down to Mexico. If the land was settled, with towns and high-   9 ways and accessible markets, he could better himself. He saw his fate in terms of the nation's own destiny. As its horizons expanded, so did his. He had, in other words, an acute dollars-and-cents stake in the continued growth and development of his country.

And that, perhaps, is where the contrast between Grant and Lee becomes most striking. The Virginia aristocrat, inevitably, saw himself in relation to his own region. He lived in a static society which could endure almost anything except change. Instinctively, his first loyalty would go to the locality in which that society existed. He would fight to the limit of endurance to defend it, because in defending it he was defending everything that gave his own life its deepest meaning. 10

The Westerner, on the other hand, would fight with an equal tenacity for the broader concept of society. He fought so because everything he lived by was tied to growth, expansion, and a constantly widening horizon. What he lived by would survive or fall with the nation itself. He could not possibly stand by unmoved in the face of an attempt to destroy the Union. He would combat it with everything he had, because he could only see it as an effort to cut the ground out from under his feet. 11

So Grant and Lee were in complete contrast, representing two diametrically opposed elements in American life. Grant was the modern man emerging; beyond him, ready to come on the stage, was the great age of steel and machinery, of crowded cities and a restless, burgeoning vitality. Lee might have ridden down from the old age of chivalry, lance in hand, silken banner fluttering over his head. Each man was the perfect champion of his cause, drawing both his strengths and his weaknesses from the people he led. 12

Yet it was not all contrast, after all. Different as they were—in background, in personality, in underlying aspiration—these two great soldiers had much in common. Under everything else, they were marvelous fighters. Furthermore, their fighting qualities were really very much alike. 13

Each man had, to begin with, the great virtue of utter tenacity and fidelity. Grant fought his way down the Mississippi Valley in spite of acute personal discouragement and profound military handicaps. Lee hung on in the trenches at Petersburg after hope itself had died. In each man there was an indomitable quality. . . the born fighter's refusal to give up as long as he can still remain on his feet and lift his two fists. 14

Daring and resourcefulness they had; too; the ability to think faster and move faster than the enemy. These were the qualities which gave Lee the dazzling campaigns of Second Manassas and Chancellorsville and won Vicksburg for Grant. 15

Lastly, and perhaps greatest of all, there was the ability, at the end, to turn quickly from war to peace once the fighting was over. Out of the way these two men behaved at Appomattox came the possibility of a peace of reconciliation. 16

It was a possibility not wholly realized, in the years to come, but which did, in the end, help the two sections to become one nation again . . . after a war whose bitterness might have seemed to make such a reunion wholly impossible. No part of either man's life became him more than the part he played in their brief meeting in the McLean house at Appomattox. Their behavior there put all succeeding generations of Americans in their debt. Two great Americans, Grant and Lee—very different, yet under everything very much alike. Their encounter at Appomattox was one of the great moments of American history.

1958

Section VI:
The Integrated
Essay

CHAPTER 10

Writing in the Real World: The Integrated Essay

When a person needs to write in the world outside of the English classroom—in other classes, in the workplace, and in one's personal and financial affairs, one can almost never utilize only one of the writing tactics that have been focused upon here. One is usually called upon to respond to certain questions (from employers and co-workers or from teachers on exams), seek information, provide certain information, or solve—or attempt to solve—certain problems. All too often, one must write on the basis of the very limited information one has. Nevertheless, one must respond to the writing situation in which one finds oneself.

To write effectively in situations such as these—in school, in business, professional, and technical situations, in one's personal business transactions, and in one's personal life—a writer will want to have at his or her command all of the kinds of developmental material, organizational tactics, coherence devices, and secondary discourse that have been presented in this book.

One must nearly always use a variety of these tactics. No matter what one's writing situation is, one always must present ideas and nearly always must present evidence and perhaps reasons as well. One must always decide on a method of organization and an order in which to present one's ideas. Then, depending on the requirements of the particular writing situation, one may need to utilize various secondary discourse to make what one is writing more interesting and more persuasive.

A writer needs to utilize whatever will be the most effective in a particular situation and often the most effective essay is eclectic. One may have to write an essay which has some paragraphs based on classification, others utilizing description, perhaps another paragraph of

definition, and still another developed by a list of examples. One may
have to utilize one kind of organizational method in one paragraph and
another method in another paragraph. One may find that certain parts
of what one is writing needs secondary discourse (such as definition or
comparison or analogy). And one usually needs to utilize some coherence devices.

A writer nearly always wishes he or she 1) had more information,
2) wrote more easily, faster, or more grammatically, 3) had more time,
4) had someone to help with the writing (or, better yet, to do the writing), 5) had a larger vocabulary, 6) spelled perfectly, 7) wrote with
greater stylistic power and maturity, or even 8) were wittier. Nearly
everyone who ever has to write, including professional writers or teachers of writing, entertains such longings. We also wish we were thin,
handsome, athletic, rich, and famous. But we all have to make do with
the bodies, bank accounts, and degree of fame we already have. And,
when we are called on to write, we have to rely on the knowledge, the
vocabulary, and the writing skills we already have. We have to make
do with what we have.

This book has tried to help you understand the basic elements and
components, organizational and ordering methods, coherence devices,
and secondary discourse of which all writing is constructed. The
assumption has been—as was said in the introduction—that, just as one
will play the piano better and more easily if one knows how to read
music, understand basic scale, chord, and rhythm principles, and certain
fingering tactics, one will write better and more easily if he or she
understands these basic principles of writing.

Public Statement by Eight Alabama Clergymen

(The statement to which King's following "Letter" responds)

April 12, 1963

We the undersigned clergymen are among those who, in January, issued "An   1
Appeal for Law and Order and Common Sense," in dealing with racial problems
in Alabama. We expressed understanding that honest convictions in racial matters could properly be pursued in the courts, but urged that decisions of those
courts should in the meantime be peacefully obeyed.

Since that time there have been some evidence of increased forbearance   2
and a willingness to face facts. Responsible citizens have undertaken to work
on various problems which cause racial friction and unrest. In Birmingham,

recent public events have given indication that we all have opportunity for a new constructive and realistic approach to racial problems.

However, we are now confronted by a series of demonstrations by some of   3
our Negro citizens, directed and led by outsiders. We recognize the natural impatience of people who feel that their hopes are slow in being realized. But we are convinced that these demonstrations are unwise and untimely.

We agree rather with certain local Negro leadership which has called for   4
honest and open negotiation of racial issues in our area. And we believe this kind of facing of issues can best be accomplished by citizens of our own metro-politan area, white and Negro, meeting with their knowledge and experience of the local situation. All of us need to face that responsibility and find proper channels for its accomplishment.

Just as we formerly pointed out that "hatred and violence have no sanction   5
in our religious and political traditions," we also point out that such actions as incite to hatred and violence, however technically peaceful those actions may be, have not contributed to the resolution of our local problems. We do not believe that these days of new hope are days when extreme measures are justified in Birmingham.

We commend the community as a whole, and the local news media and   6
law enforcement officials in particular, on the calm manner in which these demonstrations have been handled. We urge the public to continue to show restraint should the demonstrations continue, and law enforcements to remain calm and continue to protect out city from violence.

We further strongly urge our own Negro community to withdraw support   7
from these demonstrations, and to unite locally in working peacefully for a better Birmingham. When rights are consistently denied, a cause should be pressed in the courts and negotiations among local leaders, and not in the streets. We appeal to both our white and Negro citizenry to observe the principles of law and order and common sense.

Signed by:

C. C. J. CARPENTER, D.D., LL.D., Bishop of Alabama

JOSEPH A. DURICK, D.D., Auxiliary Bishop, Diocese of Mobile-Birmingham

Rabbi MILTON L. GRAFMAN, Temple Emanu-El, Birmingham, Alabama

Bishop PAUL HARDIN, Bishop of the Alabama-West Florida Conference of the Methodist Church

Bishop NOLAN B. HARMON, Bishop of the N. Alabama Conference of the Methodist Church

Bishop GEORGE M. MURRAY, D.D., LL.D., Bishop Coadjutor, Episcopal Diocese of Alabama

EDWARD V. RAMAGE, Moderator, Synod of the Alabama Presbyterian Church in the United States

EARL STALLINGS, Pastor, First Baptist Church, Birmingham, Alabama

"Letter from Birmingham Jail"
Martin Luther King, Jr.

MY DEAR FELLOW CLERGYMEN:

While confined here in the Birmingham city jail, I came across your recent   1
statement calling my present activities "unwise and untimely." Seldom do I
pause to answer criticism of my work and ideas. If I sought to answer all the
criticisms that cross my desk, my secretaries would have little time for anything other than such correspondence in the course of the day, and I would
have no time for constructive work. But since I feel that you are men of genuine good will and that your criticisms are sincerely set forth, I want to try to
answer your statement in what I hope will be patient and reasonable terms.

I think I should indicate why I am here in Birmingham, since you have   2
been influenced by the view which argues against "outsiders coming in." I
have the honor of serving as president of the Southern Christian Leadership
Conference, an organization operating in every southern state, with headquar-
ters in Atlanta, Georgia. We have some eighty-five affiliated organizations
across the South, and one of them is the Alabama Christian Movement for
Human Rights. Frequently we share staff, educational, and financial resources
with our affiliates. Several months ago the affiliate here in Birmingham asked
us to be on call to engage in a nonviolent direct-action program if such were
deemed necessary. We readily consented, and when the hour came we lived up
to our promise. So I, along with several members of my staff, am here
because I was invited here. I am here because I have organizational ties here.

But more basically, I am in Birmingham because injustice is here. Just as   3
the prophets of the eighth century B.C. left their villages and carried their "thus
saith the Lord" far beyond the boundaries of their home towns, and just as the
Apostle Paul left his village of Tarsus and carried the gospel of Jesus Christ to
the far corners of the Greco-Roman world, so am I compelled to carry the
gospel of freedom beyond my own home town. Like Paul, I must constantly
respond to the Macedonian call for aid.

Moreover, I am cognizant of the interrelatedness of all communities and   4
states. I cannot sit idly by in Atlanta and not be concerned about what happens
in Birmingham. Injustice anywhere is a threat to justice everywhere. We are
caught in an inescapable network of mutuality, tied in a single garment of destiny. Whatever affects one directly, affects all indirectly. Never a gain can we
afford to live with the narrow, provincial "outside agitator" idea. Anyone who
lives inside the United States can never be considered an outsider anywhere
within its bounds.

You deplore the demonstrations taking place in Birmingham. But your   5
statement, I am sorry to say, fails to express a similar concern for the condi-

tions that brought about the demonstrations. I am sure that none of you would want to rest content with the superficial kind of social analysis that deals merely with effects and does not grapple with underlying causes. It is unfortunate that demonstrations are taking place in Birmingham, but it is even more unfortunate that the city's white power structure left the Negro community with no alternative.

In any nonviolent campaign there are four basic steps: collection of the 6 facts to determine whether injustice exist; negotiation; self-purification. and direct action. We have gone through all these steps in Birmingham. There can be no gainsaying the fact that racial injustice engulfs this community. Birmingham is probably the most thoroughly segregated city in the United States. Its ugly record of brutality is widely known. Negroes have experienced grossly unjust treatment in the courts. There have been more unsolved bombings of Negro homes and churches in Birmingham than in any other city in the nation. These are the hard, brutal facts of the case. On the basis of these conditions, Negro leaders sought to negotiate with the city fathers. But the latter consistently refused to engage in good faith negotiation.

Then, last September, came the opportunity to talk with leaders of 7 Birmingham's economic community. In the course of the negotiation, certain promises were made by the merchants—for example, to remove the stores' humiliating racial signs. On the basis of these promises, the Reverend Fred Shuttlesworth and the leaders of the Alabama Christian Movement for Human Rights agreed to a moratorium on all demonstrations. As the weeks and months went by, we realized that we were the victims of a broken promise. A few signs, briefly removed, returned; the others remained.

As in so many past experiences, our hopes had been blasted, and the 8 shadow of deep disappointment settled upon us. We had no alternative except to prepare for direct action, whereby we would present our very bodies as a means of laying our case before the conscience of the local and the national community. Mindful of the difficulties involved, we decided to undertake a process of self-purification. We began a series of workshops on nonviolence, and we repeatedly asked ourselves: "Are you able to accept blows without retaliating?" "Are you able to endure the ordeal of jail?" We decided to schedule our direct-action program for the Easter season, realizing that except for Christmas, this is the main shopping period of the year. Knowing that a strong economic-withdrawal program would be the by-product of direct action, we felt that this would be the best time to bring pressure to bear on the merchants for the needed change.

Then it occurred to us that Birmingham's mayoral election was coming up 9 in March, and we speedily decided to postpone action until after election day. When we discovered that the Commissioner of Public Safety, Eugene "Bull" Connor, had piled up enough votes to be in the run-off, we decided again to postpone action until the day after the runoff so that the demonstrations could not be used to cloud the issues. Like many others, we wanted to see Mr. Connor defeated, and to this end we endured postponement after postponement. Having aided in this community need, we felt that our direct-action program could be delayed no longer.

You may well ask, "Why direct action? Why sit-ins, marches, and so forth? Isn't negotiation a better path?" You are quite right in calling for negotiation. Indeed, this is the very purpose of direct action. Nonviolent direct action seeks to create such a crisis and foster such a tension that a community which has constantly refused to negotiate is forced to confront the issue. It seeks so to dramatize the issue that it can no longer be ignored. My citing the creation of tension as part of the work of the nonviolent-resister may sound rather shocking. But I must confess that I am not afraid of the word "tension." I have earnestly opposed violent tension, but there is a type of constructive, nonviolent tension which is necessary for growth. Just as Socrates felt that it was necessary to create a tension in the mind so that individuals could rise from the bondage of myths and half-truths to the unfettered realm of creative analysis and objective appraisal, so must we see the need for nonviolent gadflies to create the kind of tension in society that will help men rise from the dark depths of prejudice and racism to the majestic heights of understanding and brotherhood. 10

The purpose of our direct-action program is to create a situation so crisis-packed that it will inevitably open the door to negotiation. I therefore concur with you in your call for negotiation. Too long has our beloved Southland been bogged down in a tragic effort to live in monologue rather than dialogue. 11

One of the basic points in your statement is that the action that I and my associates have taken in Birmingham is untimely. Some have asked: "Why didn't you give the new city administration time to act?" The only answer that I can give to this query is that the new Birmingham administration must be prodded about as much as the outgoing one, before it will act. We are sadly mistaken if we feel that the election of Albert Boutwell as mayor will bring the millennium to Birmingham. While Mr. Boutwell is a much more gentle person than Mr. Connor, they are both segregationists, dedicated to maintenance of the status quo. I have hoped that Mr. Boutwell will be reasonable enough to see the futility of massive resistance to desegregation. But he will not see this without pressure from devotees of civil rights. My friends, I must say to you that we have not made a single gain in civil rights without determined legal and nonviolent pressure. Lamentably, it is an historical fact that privileged groups seldom give up their privileges voluntarily. Individuals may see the moral light and voluntarily give up their unjust posture; but, as Reinhold Niebuhr has reminded us, groups tend to be more immoral than individuals. 12

We know through painful experience that freedom is never voluntarily given by the oppressor; it must be demanded by the oppressed. Frankly, I have 13 yet to engage in a direct-action campaign that was "well timed" in the view of those who have not suffered unduly from the disease of segregation. For years now I have heard the word "Wait!" It rings in the ear of every Negro with piercing familiarity. This "Wait" has almost always meant "Never." We must come to see, with one of our distinguished jurists, that "justice too long delayed is justice denied."

We have waited for more than 340 years for our constitutional and God-given rights. The nations of Asia and Africa are moving with jetlike speed toward gaining political independence, but we still creep at horse-and-buggy pace toward gaining a cup of coffee at a lunch counter. Perhaps it is easy for those who have never felt the stinging darts of segregation to say, "Wait." But when you have seen vicious mobs lynch your mothers and fathers at will and drown your sisters and brothers at whim; when you have seen hate-filled policemen curse, kick, and even kill your black brothers and sisters; when you see the vast majority of your twenty million Negro brothers smothering in an airtight cage of poverty in the midst of an affluent society; when you suddenly find your tongue twisted and your speech stammering as you seek to explain to your six-year-old daughter why she can't go to the public amusement park that has just been advertised on television, and see tears welling up in her eyes when she is told that Funtown is closed to colored children, and see ominous clouds of inferiority beginning to form in her little mental sky, and see her beginning to distort her personality by developing an unconscious bitterness toward white people; when you have to concoct an answer for a five-year-old son who is asking, "Daddy, why do white people treat colored people so mean?"; when you take a crosscountry drive and find it necessary to sleep night after night in the uncomfortable corners of your automobile because no motel will accept you; when you are humiliated day in and day out by nagging signs reading "white" and "colored"; when your first name becomes "nigger," your middle name becomes "boy" (however old you are) and your last name becomes "John," and your wife and mother are never given the respected title "Mrs."; when you are harried by day and haunted by night by the fact that you are a Negro, living constantly at tiptoe stance, never quite knowing what to expect next, and are plagued with inner fears and outer resentments; when you are forever fighting a degenerating sense of "nobodiness"—then you will understand why we find it difficult to wait. There comes a time when the cup of endurance runs over, and men are no longer willing to be plunged into the abyss of despair. I hope, sirs, you can understand our legitimate and unavoidable impatience.

You express a great deal of anxiety over our willingness to break laws. This is certainly a legitimate concern. Since we so diligently urge people to obey the Supreme Court's decision of 1954 outlawing segregation in the public schools, at first glance it may seem rather paradoxical for us consciously to

14

15

break laws. One may well ask: "How can you advocate breaking some laws and obeying others?" The answer lies in the fact that there are two types of laws: just and unjust. I would be the first to advocate obeying just laws. One has not only a legal but a moral responsibility to obey just laws. Conversely, one has a moral responsibility to disobey unjust laws. I would agree with St. Augustine that "an unjust law is no law at all."

Now, what is the difference between the two? How does one determine   16
whether a law is just or unjust? A just law is a man-made code that squares with the moral law or the law of God. An unjust law is a code this is out of har-mony with the moral law. To put it in the terms of St. Thomas Aquinas: An unjust law is a human law that is not rooted in eternal law and natural law. Any law that uplifts human personality is just. Any law that degrades human per-sonality is unjust. All segregation statutes are unjust because segregation dis-torts the soul and damages the personality. It gives the segregator a false sense of superiority and the segregated a false sense of inferiority. Segregation, to use the terminology of the Jewish philosopher Martin Buber, substitutes an "I-it" relationship for an "I-thou" relationship and ends up relegating persons to the status of things. Hence segregation is not only politically, economically, and sociologically unsound. it is morally wrong and sinful. Paul Tillich has said that sin is separation. Is not segregation an existential expression of man's tragic separation, his awful estrangement, his terrible sinfulness? Thus it is that I can urge men to obey the 1954 decision of the Supreme Court, for it is morally right; and I can urge them to disobey segregation ordinances, for they are morally wrong.

Let us consider a more concrete example of just and unjust laws. An   17
unjust law is a code that a numerical or power majority group compels a minor-ity group to obey but does not make binding on itself. This is difference made legal. By the same token, a just law is a code that a majority compels a minori-ty to follow and that it is willing to follow itself. This is sameness made legal.

Let me give another explanation. A law is unjust if it is inflicted on a   18
minority that, as a result of being denied the right to vote, had no part in enact-ing or devising the law. Who can say that the legislature of Alabama which set up that state's segregation laws was democratically elected? Throughout Alabama all sorts of devious methods are used to prevent Negroes from becom-ing registered voters, and there are some counties in which, even though Negroes constitute a majority of the population, not a single Negro is registered. Can any law enacted under such circumstances be considered democratically structured?

Sometimes a law is just on its face and unjust in its application. For   19
instance, I have been arrested on a charge of parading without a permit. Now, there is nothing wrong in having an ordinance which requires a permit for a parade. But such an ordinance becomes unjust when it is used to maintain

segregation and to deny citizens the First-Amendment privilege of peaceful assembly and protest.

I hope you are able to see the distinction I am trying to point out. In no sense do I advocate evading or defying the law, as would the rabid segregationist. That would lead to anarchy. One who breaks an unjust law must do so openly, lovingly, and with a willingness to accept the penalty. I submit that an individual who breaks a law that conscience tells him is unjust, and who willingly accepts the penalty of imprisonment in order to arouse the conscience of the community over its injustice, is in reality expressing the highest respect for law. 20

Of course, there is nothing new about this kind of civil disobedience. It was evidenced sublimely in the refusal of Shadrach, Meshach, and Abednego to obey the laws of Nebuchadnezzar, on the ground that a higher moral law was at stake. It was practiced superbly by the early Christians, who were willing to face hungry lions and the excruciating pain of chopping blocks rather than submit to certain unjust laws of the Roman Empire. To a degree, academic freedom is a reality today because Socrates practiced civil disobedience. In our own nation, the Boston Tea Party represented a massive act of civil disobedience. 21

We should never forget that everything Adolf Hitler did in Germany was "legal" and everything the Hungarian freedom fighters did in Hungary was "illegal." It was "illegal" to aid and comfort a jew in Hitler's Germany. Even so, I am sure that, had I lived in Germany at the time, I would have aided and comforted my Jewish brothers. If today I lived in a Communist country where certain principles dear to the Christian faith are suppressed, I would openly advocate disobeying that country's anti-religious laws. 22

I must make two honest confessions to you, my Christian and Jewish brothers. First, I must confess that over the past few years I have been gravely disappointed with the white moderate. I have almost reached the regrettable conclusion that the Negro's great stumbling block in his stride toward freedom is not the White Citizen's Councilor or the Ku Klux Klanner, but the white moderate, who is more devoted to "order" than to justice; who prefers a negative peace which is the absence of tension to a positive peace which is the presence of justice; who constantly says, "I agree with you in the goal you seek, but I cannot agree with your methods of direct action"; who paternalistically believes he can set the timetable for another man's freedom; who lives by a mythical concept of time and who constantly advises the Negro to wait for a "more convenient season." Shallow understanding from people of good will is more frustrating than absolute misunderstanding from people of ill will. Lukewarm acceptance is much more bewildering than outright rejection. 23

I had hoped that the white moderate would understand that law and order exist for the purpose of establishing justice and that when they fail in this purpose they become the dangerously structured dams that block the flow of social progress. I had hoped that the white moderate would understand that the 24 present tension in the South is a necessary phase of the transition from an obnoxious negative peace, in which the Negro passively accepted his unjust plight, to a substantive and positive peace, in which all men will respect the dignity and worth of human personality. Actually, we who engage in nonviolent direct action are not the creators of tension. We merely bring to the surface the hidden tension that is already alive. We bring it out in the open, where it can be seen and dealt with. Like a boil that can never be cured so long as it is covered up but must be opened with all its ugliness to the natural medicines of air and light, injustice must be exposed, with all the tension its exposure creates, to the light of human conscience and the air of national opinion, before it can be cured.

    In your statement you assert that our actions, even though peaceful, must   25 be condemned because they precipitate violence. But is this is logical assertion? Isn't this like condemning a robbed man because his possession of money precipitated the evil act of robbery? Isn't this like condemning Socrates because his unswerving commitment to truth and his philosophical inquiries precipitated the act by the misguided populace in which they made him drink hemlock? Isn't this like condemning Jesus because his unique God-consciousness and never-ceasing devotion to God's will precipitated the evil act of crucifixion? We must come to see that, as the federal courts have consistently affirmed, it is wrong to urge an individual to cease his efforts to gain his basic constitutional rights because the quest may precipitate violence. Society must protect the robbed and punish the robber.

    I had also hoped that the white moderate would reject the myth concerning   26 time in relation to the struggle for freedom. I have just received a letter from a white brother in Texas. He writes: "All Christians know that the colored people will receive equal rights eventually, but it is possible that you are in too great a religious hurry. It has taken Christianity almost two thousand years to accomplish what it has. The teachings of Christ take time to come to earth." Such an attitude stems from a tragic misconception of time, from the strangely irrational notion that there is something in the very flow of time that will inevitably cure all ills. Actually, time itself is neutral; it can be used either destructively or constructively. More and more I feel that the people of ill will have used time much more effectively than have the people of good will. We will have to repent in this generation not merely for the hateful words and actions of the bad people, but for the appalling silence of the good people. Human progress never rolls in on wheels of inevitability; it comes through the tireless efforts of men willing to be co-workers with God, and without this hard work, time itself becomes an ally of the forces of social stagnation. We must use time creatively, in the knowledge that the time is always ripe to do right. Now is the time to make real the promise of democracy and transform our pending national elegy into a creative psalm of brotherhood. Now is the time to lift our national policy from the quicksand of racial injustice to the solid rock of human dignity.

You speak of our activity in Birmingham as extreme. At first I was rather   27
disappointed that fellow clergymen would see my nonviolent efforts as those of
an extremist. I began thinking about the fact that I stand in the middle of two
opposing forces in the Negro community. One is a force of complacency, made
up in part of Negroes who, as a result of long years of oppression, are so
drained of self-respect and a sense of "somebodiness" that they have adjusted
to segregation; and in part of a few middle-class Negroes who, because of a
degree of academic and economic security and because in some ways they
profit by segregation, have become insensitive to the problems of the masses.
The other force is one of bitterness and hatred, and it comes perilously close to
advocating violence. It is expressed in the various black nationalist groups that
are springing up across the nation, the largest and best-known being Elijah
Muhammad's Muslim movement. Nourished by the Negro's frustration over the
continued existence of racial discrimination, this movement is made up of people who have lost faith in America, who have absolutely repudiated Christianity,
and who have concluded that the white man is an incorrigible "devil."

I have tried to stand between these two forces, saying that we need emu-   28
late neither the "do-nothingism" of the complacent nor the hatred and despair
of the black nationalist. For there is the more excellent way of love and nonviolent protest. I am grateful to God that, through the influence of the Negro
church, the way of nonviolence became an integral part of our struggle.

If this philosophy had not emerged, by now many streets of the South   29
would, I am convinced, be flowing with blood. And I am further convinced that
if our white brothers dismiss as "rabblerousers" and "outside agitators" those
of use who employ nonviolent direct action, and if they refuse to support our
nonviolent efforts, millions of Negroes will, out of frustration and despair, seek
solace and security in black-nationalist ideologies—a development that would
inevitably lead to a frightening racial nightmare.

Oppressed people cannot remain oppressed forever. The yearning for   30
freedom eventually manifests itself, and that is what has happened to the
American Negro. Something within has reminded him of his birthright of freedom, and something without has reminded him that it can be gained.
Consciously or unconsciously, he has been caught up by the *Zeitgeist*, and with
his black brothers of Africa and his brown and yellow brothers of Asia, South
America, and the Caribbean, the United States Negro is moving with a sense of
great urgency toward the promised land of racial justice. If one recognizes this
vital urge that has engulfed the Negro community, one should readily understand why public demonstrations are taking place. The Negro has many pent
up resentments and latent frustrations, and he must release them. So let him
march; let him make prayer pilgrimages to the city hall; let him go on freedom
rides and try to understand why he must do so. If his repressed emotions are
not released in nonviolent ways, they will seek expression through violence;

this is not a threat but a fact of history. So I have not said to my people, "Get rid of your discontent." Rather, I have tried to say that this normal and healthy discontent can be channeled into the creative outlet of nonviolent direct action. And now this approach is being termed extremist.

But though I was initially disappointed at being categorized as an   31 extremist, as I continued to think about the matter I gradually gained a measure of satisfaction from the label. Was not Jesus an extremist for love: "Love your enemies, bless them that curse you, do good to them that hate you, and pray for them which spitefully use you, and persecute you." Was not Amos an extremist for justice: "Let justice roll down like waters and righteousness like an ever-flowing stream." Was not Paul an extremist for the Christian gospel: "I bear in my body the marks of the Lord Jesus." Was not Martin Luther an extremist: "Here I stand; I cannot do otherwise, so help me God." And John Bunyan: "I will stay in jail to the end of my days before I make a butchery of my conscience." And Abraham Lincoln: "This nation cannot survive half slave and half free." And Thomas Jefferson: "We hold these truths to be self-evident, that all men are created equal. So the question is not whether we will be extremists, but what kind of extremists we will be. Will we be extremists for hate or for love? Will we be extremists for the preservation of injustice or for the extension of justice? In that dramatic scene on Calvary's hill three men were crucified. We must never forget that all three were crucified for the same crime—the crime of extremism. Two were extremists for immorality, and thus fell below their environment. The other, Jesus Christ, was an extremist for love, truth, and goodness, and thereby rose above his environment. Perhaps the South, the nation, and the world are in dire need of creative extremists.

I had hoped that the white moderate would see this need. Perhaps I was   32 too optimistic; perhaps I expected too much. I suppose I should have realized that few members of the oppressor race can understand the deep groans and passionate yearnings of the oppressed race, and still fewer have the vision to see that injustice must be rooted out by strong, persistent, and determined action. I am thankful, however, that some of our white brothers in the South have grasped the meaning of this social revolution and committed themselves to it. They are still all too few in quantity, but they are big in quality. Some—such as Ralph McGill, Lillian Smith, Harry Golden, James McBridge Dabbs, Ann Braden, and Sarah Patton Boyle—have written about our struggle in eloquent and prophetic terms. Others have marched with us down nameless streets of the South. They have languished in filthy, roach-infested jails, suffering the abuse and brutality of policemen who view them as "dirty nigger-lovers." Unlike so many of their moderate brothers and sisters, they have recognized the urgency of the moment and sensed the need for powerful action antidotes to combat the disease of segregation.

Let me take note of my other major disappointment. I have been so great-   33
ly disappointed with the white church and its leadership. Of course, there are
some notable exceptions. I am not unmindful of the fact that each of you has
taken some significant stands on this issue. I commend you, Reverend
Stallings, for your Christian stand on this past Sunday, in welcoming Negroes to
your worship service on a nonsegregated basis. I commend the Catholic leaders of this state for integrating Spring Hill College several years ago.

But despite these notable exceptions, I must honestly reiterate that I have   34
been disappointed with the church. I do not say this as one of those negative
critics who can always find something wrong with the church. I say this as a
minister of the gospel, who loves the church; who was nurtured in its bosom;
who has been sustained by its spiritual blessings and who will remain true to it
as long as the cord of life shall lengthen.

When I was suddenly catapulted into the leadership of the bus protest in   35
Montgomery, Alabama, a few years ago, I felt we would be supported by the
white church. I felt that the white ministers, priests, and rabbis of the South
would be among our strongest allies. Instead, some have been outright opponents, refusing to understand the freedom movement and misrepresenting its
leaders; all too many others have been more cautious than courageous and have
remained silent behind the anesthetizing security of stained glass windows.

In spite of my shattered dreams, I came to Birmingham with the hope that   36
the white religious leadership of this community would see the justice of our
cause and, with deep moral concern, would serve as the channel through which
our just grievances could reach the power structure. I had hoped that each of
you would understand. But again I have been disappointed.

I have heard numerous southern religious leaders admonish their wor-   37
shippers to comply with a desegregation decision because it is the law, but I
have longed to hear white ministers declare: "Follow this decree because inte-
gration is morally right and because the Negro is your brother." In the midst of
blatant injustices inflicted upon the Negro, I have watched white churchmen
stand on the sideline and mouth pious irrelevancies and sanctimonious triviali-
ties. In the midst of a mighty struggle to rid our nation of racial and economic
injustice, I have heard many ministers say: "Those are social issues, with which
the gospel has no real concern." And I have watched many churches commit
themselves to a completely otherworldly religion which makes a strange, un-
Biblical distinction between body and soul, between the sacred and the secular.

I have traveled the length and breadth of Alabama, Mississippi, and all the   38
other southern states. On sweltering summer days and crisp autumn mornings
I have looked at the South's beautiful churches with their lofty spires pointing
heavenward. I have beheld the impressive outlines of her massive religious-
education buildings. Over and over I have found myself asking: "What kind of
people worship here? Who is their God? Where were their voices when the

lips of Governor Barnett dripped with words of interposition and nullification? Where were they when Governor Wallace gave a clarion call for defiance and hatred? Where were their voices of support when bruised and weary Negro men and women decided to rise from the dark dungeons of complacency to the bright hills of creative protest?"

Yes, these questions are still in my mind. In deep disappointment I have wept over the laxity of the church. But be assured that my tears have been tears of love. There can be no deep disappointment where there is not deep love. Yes, I love the church. How could I do otherwise? I am in the rather unique position of being the son, the grandson, and the great-grandson of preachers. Yes, I see the church as the body of Christ. But, oh! How we have blemished and scarred that body through social neglect and through fear of being nonconformists.   39

There was a time when the church was very powerful—in the time when the early Christians rejoiced at being deemed worthy to suffer for what they believed. In those days the church was not merely a thermometer that recorded the ideas and principles of popular opinion; it was a thermostat that transformed the mores of society. Whenever the early Christians entered a town, the people in power became disturbed and immediately sought to convict the Christians for being "disturbers of the peace" and "outside agitators." But the Christians pressed on, in the conviction that they were "a colony of heaven," called to obey God rather than man. Small in number, they were big in commitment. They were too God-intoxicated to be "astronomically intimidated." By their effort and example they brought an end to such ancient evils as infanticide and gladiatorial contests.   40

Things are different now. So often the contemporary church is a weak, ineffectual voice with an uncertain sound. So often it is an archdefender of the status quo. Far from being disturbed by the presence of the church, the power structure of the average community is consoled by the church's silent—and often even vocal—sanction of things as they are.   41

But the judgment of God is upon the church as never before. If today's church does not recapture the sacrificial spirit of the early church, it will lose its authenticity, forfeit the loyalty of millions, and be dismissed as an irrelevant social club with no meaning for the twentieth century. Every day I meet young people whose disappointment with the church has turned into outright disgust.   42

Perhaps I have once again been too optimistic. Is organized religion too inextricably bound to the status quo to save our nation and the world? Perhaps I must turn my faith to the inner spiritual church, the church within the church, as the true *ekklesia* and the hope of the world. But again I am thankful to God that some noble souls from the ranks of organized religion have broken loose from the paralyzing chains of conformity and joined us as active partners in the struggle for freedom. They have left their secure congregations and walked the   43 streets of Albany, Georgia, with us. They have gone down the highways of the South on tortuous rides for freedom. Yes, they have gone to jail with us. Some have been dismissed from their churches, have lost the support of their bishops and fellow ministers. But they have acted in the faith that right defeated is stronger than evil triumphant. Their witness has been the spiritual salt that has preserved the true meaning of the gospel in these troubled times. They have carved a tunnel of hope through the dark mountain of disappointment.

I hope the church as a whole will meet the challenge of this decisive hour. But even if the church does not come to the aid of justice, I have no despair about the future. I have no fear about the outcome of our struggle in Birmingham, even if our motives are at present misunderstood. We will reach the goal of freedom in Birmingham and all over the nation because the goal of America is freedom. Abused and scorned though we may be, our destiny is tied up with America's destiny. Before the pilgrims landed at Plymouth, we were here. Before the pen of Jefferson etched the majestic words of the Declaration of Independence across the pages of history, we were here. For more than two centuries our forebears labored in this country without wages; they made cotton king; they built the homes of their masters while suffering gross injustice and shameful humiliation—and yet out of a bottomless vitality they continued to thrive and develop. If the inexpressible cruelties of slavery could not stop us, the opposition we now face will surely fail. We will win our freedom because the sacred heritage of our nation and the eternal will of God are embodied in our echoing demands. 44

Before closing I feel impelled to mention one other point in your statement that has troubled me profoundly. You warmly commended the Birmingham police force for keeping "order" and "preventing violence." I doubt that you would have so warmly commended the police force if you had seen its dogs sinking their teeth into unarmed, nonviolent Negroes. I doubt that you would so quickly commend the policemen if you were to observe their ugly and inhumane treatment of Negroes here in the city jail; if you were to watch them push and curse old Negro women and young Negro girls; if you were to see them slap and kick old Negro men and young boys; if you were to observe them, as they did on two occasions, refuse to give us food because we wanted to sing our grace together. I cannot join you in your praise of the Birmingham police department. 45

It is true that the police have exercised a degree of discipline in handling the demonstrators. In this sense they have conducted themselves rather "nonviolently" in public. But for what purpose? To preserve the evil system of segregation. Over the past few years I have consistently preached that nonviolence demands that the means we use must be as pure as the ends we seek. I have tried to make clear that it is wrong to use immoral means to attain moral ends. But now I must affirm that it is just as wrong, or perhaps even more so, to use moral means to preserve immoral ends. Perhaps Mr. Connor and his policemen 46 have been rather nonviolent in public; as was Chief Pritchett in Albany, Georgia, but they have used the moral means of nonviolence to maintain the immoral end of racial injustice. As T. S. Eliot has said, "The last temptation is the greatest treason: To do the right deed for the wrong reason.

I wish you had commended the Negro sit-inners and demonstrators of Birmingham for their sublime courage, their willingness to suffer, and their amazing discipline in the midst of great provocation. One day the South will recognize its real heroes. They will be the James Merediths, with the noble sense of purpose that enables them to face jeering and hostile mobs, and with the agonizing loneliness that characterizes the life of the pioneer. They will be old, oppressed, battered Negro women, symbolized in a seventy-two-year-old woman in Montgomery, Alabama, who rose up with a sense of dignity and with her people decided not to ride segregated buses, and who responded with ungrammatical profundity to one who inquired about her weariness: "My feets is tired, but my soul is at rest." They will be the young high school and college students, the young ministers of the gospel and a host of their elders, courageously and nonviolently sitting in at lunch counters and willingly going to jail for conscience' sake. One day the South will know that when these disinherited children of God sat down at lunch counters, they were in reality standing up for what is best in the American dream and for the most sacred values in our Judaeo-Christian heritage, thereby bringing our nation back to those great wells of democracy which were dug deep by the founding fathers in their formulation of the Constitution and the Declaration of Independence. 47

Never before have I written so long a letter. I'm afraid it is much too long to take your precious time. I can assure you that it would have been much shorter if I had been writing from a comfortable desk, but what else can one do when he is alone in a narrow jail cell, other than write long letters, think long thoughts, and pray long prayers? 48

If I have said anything in this letter that overstates the truth and indicates an unreasonable impatience, I beg you to forgive me. If I have said anything that understates the truth and indicates my having a patience that allows me to settle for anything less than brotherhood, I beg God to forgive me. 49

I hope this letter finds you strong in the faith. I also hope that circumstances will soon make it possible for me to meet each of you, not as an integrationist or a civil-rights leader but as a fellow clergyman and a Christian brother. Let us all hope that the dark clouds of racial prejudice will soon pass away and the deep fog of misunderstanding will be lifted from our fear-drenched communities, and in some not too distant tomorrow the radiant stars of love and brotherhood will shine over our great nation with all their scintillating beauty. 50

Yours for the cause of Peace and Brotherhood,

MARTIN LUTHER KING, JR.

1963

Acknowledgments

Angelou, Maya. "Graduation", from All God's Children Need Traveling Shoes. New York : Random House, c1986.

Anonymous. "Confessions of an Erstwhile Child", from The New Republic, c1974.

Arden, Harvey. "Morrocco's Ancient City of Fez" first appeared in The National Geographic. cHarvey Arden.

Arendt, Hanna. "Denmark and the Jews", from Eichmann In Jerusalem. New York: Viking Press, c1963.

Arieti, Silvano. Interpretation of Schizophrenia. New York: R. Brunner, 1955.

Arieti, Silvano. The Intrapsychic Self: Feeling, Cognition, and Creativity in Health and Mental Illness. New York: Basic Books, c1967.

Asimov, Isaac. "The Eureka Phenomenon", from The Left Hand of the Electron. Garden City, N.Y.: Doubleday, c1972.

Auden, W.H.. "Work, Labor, and Play", from A Certain World. New York: Viking Press, c1970.

Baker, Sheridan. The Practical Stylist. New York: Crowell, c1969.

Baker, Sheridan. The Complete Stylist. New York: Crowell, c1966.

Barthelme, Donald. The Dead Father. New York: Farrar, Straus, and Giroux, c1975.

Berlin, Isaiah. "Mr. Churchhill", from Mr. Churchill in 1940. Boston: Houghton Mifflin, c1964.

Bombeck, Erma. Aunt Erma's Cope Book : How to Get From Monday to Friday ... in 12 Days. New York : McGraw-Hill, c1979.

Buckley, William F. "Why Don't We Complain?", from Esquire, January, 1961. c1961 William F. Buckley. Reprinted by permission of Wallace Literary Agency.

Burmeister, Jill et al (editors). Better Homes and Gardens Complete Quick and Easy Cookbook. Des Moines, Iowa : Meredith Corp., c1983.

Capote, Truman. "Isak Dinesen", from Observations (with photography by Richard Avedon). New York: Simon and Schuster, c1957 Truman Capote and Richard Avedon.

Capote, Truman. "A Christmas Memory", New York: Random House, c1956.

Catton, Bruce. "Grant and Lee: A Study in Contrasts", from The American Story. Reprinted by permission of U.S. Capitol Historical Society.

Colinvaux, Paul. "Every Species Has Its Niche", from Why Big Fierce Animals Are Rare : An Ecologist's Perspective. Princeton, N.J. : Princeton University Press, c1978.

Corbett, Edward. Classical Rhetoric for the Modern Student. New York: Oxford University Press, c1965.

Cousins, Norman. "Pain is Not the Ultimate Enemy", from Anatomy of an Illness. New York: W.W. Norton and Co., c1979.

Cunningham, Marion. "Ingredients for Cake", "Kinds of Cake", and "Cake Recipe", from Fannie Farmer Cookbook. New York: Knopf, Dist. By Random House, c1990.

D'Angelo, Frank. Process and Thought in Composition. Cambridge, Mass.: Winthrop Publishers, c1977.

Davies, Robertson. "A Few Kind Words For Superstition", from Newsweek, November 20, 1978. c1978 Robertson Davies.

Decker, Randall. Patterns of Exposition. Boston: Little, Brown, c1966.

Didion, Joan. "Some Dreamers of the Golden Dream", from Slouching Towards Bethlehem. New York, Farrar, Straus & Giroux, c1967, 1968.

Dillard, Annie. "Sojourner", from Teaching a Stone to Talk. New York: Harper and Row, c1982.

Dobson, Terry, "Not Looking Like a Victim", from Safe and Alive. Los Angeles: Houghton Mifflin, c1981.

Du Bois, William Edward Burghardt, John Brown. New York: International Publishers, c1962.

Erikson, Kai. "Of Accidental Judgements and Casual Slaughter", from A New Species of Trouble : Explorations in Disaster, Trauma, and Community. New York : W.W. Norton & Co., c1994.

Finch, Robert. "Very Like a Whale", from Common Ground, a Naturalist's Cape Cod. Boston, Mass: David R. Godine, c1981.

Frye, Northrop. "Communications", from The Eternal Act of Creation : Essays, 1979-1990. Edited by Robert D. Denham. Bloomington : Indiana University Press, c1993.

Robert Fulghum. All I Really Need to Know I Learned in Kindergarten : Uncommon Thoughts on Common Things. New York: Villard Books, 1988.

Fussell, Paul. "Notes on Class", from The Boy Scout's Handbook and Other Observations. New York: Oxford University Press, c1982.

Gass, William. "China Still Lifes", first published in House and Garden , c1985.

Geyer, Georgie Ann. "We Must Excise Savage Behavior, Not Excuse It", Chicago Daily News Syndicate, c Georgie Ann Geyer.

Goodman, Ellen. "A Proposal to Abolish Grading", first published in The Washington Post. c1981.

Hall, Edward T., "Proxemities and the Arab World", from Proxemics: The Hidden Dimension. Garden City, NY: Doubleday, 1969, c1966.

Hardin, Garret. Biology: Its Human Implications. San Francisco: W.H. Freeman, c1949.

Hefferman, William A. and Mark Johnson (Editors). The Harvest Reader. San Diego: Harcourt Brace Jovanovich, c1991.

Huxley, Aldous. "Waterworks and Kings", from The Olive Tree. New York: Harper and Row, c1937 Aldous Huxley, renewed 1965 Laura Huxley.

Huxtable, Ada Louise. "Modern-Life Battle: Conquering Clutter", first published in The New Yorker Magazine. cThe New Yorker Inc.

Jacobson, Mark. "On Rediscovering Evil", from The Development of American Political Thought. New York, London: The Century Co., c1932.

Keillor, Garrison. "Hoppers" from We Are Still Married. Viking, c1982.

King, Larry L. "Playing Cowboys" from Of Outlaws, Con Men, Whores, Politicians, and Other Artists. New York : Viking Press, c1980.

King, Martin Luther, Jr. "Letter From Birmingham Jail", from Why We Can't Wait. Reprinted by Permission of Joan Daves. c1963, 1964, Martin Luther King.

Kinneavy, James L. Elements of Writing: 3rd Course. Austin, TX: Holt, Rinehart and Winston Inc: Harcourt Brace Jovanovich, c1993.

Kubler-Ross, Elizabeth. "On the Fear of Death", from On Death and Dying. New York: Macmillan, c1969 Elizabeth Kubler-Ross.

Lasch, Christopher. "Spectatorship", from The Culture of Narcissism : American Life in an Age of Diminishing Expectations. New York : Norton, 1978, c1979.

Lawrence, Margaret. "Where the World Began", from Heart of a Stranger. c1976 Margaret Lawrence. Reprinted by permission of VCA Literary Agency and the Canadian Publishers, Toronto: McClelland and Stewart Ltd.

Lessing, Doris. "My Father", from A Small Personal Voice. c1963 Doris Lessing. Reprinted by permission of Jonathan Clones, Ltd..

Lowes, John Livingston. "Time in the Middle Ages", from The Road to Xanadu; a Study in the Ways of the Imagination. Boston and New York: Houghton Mifflin Company, c1927.

Macaulay, David. Pyramid. Boston : Houghton Mifflin, c1975.

Markels, Robin Bell. A New Perspective on Cohesion in Expository Paragraphs. Carbondale: Southern Illinois Press, c1984.

McPhee, John. "How to Make a Nuclear Bomb", first published in The New Yorker. c John McPhee.

Mead, Margaret. "The Gift of Autonomy", from Redbook Magazine. c1966 Margaret Mead and Rhoda Metraux.

Mitford, Jessica. The American Way of Death. New York: Simon and Schuster, c1963.

Morris, Desmond. "Altruistic Behaviour" and "Sporting Behaviour", from Manwatching: A Field Guide to Human Behaviour. London : Cape, c1977.

Mowat, Farley. "The Perfect House", from People of the Deer. c1952 Farley Mowat.

Orwell, George. "Politics and the English Language", from Shooting an Elephant and Other Essays. c1946 Sonia Orwell, renewed 1974. New York: Harcourt Brace.

Petrunkevitch, Alexander. "The Spider and the Wasp", first published in Scientific American. c1952 Scientific American.

Pettit, Florence H. "How to Sharpen Your Knife" from How to Make Whirligigs and Whimmy Diddles and Other American Folkcraft Objects. Illustrated by Laura Louise Foster. New York: Crowell, c1972.

Robert M. Pirsig. "Scientific Method" and "Analysis of a Motorcycle", from, Zen and the Art of Motorcycle Maintenance: an Inquiry Into Values. New York: Morrow, c1974.

Randolph, David. "Five Basic Elements of Music", from This Is Music: A Guide to the Pleasures of Listening. New York: Cornerstone, c1964.

Rockwell, F.F. (editor) 10,000 Garden Questions Answered by 20 Experts. New Edition edited by Marjorie J. Dietz. New York : Wings Books; Avenel, N.J. : Distributed by Random House Value Pub., c1995.

Saffire, William. "Emphasis on Stress", from Language Maven Strikes Again. New York: Doubleday. First appeared in The New York Times, c1990 Cobbet Corporation.

Sagan, Carl. "The Abstractions of Beasts", c Carl Sagan.

Sale, Kirkpatrick. "The Myth of Bigness", from Human Scale. New York : Coward, McCann & Geoghegan, c1980.

Schell, Jonathan. "Nothing to Report", from <u>Fate of the Earth</u>. New York: Knopf, c1982.

Selzer, Richard. "Liver", from <u>Mortal Lessons: Notes on the Art of Surgery</u>. New York: Simon and Schuster. c1974, 1975, 1976, Richard Selzer.

Shoemaker, Robin. <u>The Peasents of El Dorado</u>. Ithica: Cornwell University Press, c1981.

Schumacher, E.F., <u>A Guide for the Perplexed</u>. London : Cape, c1977.

Stegner, Wallace. "The Town Dump", from <u>Wolf Willow</u>. c1959 Wallace Stegner. Renewed 1987. Reprinted by permission of Brandt & Brandt Literary Agents, Inc.

Stein, Sarah B. "Let's Get Botanical", from <u>Planting Noah's Garden</u>. Boston, Mass: Houghton Mifflin, c1997.

Steinem, Gloria. "Erotica and Pornography", from <u>Ms. Magazine</u>, November 1978. c1978 <u>Ms. Magazine</u>.

Sudnow, David. <u>Ways of the Hand</u>. Cambrige, Mass: Harvard University Press, c1978.

Syfers, Judy (Judy Brady). "Why I Want a Wife", from <u>Ms. Magazine</u>, December 1971. c1971, <u>Ms. Magazine</u>.

Szasz, Thomas. <u>Heresies</u>. Garden City, NY: Anchor Press, c1976.

Theroux, Alexander. "Matters of Taste", from <u>Three Wogs</u>. Boston : D. R. Godine, c1975.

Theroux, Paul. <u>The Kingdom by the Sea : a Journey Around Great Britain</u>. Boston : Houghton Mifflin, c1983.

Thomas, Lewis. "The World's Biggest Membrane", from <u>The Lives of a Cell</u>. New York: Viking Press, c1974.

Thomas, Lewis. "Ponds", from <u>The Medusa and the Snail</u>. c1979 Thomas Lewis. Reprinted by Permission of Viking-Penguin Inc.

White, E.B. "Democracy", from <u>The Wild Flag</u>. Boston, Mass: Houghton Mifflin, c1956.

Wu-Tsu Fa-Yen. "Zen and the Art of Burglary", from <u>Zen and the Japanese Culture</u>. Princeton University Press, c1959.

Author & Title Index